Raising Great Kids

$4.99

Raising Great Kids:
Ages 6 to 12

EDITOR: CHRISTINE LANGLOIS

CANADIAN LIVING'S HEALTH AND FAMILY EDITOR

In collaboration with the Canadian Paediatric Society and

The College of Family Physicians of Canada

A **Canadian Living** Family Book

Ballantine Books

A Division of Random House of Canada Limited

We are grateful to the following for permission to adapt their material.
The Alliance for Children and Television: pages 106–107
B.C. Confederation of Parent Advisory Councils: page 93
Canadian Paediatric Society: pages 48, 204–211
Dads Can: page 181
Health Canada: pages 42, 212–13
Sharon McKay: pages 29–36

PROJECT TEAM
Project Editor: Jean Stinson
Assistant Editor: Jaishree Drepaul
Preliminary Research: Quinn Ross
Fact-checking: Laurel Aziz
Cover and book design: Hambly & Woolley Inc.
Cover photograph: Chris Gordaneer, Westside Studios
Brush drawings: Bob Hambly
Photos: Courtesy of generous parents

Publisher: Caren King
Editorial Director: Bonnie Baker Cowan

CANADIAN CATALOGUING IN PUBLICATION DATA
Main entry under title:
Raising great kids: ages 6 to 12

"A Canadian Living family book"
"In collaboration with the Canadian Paediatric Society and the College of Family Physicians of Canada."
On cover: The complete guide to your child's health and development.
Includes index.
ISBN 0-345-39879-3

1. Child rearing. 2. Parent and child. 3. Child development. I. Langlois, Christine (Christine Anne).

HQ769.R34 1999 649'.124 C98-932366-8

Ballantine Books
A Division of
Random House of Canada Limited
2775 Matheson Boulevard East
Mississauga, ON L4W 4P7
Canada

Canadian Living
Telemedia Communications Inc.
25 Sheppard Avenue West
Suite 100
Toronto, ON M2N 6S7
Canada

1999 2000 01 02 03 FP 5 4 3 2 1
Printed and bound in Canada by Friesens

Writers

LYNNE AINSWORTH
CINDY BARRETT
MARCIA KAYE
JOHN KEATING
SUSAN NOAKES
SUSAN PEDWELL
LAURA PRATT
BRAMWELL RYAN
MARK WITTEN

Expert Advisors

CANADIAN PAEDIATRIC SOCIETY
Danielle Grenier MD, FRCPC
Medical Affairs Officer, Canadian Paediatric Society
Denis Leduc MD, FRCPC, CCFP
Assistant Professor of Paediatrics, McGill University
Liaison: Elizabeth Moreau

THE COLLEGE OF FAMILY PHYSICIANS OF CANADA
Cheri Bethune MD, CCFP, FCFP
Professor of Family Medicine, Memorial University of Newfoundland
Carol P. Herbert MD, CCFP, FCFP
Professor and Head, Family Practice, University of British Columbia
Inese Grava-Gubins, MA, Director of Research
Liaison: Monica Proudler

Meg Hickling RN, *Sexual Health Educator*
Rena Mendelson MS, DSc, RD, *Professor of Nutrition, Ryerson Polytechnic University*
Penny Milton, Executive Director, *Canadian Education Association*
Anne Lindsay, *Nutrition Editor, Canadian Living*

Contents

Foreword

Raising Great Kids provides advice for parents and other caregivers engaged in the challenging task of rearing children between the ages of six and twelve. This second book in the **Canadian Living Family Book** series pulls information and recommendations from a broad range of sources, from the practices of many health professionals and the experiences of many parents. The advice and opinions are essentially Canadian, and the focus is on the Canadian scene.

Raising children today is no easy task. The challenges facing parents, caregivers, teachers, and others involved with youngsters have become increasingly complex. The search for a well-conceived and accurate source of guidance poses difficulties in itself. With books, magazines, newspapers, videos, radio and television call-in programs, and the Internet offering information, how does the besieged parent choose a reliable source of facts and advice about his children's development and needs? *Raising Great Kids* offers excellent up-to-date information and sources that can simplify the task.

This **Canadian Living** book includes advice and recommendations not only on children's health and safety, but also on learning and education issues, and on emotional, social, and spiritual development. Chapter Three, "Heart and Soul," deals with the development of personality and self-esteem as well as the stress some children feel—a frequently unrecognized issue. One unique section, "Small Steps to Independence," helps parents decide when their child is ready for more freedom, such as being allowed to sleep over at a friend's house. Chapter Four, "Parenting through Family Highs and Lows," discusses how family difficulties or stresses such as illness, unemployment, or alcoholism affect a child and suggests how parents can help their child deal with these problems. Of particular help are the lists of selected Canadian resources, including organizations, Web sites, and help lines, as well as Canadian children's literature and further reading for parents.

This parenting resource has been reviewed by a subcommittee of the newly formed Joint Action Committee on Child and Adolescent Health. This first joint committee of the Canadian Paediatric Society and The College of Family Physicians of Canada has many goals, among them the goal of enhancing the relationship between pediatricians and family physicians in their care of kids and teens. That means addressing key issues such as defining physician roles in relation to other health-care professionals, enhancing physician training, assessing the policy statements of organizations, advocating for research, and increasing the collaboration between pediatricians and family physicians.

The Canadian Paediatric Society, an organization of Canadian medical specialists in child care, celebrated its 75th anniversary this year. With roughly two thousand members, this growing organization represents over 80 per cent of the pediatricians in Canada and includes other physicians who are interested in child care. The society recognizes that children are not "little adults," that the growing child has special needs—medical, social, and developmental—during her growth toward adolescence. Our challenge for the future is to involve parents and caregivers to a greater extent within the processes of medical care, and the most important means of achieving this will be the spread of medical knowledge and education. This second book in the **Canadian Living Family Book** series, *Raising Great Kids,* contributes to that goal.

David F. Smith, MD, FRCPC
Vice President, Canadian Paediatric Society
Associate Professor, Department of Pediatrics,
University of British Columbia

Introduction

Warning: You have now entered the busy years. That may surprise you because, as a parent, you probably think you've been very busy from the minute your child was born. But what changes from age six on is that your child moves out into the world of full-time school and lessons and friends. He begins to get involved in more activities, and even to direct the action. He makes time for swimming classes, school projects, a favourite TV show, and a few chores. For most kids between the ages of six and twelve, the days are so full that their parents often lament the elaborate schedules the family maintains. If it's Tuesday, it must be soccer practice. If it's Thursday, her spelling words are due. On Saturday, he has Cubs and a birthday party in the afternoon.

When editing *Raising Great Kids*, I was very aware that overloaded moms and dads will be reading it because they need fast answers to questions about their child's development and solid advice on how to parent her through the childhood years. As a busy parent, you are the one most aware of your child's subtle changes as she grows and develops. You notice your son's newfound ability to empathize with a friend as he recounts school-yard tales at the dinner table. Your daughter's ability to handle more complex assignments is apparent in the intricacies of her latest school project. But every day, you'll have questions: What kind of homework will she have in grade three? How can I help my shy son make a new friend? What should I do when my nine-year-old announces she's vegetarian? What's the appropriate response when my ten-year-old loses her baseball glove—again? *Raising Great Kids* answers questions like these with advice on physical, emotional, cognitive, and social development from both experts and parents across the country.

Raising Great Kids will help you and your partner develop as a team. To parent effectively, you need to share your expectations of family life. Tell each other about what changes you've noticed in your child: Your eight-year-old is looking for a little more privacy; your six-year-old has discovered the power of "bad" words. Discuss how you'll handle key decisions about your child's education, or the setting of limits. You'll also want to choose a healthy parenting style that will work for both of you—one that sets basic ground rules for raising your kids but acknowledges that kids are always stretching their boundaries. This is also the time in your child's life when you really begin passing on your values to your kids. But how do you do that? Maybe you want to start holding family meetings to discuss your life together and let the kids get involved in some of the decision making.

Mothers and fathers bring different perspectives to parenting, so in *Raising Great Kids*, we've looked at what's unique about each while making it clear that moms and dads are interchangeable when it comes to doing a great job of meeting their kids' needs and building strong bonds. The information in the book has been gathered by a wonderful team of **Canadian Living** writers, who have interviewed experts across the country on the many topics—from curriculum development to nutrition to sibling relationships—that need to be explored in a comprehensive resource for parents. Everything in the book reflects a Canadian perspective. When we discuss education, we're talking about Canadian schools; when we talk about how many fruits and vegetables your child needs in a day, we're referring to Canada's Food Guide; when we list an organization, it has a Canadian address.

Raising Great Kids is the second book in the **Canadian Living Family Book** series, following on from *Growing with Your Child: Pre-Birth to Age 5* and preceding *Understanding Your Teen.* I have again been fortunate to have edited the book in collaboration with both the Canadian Paediatric Society and The College of Family Physicians of Canada. Their involvement means that the advice reflects the most current thinking about children's health and development.

Parents like you who are raising kids in Canada at the turn of the millennium are living busy lives that can sometimes feel overwhelming. What *Raising Great Kids* will do for you is give you the fast answers you need along with the reassurance that just as in a simpler time, fathers and mothers do know best. It's a lot easier to parent well when you know what to expect in terms of your child's development. But it's up to you to apply the expert advice in the way that works best for your child. After all, you're the one she snuggles with and tells her secrets to. When it comes to your child, you're the expert.

Christine Langlois
Toronto, September 1998

Body

1

So much about your child's body changes between the ages of six and twelve. Both boys and girls become taller, stronger, and more coordinated. They need lots of opportunity to develop their physical prowess at running, jumping, throwing, climbing. You may see signs of puberty in your daughter as early as seven, and most girls start their period by the time they are twelve. Your son may show signs of puberty, or you may not notice changes until he's a teenager. Your child's physical growth and development are nurtured by healthy eating, good sleep habits, attention to safety, and your reassurance about the many body changes she is experiencing.

The time in your child's life when she is best able to develop her gross motor skills is the prepubescent period. As her body size and muscle strength gradually increase, her reaction time improves. Fundamental patterns of movement such as throwing and catching, kicking, hopping and jumping, skipping, running and galloping are the easiest to learn by ages seven and eight. Give her lots of opportunities to learn and practise these basic skills. It's much easier for her to increase her speed and coordination in the period from age six to twelve than it will be in her teens or later. If she leads an active life at this stage, your child will develop the skills to play many different sports and games throughout her whole life. But more than that, the same hand-eye coordination required to catch a ball contributes to developing skills in keyboarding, in sewing, in playing the piano or other musical instruments, and in any number of life activities.

Kids learn best when they're having fun and when they feel competent. They need to find a balance between the physical challenges of games and their developing skills. Because there's about a one-year lag between bone growth and muscle development, prepubescent kids go through periods of awkwardness during growth spurts. Find ways to help your young child succeed if she has difficulty with a physical skill. If she can't yet throw a ball well, have her throw a scarf instead to slow the motion down. Then try a beach ball or beanbag. Let your kids strap on some kneepads and play kneeling basketball with a big bouncy ball and kitchen pots for nets. They'll enjoy the silliness of the game while they get practice in throwing, bouncing, and catching the ball.

What Kids Can Do

Your child's balance and agility are increasing, although his flexibility has been decreasing since infancy. He can jump hurdles, tumble, and balance while walking along a narrow board. Many children's games, like skipping rope and hopscotch, help them improve their gross motor skills.

Kids between six and twelve need at least 60 minutes of physical exercise every day, according to the Canadian Fitness and Lifestyle Research Institute (CFLRI). This hour could consist of 30 minutes of vigorous play and 30 minutes of lighter activity, or it could be broken into 10-minute spurts of action and still provide health benefits.

Lots of kids don't get enough exercise. In the 1998 report of a joint study by the Heart and Stroke Foundation and the CFLRI, researchers reported that the health of more than 60 per cent of Canadian children is threatened because they are inactive. It's vitally important for your children to be regularly involved in physical activities. Not only does activity help develop their gross motor skills, it helps forestall the development of disease as your children grow older.

All kids are different. How a child's gross motor skills develop depends on many factors, including his own interest, your encouragement, and his inherited form and ability. Some kids have initial growth spurts earlier than others, so they will kick a ball farther at age ten simply because they have more strength. The following descriptions give a general idea of what the average kid might be capable of:

For many kids, individual sports and activities are as important as team sports.

At age six

Most six-year-olds are in motion almost constantly. They love climbing and rough-and-tumble play. Swinging on swings and dancing are good, too. Most six-year-olds should be able to:

- run energetically around the back yard or playground.
- skip with alternating feet.
- jump or step sideways.
- bounce a ball, probably with awkward slapping movements.
- throw a ball overhand with accuracy and direction.
- ride a two-wheeled bicycle.
- learn to skate.

At ages seven and eight

Seven- and eight-year-olds are exploding with energy. Left to their own devices, they choose wild, unrestrained horseplay that includes jumping, chasing, wrestling, and tree climbing. They enjoy testing their limits and may be risk takers.

At age nine

Nine-year-olds like to play hard. They often exert themselves to the point of exhaustion. They perform the same activities repeatedly. At this age, they're often interested in improving their athletic skills, and may become obsessed with improving their record of personal bests. They may also become interested in professional sports like baseball and soccer, and get involved in local teams for youngsters.

At age ten

Active play is still a fun part of life for most ten-year-olds, who are active just for the sheer joy of movement. Their skills and stamina have improved to the point where they get real enjoyment from games and activities that put their skills to use. They may have become quite competent on their bikes, and usually prefer to play at outdoor activities, not indoors.

At age eleven

By age eleven, when most children are going through one of the stages of puberty and are growing more quickly, they may become more inhibited physically. They may appear both more agile and more awkward.

At age twelve

By age twelve, your children may want to concentrate only on the sports and activities that they're good at. Most parents should be careful not to emphasize team sports and "winning at any cost," because kids still benefit most from generalized physical activity and games. Parents should try to maintain their kids' involvement in a variety of activities just for the pleasures of being active—and the lifelong benefits such physical activity brings.

A twelve-year-old has the stamina to test her limits on an overnight hike.

Remember that all children develop their gross and fine motor skills at their own speed, so take these descriptions as rough guidelines for assessing children's increasing skills. There are several organizations that offer training programs of different levels that are not tied solely to age. The Canadian Red Cross has three programs to train children and adults in water safety. AquaTots has three levels for infants to preschoolers and their parents or caregivers. The AquaQuest program, which offers twelve levels starting as early as age three, teaches children to stay safe on, in, and around the water. The AquaAdults program offers three stages in swimming and water safety measures that are appropriate for both adolescents and adults.

Active Family Games

Only about one-third of Canadian kids are as physically active as the CFLRI recommends for their minimum level of health. Such a statistic means that there are lots of kids sitting in front of the TV set or playing video games when they should be out in the playground, or on the bike path, or wrestling with the dog in the family room.

SEE PAGE 105

In most Canadian schools, physical education doesn't rank high on the priorities for the curriculum. In New Brunswick, for example, only 56 minutes per week of phys. ed. are scheduled into the average elementary school timetable. That's barely 11 minutes a day of purposeful training, apart from any recess and lunch-hour activity. If parents want their kids to reach the CFLRI's recommended minimum of 60 minutes a day, it's up to them to get their kids moving.

Canadian kids are four times less active today than kids of the same age were forty years ago in the pre-TV-invasion 1950s, and the reasons are well documented. On average, Canadian kids spend nearly as much time sitting in front of the television set as they do sitting in school. Other technological toys take up more of their time—and adults' time, too. Kids walk to school less; parents drive their kids and themselves to more places.

Really listen to what your children like to do. Involve their friends or other families in your neighbourhood in your games. Provide the equipment and a safe environment at home, or take everybody to the park and make sure there are enough balls or Hula-Hoops to go around. Suggest games that appeal to the children's activity level and imagination. State the object of the game in a few simple words. Then step back and let the kids take the lead.

Don't let them get bogged down with too many rules. It's better to bend the rules to fit the kids than to bend the kids to fit the game. Modify outdoor games for indoors and vice versa. The idea is to make the activity a game, not a competition, and your child's skills will follow naturally.

How do you stir your sedentary child from the couch? First, assess your own activity level. Not surprisingly, the children of active parents spend more time on physical activity than the children whose parents are inactive. You may need to get moving yourself. The next step is to put limits on the amount of time you and your children spend in front of the TV set or the computer. Third, consider the ways that you can add more physical activity to your and their day-to-day life. Would it be safe for your daughter to walk to and from school every day rather than be driven, if she walked with an older child in the neighbourhood? Could your son help one or both parents with household chores—perhaps cleaning the lowest windows, doing some of the laundry tasks, helping wash the car or dust the bookshelves?

Then, look for ways to spark their interest in new activities that will get them moving. When you play boisterous, rough-and-tumble physical games with them, you all have fun together. Your child learns the skills of teamwork and develops more enthusiasm for physical activity at the same time as he gets his daily quota of exercise. And you get more exercise yourself, and become a better model for your child.

Consider your children's personalities, but look for ways to involve them in something active. Your daughter may be shy and prefer not to join the games of the neighbourhood kids outside. But if she loves animals, suggest that she and a friend offer to walk the neighbour's dog every other day. Follow the children's interests, rather than impose your ideas on them, but they may need your guidance and suggestions at first. If they show an interest in team sports, look for an organized sport in the community, but also consider other groups whose activities are appropriate to their ages, and keep your children on the move.

When you play rough-and-tumble physical games, you all have fun together.

Activities for kids six and under

Colour Tag Everyone wearing one particular colour chases after those wearing the other colours, and tags them.

Monkey in the Middle Everyone stands in a circle, with one person in the middle as the "monkey." Those in the circle toss a soft ball or beanbag from one to the other. As the beanbag flies through the air, the monkey tries to grab it. If successful, he joins the circle, and the one who didn't catch the beanbag becomes the monkey.

Counting Games Count how many volleys the two teams can get back and forth across the net, how many Hula-Hoop rotations each of you can do, or how many seconds a child can stay poised in a handstand. Challenge each other to better the numbers at every go.

Pretend Games You all become a herd of wild horses, or a track full of race cars, or a tag team of wrestlers.

Wallyball This is like volleyball, except it's played on a racquetball court. You bounce the ball off the walls, or kick it with your feet. Play with as many people as you like, divided into two teams.

Nuke-'em This is also like volleyball, but you're allowed to catch the ball, which slows the game down and makes it easier for small kids to participate.

Soccer Play three on three with an oversize bouncy ball.

Bonky Baseball Use a big plastic bat and a big bouncy ball.

Kickball In this variation on baseball, the pitcher (you) rolls the bouncy ball to the child, who kicks it, rather than bats it.

Activities for seven- to nine-year-olds

- Don't underestimate the power of a new toy. It doesn't have to be expensive—marbles, a skipping rope, a Hula-Hoop, liquid soap bubbles, or a plastic snow slider may be enough. Once you've brought it home, suggest that your daughter invite a friend over and try it out.
- Plan a hike for the family that gives the children an opportunity to explore nature, to watch tadpoles and frogs in their natural habitat, or to collect samples of different leaves or nuts and pine cones.
- Plan an outdoor scavenger hunt. It's like hiking, but with the added thrill of the hunt.
- Take your child wall climbing at an indoor facility. It's popular, it's safe (they'll be in a harness), and it's an adventure.
- Offer to enroll them in dance classes, which require a fair amount of exercise and movement with a purpose. Many cultural groups offer classes to teach their traditional folk dances, which are very energetic.

Activities for ten- to twelve-year-olds

- Offer to take them snowboarding and provide instruction.
- Try in-line skates for the family, but be sure to get the appropriate protective gear at the same time.
- Suggest a water balloon fight in the playground.
- Take your daughter and her friend to play laser tag.
- Take your son door-to-door canvassing with you, on the Terry Fox Run, or on a bike-a-thon for the Canadian Cancer Society.

When kids are learning a new sport, go at their pace. Let them take the lead.

Picking the Right Team Sport

Between the ages of seven and twelve, most kids want games that have tactics and strategies. During the elementary school years, depending on the curriculum and the facilities available, your child may have the opportunity to try a variety of sports—indoor and out, summer and winter, unstructured and organized, recreational and competitive. Swimming, soccer, baseball, and hockey are four of the most popular organized sports at this age. A couple of million Canadian kids head to arenas, to pools, or to playing fields every week to have fun, learn new skills and teamwork, and get their exercise.

Kids love the excitement of sports and the sense of personal accomplishment that comes with their participation on the team. They also enjoy the social aspect. If all the eight-year-olds in your neighbourhood are starting soccer in the spring, your eight-year-old may want to go with them. Lots of children who may have difficulties in other parts of their lives, at school or with friends, build confidence and gain self-esteem on the ice, on the soccer field, or on the baseball diamond.

As a parent, you walk a fine line in guiding your child to the right sports for him. If your child is interested in trying a particular sport, by all means sign him up. But before you do, investigate the league and its coaching style to be sure you're comfortable with the approach. There is an ongoing debate about how appropriate organized competitive sports are for this age group.

If all the other eight-year-olds are starting soccer, yours will want to go with them.

Kids between seven and twelve need, more than anything, to have opportunities for broad-based skill development. Heavy practice and game schedules and serious competition can be stressful for your child and require specialization at too early an age. Also, a competitive environment may emphasize applying skills instead of acquiring or improving them. Specializing in one sport during the prepubescent years is inappropriate for the majority of kids. There's little guarantee that a hockey player who's great at the age of ten will still be great at fifteen or sixteen. And specialization can put too much stress on young bodies. Early burnout is not uncommon.

Take into account your child's stage of development when deciding how much competition he's ready for.

Take into account the stage of development your child has reached. Competition will favour early developers at this age for the simple reason that they are bigger, taller, and better coordinated physically than later-maturing kids. Your early-developing ten-year-old daughter may be stronger and faster than her late-developing twelve-year-old brother. This is initially tough on late developers, who tend to occupy the bench while the early developers fill the team's starting positions. But this experience can skew both kids' attitudes over time. The late developers may not have the chance to acquire skills or confidence, even though they have the same potential to enjoy sports as a teen or adult. The early developers, after a burst of success, may lose confidence in their teens when they're no longer automatically a star on the team.

"For now, I know Kieran is mostly interested in playing the kinds of sports I'm playing, which these days seems to be a lot of road hockey. That's fine with me, because I can see he's genuinely interested and his skills are improving all the time. But I'm increasingly trying to expose him to other types of activities, like swimming and soccer, because I don't want him to get locked into hockey. The other day, I looked into joining a tennis club with him. And I want him to give volleyball a try on the beach this summer.

I remember my childhood as being filled with a huge variety of sports, and I loved it. To this day, I go through stages, and have never really settled on a particular athletic passion. Variety is the spice of life, right? I want him to have a similar kind of experience."

GORD, FATHER OF TWO

As a parent, you need to explain to your child that her sports experiences at this age are not necessarily an indicator of her sports experiences a few years later. And as a parent, you need to remember the same thing. Don't get too caught up in your child's early successes or show disappointment at a less than stellar performance, except to support your child's reactions. Keep looking for ways to involve your child in an active lifestyle that emphasizes many activities—whether she is the current star of the baseball team or still practising catching the ball. Let your child set the pace.

"Cathy and Laurie do soccer and swimming. And Cathy enjoys figure skating. But she got to a level in skating about a year ago where it was going to require a significant financial commitment. She was at the point where she was going to have to go three times a week and have professional lessons each time, along with $500 skates. She would have liked to go on, but we had to evaluate what we thought. Was her ability outstanding? Did it outweigh the cost commitment? It didn't so we let it go. She doesn't do it at all anymore. Once you reach a certain point, you have to either buy in or not. She was disappointed initially, but she understood. I think she recognized, too, that she wasn't as inclined as some other kids. If they don't see themselves in that group, they can rationalize.

It's just a big balancing act. You have recreational dollars that have to be distributed among several kids and several sports. You have to make the best choices you can."

PAM, MOTHER OF THREE

Before allowing your child to commit to a team sport, calculate the financial cost and the cost in time to the child and the rest of the family. Talk to other parents about their experiences and where to find up-to-standard secondhand equipment before you sign on the dotted line.

Is the coach right for your child?

The coaches for the teams that interest your child should be focused on the fun of the game and on encouraging each team member to build his or her skills. Spend time watching the coach in action both at a practice and at a game to assess whether you're comfortable with his coaching style. Talk with him about what he values for his team members. Is he focused primarily on winning? Ask how he deals with children's different skill levels. Try also to talk with the parents of the other kids to find out what their contributions are to the team. If you let your child try out for and join the team, monitor her attitude—how much she looks forward to participating, whether she wants to arrive at the program on time, and how interested she is in talking with you about her experiences.

SEE PAGE 36

The talented athlete

The exceptional kids who show a real talent for a particular sport or activity usually stand out not only in their parents' view but in the more objective view of coaches and sports organizations. Parents should let their talented child decide whether to practise and develop specialized skills in order to participate in organized local or national competitive games and professional sports. But you can help your son or daughter think through the pros and cons of such involvement by researching as much as possible, by discussing it, and by providing your continuing love and support. Both will be necessary throughout the many ups and downs your youngster will experience over the years of practice and training usually required.

If your child's coach sees exceptional talent in your child, he will let you know.

Physical Awkwardness

Your son never makes it across the room without tripping over the dog. Or he still spills his milk at the breakfast table long after most kids can pour from the container without spilling. Such physical awkwardness may stem from one of many causes. Before your child started school, you and your family doctor would have spotted and dealt with any obvious cause. Most often, the new awkwardness shows that your child is somewhat slower in developing some of the gross motor skills. Or he may be going through a rapid growth spurt that temporarily affects his coordination. It's rare, but the child may have a diagnosable condition called developmental coordination disorder (DCD).

If your child's awkwardness affects all his physical activities, discuss with your family doctor the possibility of DCD. It affects about 6 per cent of children and is difficult to diagnose before the child becomes more physically active. Your doctor may decide on a referral to a neurologist to determine if DCD is at the root of the problem. More likely, though, there is a more common cause. The awkwardness may be genetic, or your child may simply not have had enough opportunities to be involved in the physical activities that develop his gross motor skills.

When a child is going through a growth spurt, his coordination may be temporarily affected.

If your kid shies away from organized sports because he feels incompetent, don't push him. Too much pressure from his parents might cause him to withdraw even more from physical activity. Let him go at his own speed, but help by simplifying games to suit his skill level. In other words, help keep his options open, rather than choose one sport. He might be interested in sports that initially require less precise movements and coordination. Swimming might be preferable to hockey, and soccer to tennis, or he might enjoy individual physical activities that emphasize repetition—yoga or karate, for example.

It would be best to give this child many low-stress, noncompetitive opportunities to work on his gross motor skills. "Where another child needs one hundred practices to be able to catch the ball, these kids are going to need five hundred," says Graham Fishburne, a professor of elementary education at the University of Alberta in Edmonton. "They're going to need mega-practice." The key is for parents to be creative in adapting games or sports so that the child can succeed. If they're motivated, they will stick with it, so it's important to choose activities that are appropriate to their developmental level.

Activities for six- to nine-year-olds

Skating Let him learn to skate with a hockey stick. It provides support and brings his centre of gravity lower.
Tandem biking Letting your child ride on a tandem bike attachment behind you introduces her to the pleasures of the open road before she's mastered the turning and stopping skills.
Water slides Going up and down those stairs is a good workout. It's fun to do with friends.
Paddleboating There's no arm movement required. The legs get good exercise in a very easy motion.
Beanbag throwing Set up targets (pizza boxes are a good size) and let your child toss away.
Mini-golf Make your own course in the back yard or head out to one in your community.

Activities for nine- to twelve-year-olds

Rowing It's very rhythmical and repetitive, making it easy to learn.
Cross-country skiing Start with short skis, which are easier to control.
Bowling It's fun and social.
Creative dance If your child enjoys music, she may enjoy dancing in a no-rules environment.
Badminton Set the net higher than regulation—about 2 m (6 ft.)—so that players must hit the birdie higher, thus slowing the action. Give your child a large racquet with a shorter handle. Try setting up a narrower court with less area for players to cover.

At school

Traditional physical education classes and outdoor games at school are difficult for awkward kids. Most provinces now include differently abled kids in the regular classroom, so teachers are more accustomed to making changes in sports or other activities to include a range of abilities. To make up for physical deficiencies, children need the same parental and school support that they would need to overcome academic deficiencies. Ask your child's teacher how she modifies the phys. ed. activities so that all kids can participate without the pressure of competition. Perhaps the teacher might invite a parent with a strong arm to throw out ball after ball so that these kids can practise catching a ball and throwing it back. This one-on-one activity gives them more opportunity for participation than a game of baseball in which most players on the teams sit on the bench.

Practice, without pressure, will keep your child smiling as he learns a new skill.

Growth Spurts

Canadian children of recent generations are growing taller than did previous generations because of better nutrition and health care. Today, the range of normal for six-year-olds is 105–122 cm (42–49 in.) tall with a mass or weight of 15–26 kg (33–57 lb.). Through the prepubescent years, this average child grows approximately 5–6 cm (2–2.5 in.) a year, and mass or weight increases by about 2 kg (4.5 lb.) per year.

How your child compares to this average, however, depends on several factors, including his ethnic background and genetic inheritance. In Canada, where many racial and ethnic groups are represented, children and their parents come in different sizes—their height and weight are determined by the norms for the two families of origin. There is a wide range of normal, so the difference in height among children in a typical elementary school classroom can be as much as 12.5 cm (5 in.).

Girls may have small growth spurts at the ages of six-and-a-half, eight-and-a-half, and ten; boys at seven, nine, and ten-and-a-half. In between these spurts, growth continues, but less visibly. During the prepubescent years, the extremities of the body grow faster than the torso, giving kids a long-legged appearance. As kids' bones grow, they pull the tendons and muscles along, and the ligaments to which the bones are attached become stretched.

Kids grow at individual rates. Some parents see their children bursting out of their clothes with regularity every season. Other kids never experience a spurt but grow at a steady pace. Just as adult bodies come in many shapes and sizes, so too do children's bodies. Most children are slimmer during these years than they were as preschoolers. Some youngsters are gangly, especially eight- and nine-year-olds, whose body mass increases more slowly than the lengthening of their skeletons. Other kids—particularly girls—remain rounder, keeping the female fat they carry throughout their lives.

When puberty begins, the hormones of estrogen and testosterone have a major impact on development. Girls may begin puberty as early as the age of seven, although most will begin their growth in height at ten-and-a-half. Boys may begin puberty at the age of eight, although most will experience their growth in height at the age of thirteen. Both boys and girls may experience nighttime "growing pains," although these nonspecific lower leg pains may occur even before the onset of puberty. Warm baths, hot milk, and liniment can help.

Because most girls begin puberty before boys do, their major growth spurts happen earlier, which is why many girls feel that they "tower" over boys in the last years of elementary school. Boys do catch up and then surpass girls in height by the mid-teens, around fifteen or so.

Puberty in Girls

The changes that puberty brings occur normally between the ages of seven and seventeen. The journey takes three to five years as your daughter passes through predictable stages of physical development.

Stage One The first outward sign you may notice is a slight growth spurt that could start when your daughter is about eight. Her hips and thighs begin to get wider. She will develop a potbelly that is her energy store for puberty. The increased growth has been triggered by an increase in hormone production, which is also causing her ovaries to enlarge.

Stage Two Breast development begins. Called "budding," this breast growth begins with buds of enlarged tissue underneath the nipples. These buds are often tender to the touch and easily irritated by rough clothing or by jumping up and down. It's common for the two breasts to grow unevenly. One might begin to grow before the other, or one might grow faster than the other. Let your daughter know that this may happen so that she's not alarmed. She may also worry that breast swelling is a sign of breast cancer. Reassure her.

Also during this stage, your child will continue to grow more quickly in height, and her weight will increase. Fat deposits will continue to round out her hips and give the appearance of a smaller waist. She will begin to grow pubic hair. Her sweat glands will increase her production of sweat, and she will begin to produce body odour.

Stage Three Breasts grow larger. Pubic hair growth continues and the hair becomes curlier. Armpit hair starts to grow, and the hair on legs and arms becomes darker and thicker. She begins to discharge into her underwear a clear or white fluid from her vagina.

Stage Four Your daughter will likely have her first period during this stage. Often, a thick white vaginal discharge precedes her period. Also, her nipples become raised and separated from the breast areolae. The growth pattern of her pubic hair takes on its distinct triangular shape. Her skin and hair may become oilier.

"I was one of the first ones to go through puberty. I remember it because it was kind of embarrassing. I was one of only three girls in my class to have breasts. I started to get breasts in grade five, and then I got my period when I was in grade six. When I was one of only three, I kind of felt abnormal. I used to wear baggy clothing to try and hide them. But it's fine now. Right after grade six, right when I went into grade seven, I felt like everyone evened out. That was a great relief."

CATHY, AGE 12

Stage Five At this stage, a girl's breasts have reached full development, and her pubic hair growth is complete. Her growth in height slows, then eventually stops. At this stage, your daughter has probably attained her full height, but her menstrual periods may not follow a regular pattern for a year or two.

Are children starting puberty earlier than they used to? Yes and no. Exposure to light is thought to be a contributing factor to when puberty starts. Children in equatorial countries have always begun puberty between the ages of seven and eleven. Once people in the Northern Hemisphere began lighting their homes with first gas, then electric light, thus extending the hours that children are exposed to light, the signs of puberty began earlier. However, that change has been taking place over the last hundred years. Other factors, such as improved nutrition, may also have affected the age at which the first stage of puberty begins.

Menstruation

Help your daughter get ready for her first period by explaining to her exactly what will happen and making sure she has all the supplies she needs. Once her breasts begin to develop, her first period may still be one to four years away. The average age for girls to begin their periods is between ten and twelve-and-a-half.

Knowing what to expect helps your daughter accept her changing body.

What your daughter needs to know

She needs to know that her period may start during the day or at night, that it will usually start with a spotting of blood, but that it might start with a heavier flow, so that she won't be totally surprised when she first sees the reddish or brownish menstrual blood on her underwear.

Let her know also that it's common to experience some abdominal cramps before and during her period. She may have already felt them. Some girls have such cramps for several months before their first period actually begins. If the cramping really bothers her, she may want to discuss this with your family doctor. There are specific pain relievers, but she shouldn't get to rely on them. Encourage your daughter to eat a variety of nutritious foods. Dairy products (or calcium supplements, if she's lactose-intolerant) and other minerals found in a good, balanced diet may help.

Let her know that she may experience mood swings. Her feelings—both positive and negative—may be more intense than earlier in her life. She may cry or laugh more easily, or have more difficulty controlling her anger. She may find it harder to concentrate. Suggest that she record some of the emotional and physical experiences of her period so that she gets to know what to expect of her own body's menstrual cycle.

Buy her a variety of tampons and sanitary pads well before you expect that her period might start. Show her the instructions on how to attach sanitary pads or how to insert a tampon, and suggest that she experiment to find out which is most comfortable so that she knows what she's doing before her period starts. Suggest that she keep a couple of pads or tampons in her school bag or purse, and be sure she has supplies with her when she goes away overnight. Let her know that if she chooses tampons, she should usually replace one at least every four hours. Health Canada suggests that a girl not use a tampon overnight.

Let her know that her first periods may be irregular. She may have one period and then not have another one for a few months, or she may get them more frequently until her body adapts to the hormonal changes. Most girls' periods last about four days, but anything from two to eight days is considered normal at this age.

Feelings

Much has been written in recent years about girls in early adolescence. Because our society tends to value a very limited and mostly unattainable ideal of female attractiveness, the pubertal changes that turn girls into women can frighten some girls, and they may not welcome the changes at all. Others may find that their self-esteem is shaken, and they may be prone to depression, suicide, eating disorders, and addictions. Parents may find they need to help their daughters talk through their volatile emotions during this time so that they not only accept the inevitable changes of puberty, but also welcome and celebrate them.

A girl and her parents may all have mixed feelings about the beginning of her period. Your daughter will be curious and a little excited about this mysterious new level of physical maturity. At the same time, she may not be happy about the physical discomforts and inconveniences. She may feel irritated or even intensely embarrassed by the necessity of changing pads or tampons regularly and making sure she has everything she needs with her all the time. These feelings may increase if she's an early bloomer whose period starts at age nine, or just earlier than her friends. Let her know that you understand her feelings.

Your daughter will be a little excited about this mysterious new level of physical maturity.

A girl's reactions to her first period depend largely on what she learns about it beforehand and on the support she receives from family members. Mothers and fathers have mixed feelings as well. Your daughter's first period is an important rite of passage. You may feel sad that your child is no longer "a little girl." She likely will become more emotionally independent as well as physically mature. Some mothers find they have a strong emotional reaction to their daughter's first period. If as a mother you have had difficult menstrual periods yourself, you may worry that your daughter may experience the same discomfort. You should be aware that your own menses history is not necessarily a reliable predictor of your daughter's experiences.

Dads may also feel unsure of how to relate to their daughters. In some families, menstruation may be a taboo topic between the females and males. But daughters need to know at least that their fathers know about menses, and that they can help. If your daughter wants to tell her mother when her period starts, but Mom's not available, Dad needs to be prepared to support his daughter, even to go out and buy sanitary pads if she needs them. Even when Mom is available, Dad can acknowledge his daughter's first period. Or, as a family, you might decide to celebrate this rite of passage. Some cultural traditions mark the event with a special ceremony. But you could just make her favourite dinner or take her out to dinner. Respect her privacy, but at the same time, let her know in some way that you're happy for her at this significant stage in her growth and development.

Your daughter may share more with her friends than with her family. Respect her privacy.

Puberty in Boys

Puberty begins for boys as early as the age of eight or as late as age thirteen; it usually takes a boy four to six years to pass through all five stages of puberty development.

Stage One Internally, male hormones are beginning to flow. Outwardly, you may not notice any growth in height yet.

Stage Two Your son's body shape begins to change as new layers of muscle tissue and fat are formed. His physique starts to become that of a young man, rather than a child. Some boys may gain weight before they grow taller, which might cause them embarrassment. Let your child know that plumpness at this age is normal for lots of boys.

Another source of concern or embarrassment may be their breast development. Let your son know that men have mammary tissue, too, and that he can expect some swelling under his nipples. Some boys worry that they're growing breasts or that they have breast cancer. The areolae of their breasts will also darken and increase in size.

Pubic hair first appears at this stage. A boy's testicles and scrotum begin to grow, and they're the first to grow to full size—in about three years. His penis begins to grow later and takes about six years of puberty to reach full adult size. Let your son know about the time difference so that he doesn't worry that his penis will never grow.

Stage Three The penis begins growing, more in length than in width, during this stage. His pubic hair becomes thicker and coarser. His testicles and scrotum continue to develop. Sometimes one testicle grows faster than the other. Assure your son that the difference in growth is normal. Because his testicles begin to produce sperm and his prostate produces semen, your son will experience nocturnal emissions called "wet dreams," that is, the ejaculation of semen while asleep. Some boys may be frightened when they first encounter the wet, sticky fluid in their bed, or they may try to keep the news of their nocturnal emissions a secret. During this stage, too, your son will experience spontaneous erections more frequently, not all of them for sexual reasons. He will likely wake with an erection every morning, but often they happen at inconvenient or embarrassing times. Either his father or mother should talk with him and help him understand what his body is going through.

Some boys may begin to show a light sprinkling of facial hair on their upper lip. As his larynx enlarges, a boy's voice also begins to change. As his muscle tissue increases and his shoulders broaden, he becomes taller and stronger. He has his most significant growth in height during this stage.

Stage Four During Stage Four, a boy's penis begins to broaden, and his testicles and scrotum may continue to grow. Underarm and facial hair increase and a boy's skin might become more oily. His sweat glands will increase their production of sweat and may begin to produce body odour.

Stage Five Your son's testicles and penis will have grown to their full size. For most boys, physical growth in height slows, then stops, but for some it continues slightly. Some boys develop more body hair, and many begin shaving off facial hair now.

Feelings

Our society is kinder to boys during puberty, and most boys welcome the changes they're experiencing. They're happy to display bigger muscles, to show off their height and larger sex organs, if only in the locker room. Parents, too, are pleased to see their boys transform into young men and are less ambivalent toward changes in their sons than they are to the changes in their daughters. However, that doesn't mean parents do a better job of explaining puberty to their boys or of discussing the changes as they occur. Penis growth and wet dreams are much less discussed than breast growth and menstruation. Mothers tend to do most of the talking with kids about pubertal changes, but mothers don't have personal knowledge about how boys change at puberty. Just as fathers may feel awkward discussing menstruation with their daughters, some mothers find themselves uncomfortable talking about wet dreams with their sons. Both parents should find ways to let their son know how his body will change. He needs to know that he can ask either of you any of the questions that concern him. There are also several books for youngsters that describe the physical and emotional changes of puberty.

Sometimes sons don't get as much information about puberty as daughters do.

Boys who begin puberty later than their peers may find the experience very difficult. Assure your son that a late start has no bearing on how he will eventually develop. Also let him know that once he begins puberty, it may unfold more quickly; he may reach full size and maturity at about the same time as his friends, even though they started sooner. Late-maturing boys may develop a poor body image and develop negative self-esteem, since they are usually shorter than their peers.

While preparing your son for the physical changes of puberty, prepare him as well for the emotional changes. Boys have mood swings, too, although our society doesn't always acknowledge that. Let him know that he won't always feel such intense emotions. Find ways to show him that you care when he's feeling low. Most kids appreciate a back rub or a foot rub just for the physical contact—even when they won't let you kiss them goodbye anymore.

Talking about Sexuality

Talking about sexuality and letting your children know about sexual health can be daunting. You want to be sure that you give them the information that's appropriate for their age, and you want to let them know what your sexual values are at the same time as you explain the bodily "plumbing." Many parents find it embarrassing to talk about penises and vaginas with eight-year-olds, although the kids may not feel any embarrassment until they sense yours.

You're the Best Person to Tell

Most kids are very curious about sexual differences, and they share whatever information they acquire with their friends, but the information is often less than accurate. You can be sure that your child has the right information only if you, yourself, explain the facts. Don't count on the school to teach your child everything he needs to know. Sexual education classes are not mandatory in many Canadian schools. Although some teachers handle the topic thoroughly in their health classes, others' classes are less than comprehensive.

When you talk about sexuality with your child, you also impart your own values. If you believe that sexual intercourse is appropriate only within marriage, you can say so. Some parents worry that by telling young children about their body's physical changes and about sexual intercourse, they may encourage them to experiment at an earlier age. But you can't prevent your child from getting information about sexuality—they'll get bits and pieces from television programs and movies, from the stories and confidences of other kids, from advertising. You need to balance the media messages that bombard them, and you need to provide specific, accurate information along with your own messages about sexuality and sexual health: "Every human being is a sexual being." "Children need to know and understand how human bodies work and how our emotions affect how our body works." "Sexual intercourse with a partner is great, but it's for grownups."

You can be sure that your child has the right information only if you, yourself, explain the facts.

Young children who understand how their bodies work, what the proper names are for their various body parts, and what is appropriate sexual activity are less likely to become the victims of sexual abusers; these manipulative people tend to seek out poorly informed children who are less likely to tell their parents or other adults.

You probably had your first conversations about sexuality with your child before the age of six. Meg Hickling, a registered nurse and a sexual health educator in Vancouver, British Columbia, is the author of *Speaking of Sex: Are You Ready to Answer the Questions Your Kids Will Ask?* (Northstone Publishing Inc., 1996). She has been talking to parents and kids for more than twenty years about what kids need to know about sex and how parents should explain sex to their kids. Here are Meg Hickling's lists.

By the time they are six, children should know:

- the names of their own genitals and those of the other sex.
- that a baby grows in the woman's uterus.
- that a baby is born through the woman's vagina.
- that a baby is created when a man's sperm joins a woman's ovum through sexual intercourse.
- that sexual intercourse between a man and a woman can create a baby.
- that adults have sexual intercourse even when they don't want to create a baby, because adults who love each other also enjoy sexual intercourse. Children don't have sexual intercourse, though (which will relieve your child).
- something about menstruation.
- something about wet dreams.
- what condoms are, and that children shouldn't pick them up.

Between ages six and eight, your child needs to know:

- everything a preschooler knows, plus:
- that the digestive system is separate from the reproductive system.
- that women have menstrual periods because their bodies are practising for when they will have a baby.
- that boys have nocturnal emissions because their bodies are practising for when they will make a baby.
- that both boys and girls change in different ways when they reach puberty. Girls grow breasts and start periods. Boys grow bigger penises and have wet dreams.

Between ages nine and twelve, your child needs to know:

- everything the previous age group has learned, plus:
- detailed information about puberty changes.
- basic information about sexually transmitted diseases (STDs).
- that becoming a teenager doesn't mean having to become sexually active.

- that there are many reasons for having sexual relations, including bad reasons like peer pressure and other reasons that involve force (rape), money, alcohol, or drugs.
- that whoever says No must rule a sexual situation.
- that real women's and men's bodies are very different from the media versions of perfect bodies.

Masturbation

Some parents are uncomfortable dealing with the knowledge that their children may be engaging in acts of sexual self-satisfaction. But we're all sexual beings, and humans, right from babyhood, express their sexuality by touching themselves and fondling their own genitals, which is perfectly natural.

Sometimes parents worry about their kids masturbating because they learned as children that masturbation was "bad" and that it could cause them emotional and physical harm. Or they may think that a child who masturbates is oversexed, promiscuous, or sexually deviant. Even if you, as an adult, no longer share those views, you may still feel uneasy. Those parents whose religions consider masturbation to be morally wrong should teach their children their views in an open and nonjudgmental way.

By the time kids are at school, they're usually aware that masturbation should be a private activity. You may have already explained to your child that masturbation is something he can do when he's in his bedroom or alone in the bathroom. Tell him that it's simply not acceptable to touch his genitals in public. It's as gross as picking his nose when he's on the bus. Children who don't understand that masturbation is a personal and private act are more likely to become victims of sexual abusers. A child who is not aware that he shouldn't play with his genitals while in the family room watching TV could provide an opening for a sexual approach from a baby sitter or a relative.

SEE PAGE 36

You probably won't need to introduce the subject of masturbation. It may come up naturally in conversation with your child, who may hear a reference to masturbation in the school yard or while watching a television program. Take the opportunity to discuss it with her then. Or if you discover your child masturbating in an inappropriate place, don't get angry. Explain that you know it feels good, but that the activity is only acceptable in private. Remember that, just as with teaching good manners, you may find yourself repeating this dozens of times. One mention may not do it, so don't lose patience.

If your child wants to know why touching herself feels so good, explain that some parts of our bodies give us good feelings. You don't have to talk about erogenous zones or explain that these feelings can be sexual if you don't think your child is ready for these explanations or interested in the information, says Meg Hickling. Most young kids don't yet care.

Personal Care

A six-year-old may be losing interest in the bathtime rituals that she loved as a preschooler. Some children demand complete control over bathing their bodies at this time. By age eight, she's even more independent. But don't expect her to be thorough about washing her own ears, neck, and back.

Some kids this age are perfectly competent at shampooing their own hair, but many still require help rinsing thoroughly. Some kids have sensitive scalps, and they don't enjoy hair washing or brushing. A short haircut might be the solution.

By age nine, kids can generally look after their own baths, but the bathing may be more effective with supervision. Once in the tub, they're more likely to get down to the business of washing and less likely to play than they were a year ago.

About age ten, your child may have to be coaxed into the bathtub. Baths aren't fun anymore, and he doesn't want to take the time. You may need to set up a bathing schedule with a reward system to ensure that he's reasonably clean. Or by this time, some kids switch to showers, again to speed up the cleaning process. This distaste for baths may lessen by age eleven, but some kids show a general aversion to personal hygiene during puberty.

Unfortunately, this aversion coincides with their increasing sweat gland and oil gland production. Parents may find themselves complaining about body odour and greasy hair to no avail. Let your child know that while it's important to use deodorant, deodorant doesn't replace bathing as a

The ABCs of Hand Washing

Teach your children to wash their hands for as long as it takes them to sing the ABCS. After scrubbing with soap, they should rinse off with warm water, and dry with a clean towel. Washing their hands regularly is the best way for your kids to avoid picking up and transmitting cold and flu infections. Most kids, even up to the age of twelve, need to be reminded to wash up. Set a good example by washing your own hands:

- after using the toilet.
- after handling pets or other animals.
- after coming in the house from outside.
- before handling food.
- after preparing raw meat, especially poultry, for cooking.
- before eating food.
- after coughing or sneezing into a tissue.

way of eliminating body odour. You shouldn't have to sit at the dinner table beside someone who smells. Be firm about your own limits of tolerance. Then let nature take its course. Very soon your child will love the shower again and you'll be watching your water bills climb.

Let your child set the rules for how much privacy she needs.

The Bare Facts

Deciding how much family nudity everyone is comfortable with can be tricky. You may have felt quite at ease showering with your toddler but are unsure about what's appropriate with your six-year-old. Follow the rule that either of you can set new boundaries.

If your child says she no longer wants to bathe with a sibling or a parent, or wants to change in private, then honour her decision without any teasing or jokes. Most children won't say in words that they want more privacy. But sometime around the age of eight, they may show signs. They may squirm uncomfortably at a kissing scene on TV or insist on wearing underpants under their pyjamas.

If, as a parent, you want to change an established pattern of nudity, then say so gently, using age-appropriate language. For example, if your child is used to crawling into the tub with you and you would prefer that she no longer did, say that you'd rather cuddle on the couch when you're dried and dressed. This way, you acknowledge her desire to be close to you and at the same time teach her that it's OK to set personal boundaries.

Acne

Explain that washing one's hair and face regularly can sometimes reduce acne breakouts. But acne is often a result of hormonal changes, and some soaps can even aggravate the condition. Sometimes acne occurs early in the pubertal stages, and parents assume it will disappear. But kids are often very upset by it, so take your child to your family doctor to discuss it. The doctor may refer you to a dermatologist.

To Shave or Not to Shave?

Boys are unlikely to have to shave off facial hair before they reach their teens. But some girls decide as early as age eight that they want to shave off the hair on their legs. Shaving doesn't make the hair grow back any darker or coarser, contrary to conventional wisdom, so let her give it a try. You might want her to use a cordless razor for safety's sake rather than a regular razor with blades. She'll probably shave once or twice, then lose interest until she's in her teens.

Solo Health Care

Children are ready to take charge of their own health care when they're mature enough to ask questions of all health-care providers and to comprehend and deal in a responsible fashion with the information provided. In order to build a trusting relationship with a child, the doctor will usually make a point to mention that their discussions will remain confidential. In most Canadian provinces, minors as young as twelve can choose not to have their parents accompany them either when they go to their doctor or when they go into the doctor's examining room. They may also consent to a treatment if doctors believe them capable of understanding the implications of the treatment. In Quebec, it's fourteen years and older, and parents have to be informed if the youth is admitted to hospital for more than twelve hours.

At the Children's & Women's Health Centre of British Columbia in Vancouver, health-care professionals say that children aged twelve and older are capable of deciding whether they want to pursue a recommended treatment. This policy grew out of the efforts of health professionals to deal with STDs. If the matter is debatable, the case may go to the Ethics Committee.

Parents should have begun talking with their children at an early age about all aspects of bodily health so that nothing develops into a taboo subject between them. Single parents need to inform themselves about the health concerns of their opposite-sex child. Most kids want to talk to their parents about personal health issues that concern them–they just don't want to get a lecture.

When it seems to you that your child is mature enough to handle a visit to the family doctor on her own, discuss with her whether she would like you to accompany her or to remain in the waiting room. Let her know that you respect her privacy, and that you'll understand if she wants her discussion with the doctor to be private. You may still talk separately with the doctor about your own concerns after the examination.

Dental Habits

A child's permanent teeth start coming in between the ages of five-and-a-half and seven. The first to appear are the molars, which grow at the back of the mouth where there are no baby teeth. As the roots of your child's baby teeth dissolve, they will loosen and fall out easily with little or no bleeding. Parents can wiggle the loose teeth but should not force them out. On occasion, a baby tooth must be removed by a dentist to make way for a permanent tooth. By the time your child is twelve, he should have lost all of his baby teeth and have acquired most of his permanent teeth, except for the third molars, or wisdom teeth.

Six-Year-Olds

By about age six, your child may be able to brush her own teeth. However, she may not brush far enough back in the mouth to clean the new six-year molars. Check periodically to make sure they're getting proper attention. You may want to try plaque-disclosing tablets (GUM Red-Cote by Butler). The nighttime brushing is the most critical. When your child is asleep, the saliva that helps keep his mouth clean during the day isn't nearly so active.

This is a good age to introduce your child to dental floss, but it may take her a while to become proficient at using it. Help her out until she can floss by herself. Most kids need to be regularly reminded to brush their teeth. Left to their own devices, kids of this age may develop dental caries and bad breath as a result of poor dental hygiene. Remind your child to brush after sugary snacks, after meals, and before bed. You might also want to keep a supply of celery and carrots in the fridge as a shortcut to cleansing the mouth. Most kids are more likely to grab a celery stick than to brush their teeth after a snack.

Twelve-Year-Olds

By age eleven or twelve, most children take responsibility for their own brushing and flossing. Some kids this age actually express pride in caring for their teeth. Children should have dental checkups every six months that include examination and cleaning, fluoride treatments and application of molar tooth sealants to prevent decay. Many parents are not yet aware of dental sealants and their benefits. A dental sealant is a thin plastic resin that is painted onto molars and premolars. It prevents decay-causing bacteria from getting trapped in the pits and fissures on a tooth's surface. The ideal time to have a dental sealant applied to your children's teeth is the period when their permanent teeth have just grown through their gums and are more susceptible to decay. Dental sealants are far less expensive than treating a cavity, are safe and painless for your child, and last for years.

Periodic X-rays will be recommended, as necessary, by their dentist. Even with this regular dental care, children do get caries anyway. Around age eleven or twelve, your child might require orthodontic work to correct misaligned teeth. Sometimes these straighten out as the jaw grows and the remainder of the teeth come in.

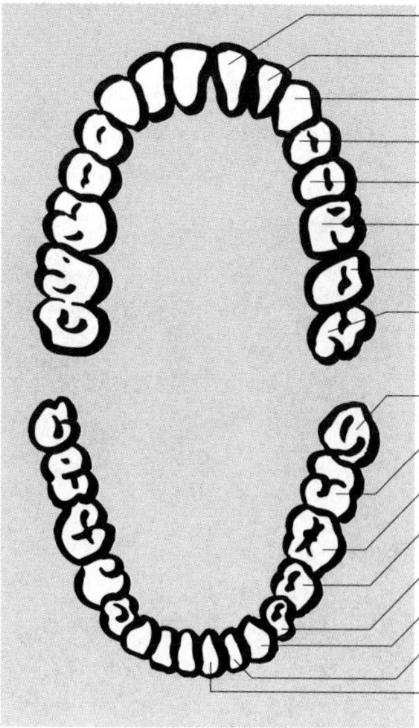

Permanent Teeth

	When teeth come in (years)
Upper	
Central incisors	7-8
Lateral incisors	8-9
Canine (cuspids)	11-12
First bicuspids	10-11
Second bicuspids	10-12
First molars	6-7
Second molars	12-13
Third molars	17-21
Lower	
Third molars	17-21
Second molars	11-13
First molars	6-7
Second bicuspids	11-12
First bicuspids	10-12
Canines (cuspids)	9-10
Lateral incisors	7-8
Central incisors	6-7

The Orthodontic Years

Jaws that shift or make sounds, poorly aligned or crowded teeth, finger sucking, mouth breathing, or difficulty chewing are just some of the indicators that your child needs an orthodontic examination. Orthodontics correct a number of dental and facial irregularities such as crooked or crowded teeth or protruding "buck" teeth.

Although orthodontic treatment is usually linked with adolescence, a child with these problems should first visit the orthodontist between the ages of seven and eleven. An early examination allows the orthodontist to determine how best to treat your child in order to minimize the length and the cost of the treatment. Depending on the severity of your child's problem, payment for a prolonged treatment can usually be handled by an initial down payment and monthly installments.

During treatment, you and your child and the orthodontist must work together as a team to ensure success. Dental care takes more time and effort when your child is wearing braces, but meticulous cleaning helps prevent swollen gums, cavities, and bad breath. Ensure that your child does a thorough cleaning at least once a day, perhaps best at bedtime. She should brush vigorously until every trace of food and plaque disappears from her teeth and braces. To finish, you might try plaque-disclosing tablets to see how well she has reached the plaque along the gum line. It's also important to rinse after brushing.

The orthodontist's aide or hygienist will show your child various cleaning techniques and may recommend special tools such as a floss threader or an interproximal brush to make cleaning between braces easier. Get your child into the habit of brushing, or at least rinsing, after every meal. Limit the sweets your child consumes, and completely eliminate sticky candy, caramels, and bubble gum.

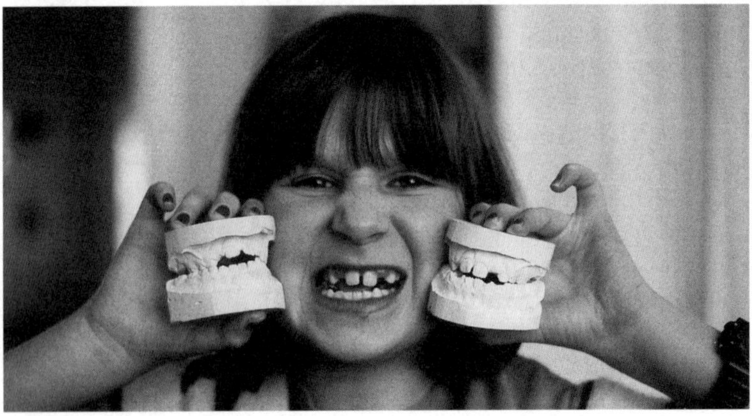

Safety

With every new stage of your child's development comes another question about safety. Is he ready to play in the back yard by himself? Is he ready to walk to school? Then, before you know it, you'll be saying Yes to his taking a bus ride to the mall. Teaching your child safety guidelines as he becomes more independent involves teaching him to evaluate risks and to avoid danger. You can't set out rules for every situation, although it's important to have general guidelines that will be helpful to your children in many different situations. You might role-play situations with them, asking what they think would be a safe course of action. Talk about the possibilities and guide them toward the action that they should follow. You want your children to eventually learn to evaluate risks on their own.

Deciding when your child is ready for more responsibility, which usually brings with it more risk, requires a balancing act. The fact that your child is eager to try something, such as riding his bike to school, doesn't necessarily mean that he has the ability and judgment to do it. Age is only one indicator of a child's readiness. Ask yourself whether your child could handle the unexpected as well as the expected in a new situation. Ask him "What if?" questions. "What if you fell off your bike and you needed help? Whom would you ask?" Role-play and practise variations on the possibilities before you let him go out on his own.

SEE PAGE 144

Check out your child's play areas and hangouts for yourself.

Rather than tell your child "Don't ever touch matches," encourage your child to be watchful for potential dangers and to tell one of you about them. Tell your child to come and get you if she finds a dangerous object or situation. When you've dealt with the problem, praise her or reward her, too, depending on the situation. You don't want her to think that a reward is the only reason to be watchful.

As your school-age child explores a wider and wider world, explore the same world yourself. Walk with her along the routes she takes to her school or to visit her friends. Ask for a tour of their hideout in the park. Meet the owner of the convenience store where she stops some days for a treat after school. The more you know about her world, the more you'll be able to help her negotiate it safely, and to know when to loosen your grip.

Safety Every Day

Here are some guidelines to discuss with your child.

- Stay away from public spaces, such as parks and school yards, when there are no other people around. You may have lots of room to practise biking skills, but you're also isolated.
- Don't visit parks at night or use deserted laneways as shortcuts.
- Identify neighbourhood Block Parent homes.
- When in an elevator, stand beside the control panel in case of an emergency.
- Appreciate the power of the voice. If someone grabs him, he should scream at the top of his lungs ("Help!" "Kidnap!"). Tell him that if he can't attract help by yelling, he should spin around as fast as he can, which makes it hard for someone to hold onto him. If he can break free, he should run as fast as he can.
- Even a small child should learn to recite back to you her full name and its spelling, telephone number, and address. It's also important to teach your children your own full names, phone numbers at work sites, and the names of the places where you work.
- Children should learn to listen to their own internal radar. If a voice inside tells them that something or someone isn't right, it's probably correct.
- Never hitchhike, and never accept a ride with strangers.
- When lost or in trouble, contact an appropriate adult. A mom with young kids is a good choice.
- Children should be wary of an adult who asks them for help, even if it's just the time or directions.
- Bypass T-shirts with personal names on them. They could provide the lure for an abductor, who would use the name to secure the child's trust.
- Never reveal to anyone who calls on the phone or comes to the door that you're alone at home, even if that's the case. Parents should role-play these situations to help their children develop some standard replies to use so that their inability to lie doesn't reveal more than they realize.
- If a school bully or other attacker threatens you and demands your money or other possessions, hand them over. When you've escaped harm, tell your teacher or a parent.
- Always tell your parents where you're going.
- Turn down job offers, rides, or gifts from any strangers.
- SEE PAGE 21 Distinguish between appropriate and inappropriate touching, and understand that no one has a right to touch you in a way that makes you uncomfortable. If someone does, tell an adult you trust.

- Refuse invitations to visit someone else's house, or refuse to invite someone into your own house without first getting parental permission.

For parents

- Guard against developing a false sense of security. Remember, children are always changing and developing.
- Keep an up-to-date photo of your children around, preferably one that is full-face, simple, and clear.
- Record changes in your child's height, weight, and hair colouring each year, perhaps when you take him in for a yearly physical examination.
- Know your children's friends and their parents and their addresses, and acquaint yourselves with their hangouts.
- Expect the unexpected. Don't be the parents who express surprise when their child who "has never done that before" has an accident.
- Understand the basics of first aid. Research shows that if people get trained in first aid, their risk of injury goes down 30 per cent over the next five years.

Traffic and Outdoor Safety

By teaching your child pedestrian safety, you help her deal with the main danger in her life. Motor vehicle accidents are the Number One cause of injury and death for children. Those in the age group between five and nine are more likely to die as pedestrians than as passengers in a vehicle. It's the responsibility of parents to teach kids how to negotiate traffic safely. Practise with your child until she knows these traffic safety rules:

- Learn and obey all signs and traffic or pedestrian signals.
- Don't walk from between parked cars to cross the street; go to the pedestrian crossing.
- Look in all directions, even at the pedestrian crossing, before you cross the street.
- Walk—don't run—when you cross the street or any road.
- When you have to walk where there's no sidewalk, walk on the left side of the road, facing toward the oncoming traffic.
- Don't play games in the street; play in a safer place away from the traffic.

When you pick outdoor clothes for your child, remember that pedestrians with retro-reflective gear are visible to motorists at a much greater distance. Remind her that a cassette/radio with headphones can be distracting and prevent her from hearing any warning horn signals from drivers.

Car safety

To protect youngsters from the danger of the sudden inflation of an air bag, Transport Canada recommends that children under twelve not ride in the front seat of vehicles equipped with air bags. Since neither you nor your child will always know whether the car you're riding in has air bags, make "kids in the back seat" the family rule for all vehicles.

Car Trip Safety

- Teach your children to adjust and fasten their seat belts before the driver starts the engine. If they undo their seat belts while you're driving, pull over and stop.
- Avoid letting your child eat in the car. Hard candies, peanuts, grapes, or any food that might cause a child to choke are particularly dangerous if there's no adult other than the driver to deal with the situation immediately.
- Never leave a child alone in the car, even if you lock it.
- Don't show a child how to start the car or to work the controls. Do show him how to honk the horn and explain when it's appropriate to use it.
- Keep all car doors locked at all times while you're travelling in the car.
- Teach your child to get out of a car on the side away from the traffic, when possible.

Bicycle safety

Teach your kids that bicycles are not toys, they are road vehicles, and bike riders must follow the same traffic rules as car drivers.

- Obey all signs and traffic lights.
- Learn how to make the hand and arm signals for turning and stopping, and use them regularly.
- Ride single file behind any cars in your lane and with the flow of the traffic; stay at least a car door's length away from the cars parked at the side of the road.
- Avoid riding your bike on streets that have heavy traffic. If you have to use one, be aware of the blind spots that car and truck drivers might have for a cyclist. Parents might put their child in the driver's seat of their own car to demonstrate what a blind spot is and how dangerous it would be when the vehicles are in motion.
- Keep off the sidewalks.
- The best routes for kids on bikes are the bike trails through parks or for distance sport riding.

- Make sure your children's bikes have the proper safety equipment, including a headlight and reflectors for biking at night.
- Cyclists should always wear a CSA-approved helmet. Let your child select his own headgear—he's more likely to wear one if he has chosen it. Three-quarters of cycling fatalities involve head injuries; 85 per cent of all cycling injuries could have been prevented if the riders had been wearing helmets. Since kids learn by example, wear your own helmet when you go biking with your kids.

Look over your child's playground equipment. Not all of it is safe.

In-line skating and skateboarding

If you think your child is ready for either a skateboard or in-line skates, be sure that you also purchase all the necessary protective gear. These skaters should protect their heads with helmets, their knees and elbows with protective pads, and their wrists with wrist guards. Wrist injuries are the most common of all the injuries that skaters face. Wearing the wrist guards, your child will be ten times less likely to break his wrist in a fall.

Playgrounds

Because playgrounds are designed for kids and are often on public property, parents expect that their children will be safe in them. But not all playgrounds are safe, not all the equipment is kept in safe condition, and not all kids play safely on the equipment or in the playground. Most often, injuries occur because kids use the equipment in ways no one expected it to be used. Few playgrounds have supervision, so parents have to monitor their children's playground activities until they reach an age for independent play with other children. If your child doesn't use the equipment properly, it may be because he's bored with it and it's time for him to move on to other sports or activities. Here's what kids should know about playing in playgrounds.

- Always slide, hang, or jump feet first.
- Use the equipment one person at a time, and move away when you've finished your turn.
- Don't climb onto the roof of a covered slide.
- Use only the equipment that you're big enough to reach.

Make "feet first" the rule when sliding, hanging, or jumping.

- Don't stand on swings, don't climb on the supports, don't ride double, and don't jump off in mid-swing. Don't walk in front of or behind someone who is swinging.
- Remove your bike helmet when you play on equipment.
- Remove scarves and mittens on cords, any outer clothing with drawstrings, hoods, or any features that could easily get caught in the mechanisms of playground equipment and cause strangulation.

Before you allow your child to use a playground or a particular piece of equipment, look it over and even give it a shake to make sure the equipment is in good repair. Look for sharp points and edges or any loose pieces or protrusions that could catch on clothes and pinch little fingers. If repairs are needed, call the park management or agency responsible for keeping the equipment in good repair.

If necessary, get together with other parents to clear the area of debris and branches, to make sure the apparatus is well spaced and safe for use by several children. Ensure kids leave their bikes and toys at a safe distance from the playground equipment. Above all, make sure that your child is strong enough and agile enough to climb on the apparatus he chooses. Falls from equipment account for 59 per cent of all playground injuries.

Apply all the guidelines for protection from the sun when your children will be outside for any length of time in a playground. Children should be protected from the sun's direct rays by wearing a cap or hat and having a long-sleeved shirt available. They should apply a sunscreen with SPF15 or higher, and frequently reapply it as long as they stay outside.

Home Pool Safety

Half of all the deaths by drowning that occur in Canada take place in home pools. If you have a backyard pool, it's your responsibility to keep everyone who uses it safe. Here's what to remember.

- The fence around the pool must meet your municipality's bylaws. Usually, the fence must be at least 1.5 m (5 ft.) high and go around all four sides, including the side that leads to the deck or patio doors.
- Keep furniture away from the fence so that kids can't use the furniture to climb over the fence.
- Put two locks on the gate, a day lock and a heavy-duty night lock.
- Install night lighting.
- Have a phone available beside the pool.
- Be very careful about the toys you let children bring to the pool. If a toy rolls into the water, children might reach for it and fall into the water.
- Store pool chemicals under lock and key.
- Write out pool rules to reduce the risks of injury or drowning. Post them and teach your child and visiting friends to follow them. Let them know that banishment is the punishment for not following the rules!

Pool Rules

- No running.
- No pushing.
- No jumping in at the deep end.
- No jumping on another swimmer.
- No swimming without an adult.

Swimming classes are a good idea for any children who haven't yet learned to swim. If you're planning a children's pool party, hire a qualified lifeguard. There may also be a teenager in your neighbourhood who has her lifeguard certification. But when you're away from home, it may not be wise to let a teenage baby sitter supervise the kids in the pool. It's a huge responsibility.

SEE PAGE 4

Fire Safety

Every year in Canada about 1,300 fires are started by children. These fires result in an average of 20 deaths and 150 burn injuries. Kids need to know that matches and lighters are not toys. Instruct your children to let you know when they find either matches or lighters. Set a good example. Don't ever let your children see you horsing around with fire or candles and matches, with lighters or lighter fluid, with barbecue equipment or any other flammable materials.

Be sure to have smoke detectors and a carbon monoxide detector installed on each floor, especially near the sleeping areas. Replace the batteries regularly—using the same schedule for changing clocks at the beginning and end of Daylight Saving Time is a good idea. Have a family plan for escaping from a home fire, and practise it as a family at regular intervals, even making the alarm ring so kids know what it sounds like. The escape plan should have two routes for getting off each floor, and should identify a place for everyone to meet when they get out. Everyone should know to call 911, but the kids should know that this is primarily the responsibility of the adults in the family. Teach kids:

- to call out to or awaken the rest of the family if they're the first to notice the fire or hear the alarm.
- to never hide in a closet or in another room.
- to get out of the house as fast as possible.
- to call 911 and give their address as soon as they are outside.
- to never try going through the flames.
- to get down on the ground if they see smoke, and crawl under the smoke.
- to cover their nose and mouth with a wet facecloth, if there's time to get one.
- to drop to the ground outside if their clothes have caught fire, and roll over and over to smother the flames.
- to not go back inside to save pets, video games, or any other valuables.
- to learn how to use a home fire extinguisher for small fires.
- to learn that putting a lid on a burning pot or pan will help to smother a small fire.

Safety from Sexual Abuse

Studies show that the person most likely to abuse a child sexually is a family member, a close family friend, or someone with authority over the child. How can you protect your child? First of all, monitor your world and the people in it. We ask kids to trust their intuition; parents should do the same. If a situation doesn't feel right, then it probably isn't. Err on the side of caution when you give other adults access to your child, even if they are adults you have trusted up to now.

Talk to your child about what's appropriate touching and what's inappropriate. However, don't make him feel that he's totally responsible for his own safety. Saying "If anyone touches you, tell them No" isn't always helpful. Any child in an abusive situation is not free to say No. He's too frightened and alone. Let your child know that he can come to you with any concern about his body, about someone touching him in a way that doesn't feel right, or about any sexual question and that you will not be angry with him. He needs to know that there are no taboo subjects in your family so that he'll feel safe enough to confide in you if anyone tries to involve him in sexual acts.

SEE PAGE 21

Sleep Needs

By the time children are five or six years of age, most of the sleep problems of early childhood have all but vanished. Unfortunately, it's often more difficult to get them into bed at a decent hour. Your child may not complain if she doesn't get a good night's sleep, but you will—when your child stays up late, you're up late, too, and you lose your private time.

When parents aren't consistent about bedtime, kids stay up as long as they can. They don't yet recognize how important sleep is to their well-being, so parents have to take responsibility for ensuring that their children get adequate sleep. Be firm. Resist entreaties for "one more show." Avoid rewarding your child with a later bedtime as a special treat.

Sleep is vital to your child's good health and ability to learn. A child who gets adequate sleep is more alert, better able to learn, less accident-prone, and more cheerful. After the initial drowsy period, the normal sleep pattern alternates between two states: deep, or delta-wave, sleep, and rapid-eye-movement (REM) sleep. During the night, REM sleep periods (during which we dream) follow the non-REM periods, occur from three to six times, and range from five to twenty minutes in length. Inadequate sleep of both types can be detrimental to the immune system and make a child more susceptible to colds and disease.

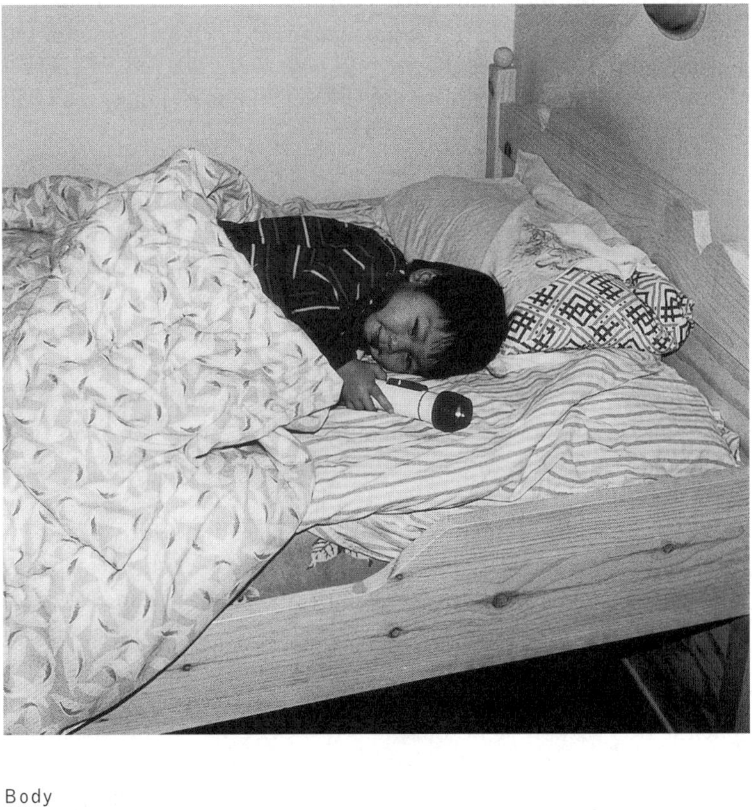

Is there a book hiding under that comforter?

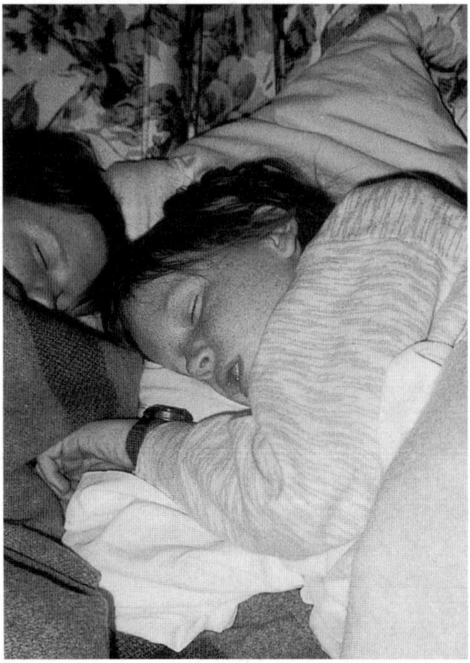

Why do kids resist going to sleep? One reason may be that, alone in the dark, children confront their fears. To push this confrontation away, kids choose bedtime to pick a major battle with a sibling. Or they stall by requesting glasses of water. They ask you to check the closet for monsters and under the bed for goblins, when really it's their inner fears they want you to keep in check.

Bedtime may seem like the right time to sit by your child in bed to discuss his concerns, but your child is usually too tired to solve problems. A child may choose to mention at bedtime an important issue that has been troubling him, just because that's when he remembers it and it frightens him. Your appearance at his side to say good night may be the first time he's had you to himself. You might choose to talk with him for a bit to resolve the problem. But if you let bedtime discussions about problems become part of your child's evening routine, you could be establishing a habit. Make sure you spend time with your child during the day to discuss anything that might worry him.

Your kids need their sleep, although they often don't agree at bedtime.

For a younger child, limit the bedtime routine to a bath, a story, and a goodnight kiss. An older child may choose to read in bed for another 15 minutes. The whole bedtime routine should last no longer than half an hour. Then lights out.

Six-year-olds need about 11 hours of sleep, which will decrease to 9 or 10 hours by the time they turn twelve. However, as with adults, children's individual sleep needs vary. Watch your child first thing in the morning. You'll know he's getting enough sleep if he awakes feeling refreshed. If he's hard to wake in the morning, or if he's nodding into his cereal bowl at the breakfast table, he isn't getting enough sleep.

During the day, your child may not act sleepy even if he is. Some overtired children appear hyperactive or "wired." Chronically tired kids can be impulsive, with emotions swinging from one extreme to another. If your child is overtired, move his bedtime back about 15 minutes every few nights until he begins to wake up feeling refreshed.

This can be difficult to accomplish, however. Kids associate a late bedtime with your acknowledgment of their maturity. At school, they may even brag about being able to stay up until 9:30 p.m. But remember, you set the time for lights out. Stand firm through the tears, but be willing to accommodate your child's concerns. If an earlier bedtime means that your child will miss a favourite TV program, offer to tape it so that he can watch it after school the next day.

The irritability that can come after a late night is easily cured by an earlier bedtime the next evening. The extra sleep doesn't have to equal the time lost. It can be less, but strive to pay down the sleep debt as soon as possible. Once your child starts having sleepovers, let her know that she needs to make up for a late night with more sleep the next night.

Sleep Problems

Anticipate sleep problems at times of change—before your child goes away to camp, after the birth of a new sibling, when a parent falls ill. Another time your child may experience sleep disturbances is when he's overtired. You might expect an exhausted child to sleep like a log, but exhaustion can contribute to a propensity to sleepwalk or experience a night terror.

"Once I dreamt that a girl in my class got pregnant—that was weird. In another dream, I dreamt that my dad died, and I woke up crying. Another time I dreamt that a witch flooded everyone's house. But usually I have good dreams."

EMMA, AGE 12

If your child's sleep difficulties are frequent or intense, discuss them with his physician. For information on sleep problems, consult Sleep/Wake Disorders Canada. SEE PAGE 231

Bedwetting

Bedwetting can be a tough problem for school-age kids. The Canadian Sleep Society reports that 1 in 10 six-year-olds and 1 in 20 ten-year-olds has problems staying dry consistently at night. For the older child, bedwetting is a threat to self-esteem. The erroneous expectation is that big kids don't wet the bed. But when they're invited to sleepovers or their group attends an overnight camp, these older kids can't hide their "little secret." Most often, bedwetting is caused by a developmental lag. The part of the nervous system controlling your child's bladder may be slow to mature. Over time, as the nervous system matures, the problem simply disappears.

If an older child suddenly starts to wet the bed, it may be because of a urinary-tract infection. Check it out with your family doctor, because generalized anxiety can also cause bedwetting. SEE PAGE 206

Nightmares

All children have occasional nightmares, but frequent nightmares are uncommon between ages seven and eleven. Nightmares usually reflect emotional conflicts and struggles. If your child is having frequent nightmares, work with him during the day to solve his problems.

Virtually all dreaming occurs during REM sleep. While you're dreaming, you don't call out. A child's crying and calling out occur after a bad dream when the child is awake. Attend to her quickly. She needs your full assurance because she is genuinely frightened. Be supportive in a firm way that shows that you, not the monster in her nightmare, are in control.

Night terrors

It's 10:00 p.m. and your child has been asleep since 8 o'clock. Suddenly her scream pierces the night. That's a night terror, experienced as the child partially awakens from a deep sleep cycle. Don't be alarmed; night terrors are very common in children. The Canadian Sleep Society reports that night terrors peak between the ages of four and twelve. Extreme fatigue or sleep deprivation can contribute to their occurrence.

Night terrors usually occur one to four hours after falling asleep. Your child may sit up, grind her teeth, and open her eyes, seeming to look through you rather than at you. After a few minutes, she'll lie back down and go back to a full sleep.

Or your child may screech, appear frightened, run around the room, or frantically try to leave the house. Usually you can't wake the child, and you shouldn't try, since it will only further aggravate her. Gently guide her back to bed. In the morning she won't remember a thing.

Sleepwalking

The most important thing you can do for a sleepwalking child is to prevent her from injuring herself. Although sleepwalkers are remarkably deft, they are clumsier than when awake. Keep doors and windows closed and locked. Consider a gate for across the stairway. The Canadian Sleep Society recommends attaching a bell to the child's door to alert you to nocturnal wanderings.

During sleepwalking, your child partly wakes from deep sleep, usually within three hours of falling asleep. If you talk to your child, she usually won't answer. If she does, her speech may be garbled. As she roams, she may perform purposeful tasks, such as eating, brushing her teeth, or looking for a book. Neither awake or fully asleep, she's confused and may urinate in a different place. Simply guide her back to bed. In the morning, she'll have no memory of the experience. Don't ask her about it. It will only embarrass her. Most children who sleepwalk don't have emotional problems. Your child will outgrow sleepwalking, usually by age fifteen.

Daily Nutritional Requirements

Children list eating among their favourite activities. They usually choose foods based on their immediate desires and what they think tastes good. But left to their own devices, kids do not stop to consider whether a food is good for their health. If your child follows what TV commercials and friends tell him to eat, then his diet may not be what you would prefer. By following Canada's Food Guide to Healthy Eating, you know what your child needs to eat to grow healthy and strong. And kids do say that their parents are the most important influence on their developing healthy eating habits.

Your child, however, is the best judge of how much she can eat. Like adults, children have built-in cues—thirst, hunger, and feeling full—to help them decide what and when to eat. If your child feels full after one piece of pizza, that may be all she needs at that time. If your child is growing well, she's probably getting enough food throughout the day's meals and snacks.

Children list eating as one of their favourite activities.

Health, growth, and activity all influence appetite, so expect your child's hunger to vary from day to day, and from month to month. During their individual growth spurts, children are hungrier and eat more. As they grow taller, they may become skinnier even though they're eating more. Or they may put on weight first, then grow an inch or three in a short space of time.

The Food Guide suggests a range of servings from each food group. Girls between ages seven and nine tend to eat the lower to middle number of servings. Girls ten to twelve and boys seven to twelve are likely to eat the largest number of servings. You may wonder how your child has room to eat the suggested 5 to 12 servings of grain products a day. But one serving size isn't large; 125 mL (½ cup) of spaghetti, half a bagel or a hamburger bun each count as one serving of grain products. The recommended 5 to 10 servings of vegetables and fruit may also seem a lot. But a 250-mL (1-cup) juice box is an easy way to score two servings.

The 1998 Heart and Stroke Report Card on the Health of Canada's Kids, which surveyed over four hundred families coast to coast, gave six- to twelve-year-olds a failing grade on their consumption of fruits and vegetables. The survey found that only 20 per cent of Canadian children eat the recommended daily minimum of 5 servings. Fruit drinks, punches, cocktails, and beverages are little more than expensive sweetened water, containing no fruit juice at all.

Canada's Food Guide to Healthy Eating

Enjoy a variety of foods from each group every day. Choose lower-fat foods more often.

	Daily Servings	
Grain Products	5–12	Choose whole grain and enriched products more often.
Vegetables & Fruit	5–10	Choose dark green and orange vegetables and orange fruit more often.
Milk Products		Choose lower-fat milk products more often.
Ages 4–9	2–3	
Ages 10–16	3–4	
Meat & Alternatives	2–3	Choose leaner meats, poultry, and fish, dried peas, beans, and lentils more often.

Note: Taste and enjoyment can also come from other foods and beverages that are not part of the four food groups. This category includes higher-fat, higher-calorie foods like soft drinks and chocolate bars that add little more than energy to a diet, so use these foods in moderation.

Different People Need Different Amounts of Food

The amount of food you need every day from the four food groups depends on your age, body size, activity level, growth rate, appetite, and whether you are male or female. For example, young children can choose the lower number of servings, while male teenagers can go to the higher number.

Examples of one serving:

Grain Products
1 slice of bread
30 g cold cereal
175 mL (¾ cup) hot cereal
½ bagel, pita, or bun
125 mL (½ cup) pasta or rice

Milk Products
250 mL (1 cup) milk
50 g (2 oz. or 2 slices) cheese
175 g (¾ cup) yogurt

Vegetables & Fruit
1 medium-size vegetable or fruit
125 mL (½ cup) fresh, frozen, or canned
250 mL (1 cup) salad
125 mL (½ cup) juice

Meat & Alternatives
50–100 g (2–4 oz.) meat, fish or poultry
1–2 eggs
125–250 mL (½–1 cup) beans
100 g (⅓ cup) tofu
30 mL (2 tbsp.) peanut butter

Adapted from Canada's Food Guide to Healthy Eating, Health Canada, 1992. With permission of the Minister of Public Works and Government Services Canada, 1998.

Through a child's eyes

A Health Canada survey revealed that children aged six to nine tend to label foods as either "good" or "bad." Apples, bananas, vegetables, and milk are "good." Chocolate bars and potato chips are "bad." Assure your child that no food is bad—labelling some food bad may lead kids to feel guilty about food. Your child may say, "I was bad today. I ate a doughnut." She might feel so ashamed about eating a "bad food" that she becomes secretive about it. More than one parent has found a pile of chocolate bar wrappers hidden under a child's bed.

Your child's overall eating pattern is what's important. Health Canada advises parents to encourage their children to think of foods as "everyday" foods or "sometimes" foods. The everyday foods are those in the four food groups of the Food Guide; the sometimes ones are foods like chips, chocolate bars, and pop—to be enjoyed less frequently. By the age of ten, most children have become familiar with Canada's Food Guide to Healthy Eating through school, and they may begin associating healthy eating with balanced eating of foods from the four groups.

Check Your Attitude

Your child looks to you for guidance about what, when, and where to eat. Check how you're guiding your kids.

- Trust your child's appetite. Even if she hasn't eaten much or anything at all at dinner, remove her plate without comment. One skipped meal won't hurt her.
- Don't offer dessert as a reward to your children for eating wholesome foods. By offering dessert only after all the vegetables are eaten, you teach your child that vegetables taste so bad that you have to be rewarded for eating them.
- Don't praise your child for eating a lot. Attention for eating large quantities could lead to overeating.
- Give your child your undivided attention, not a cookie, if she's had a rough day. If you use food to calm or cheer up kids, they'll associate food with emotions, not with hunger.
- Reward your child with a smile, a hug, or a few words of praise. If you use chocolate as a reward, it will reinforce your child's desire for treats.
- Turn off the TV and spend some time with your child if he's eating out of boredom. Address the problem of boredom, not the problem of his munching through all the snack food.

Ever wondered why you love Aunt Edna's cabbage rolls but your kids gag at the thought of them? Your kids have more taste buds than you do, so they prefer mild flavours. Some children naturally turn up their noses at strong-flavoured foods like cabbage, turnips, and meats. They also resist foods with slimy textures such as asparagus, spinach, mushrooms, and eggplant. That's not to say that kids won't eat these foods, just that they're not naturally inclined to like them.

But keep serving them, because the variety of foods helps kids meet their nutritional needs. Research shows that you may need to present a new food ten or fifteen times before a child is willing to try it. What most children like are mild flavours, sweet tastes, and crispy, crunchy textures. To kids, apples, eggs, cucumber, carrots, and celery are the best!

Calcium, Iron, and Fibre

If your family follows the recommendations in the Food Guide, your child will get all the nutrients he needs and won't be deficient in any one of them. However, the diets of many Canadian children are low in calcium, iron, and fibre. Here's how you can make sure your child meets his quota of these nutrients.

Boosting calcium

Adequate calcium intake during childhood is essential for bone formation and is a significant factor in reducing the risk of osteoporosis in later life. A calcium deficit during childhood and adolescence might never be fully overcome. Children need to increase their calcium intake mainly through milk products whenever their puberty growth spurts begin, usually earlier for girls than for boys. Believing that osteoporosis prevention must begin in childhood, the Osteoporosis Society of Canada recommends the daily calcium intakes for children shown at left.

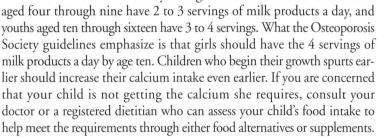

Calcium Requirements

Age	Intake
7 to 9	700 mg
10 to 12 (boys)	900 mg
10 to 12 (girls)	1200–1400 mg

To put this in perspective, these guidelines approximate those in Canada's Food Guide to Healthy Eating, which recommends that children aged four through nine have 2 to 3 servings of milk products a day, and youths aged ten through sixteen have 3 to 4 servings. What the Osteoporosis Society guidelines emphasize is that girls should have the 4 servings of milk products a day by age ten. Children who begin their growth spurts earlier should increase their calcium intake even earlier. If you are concerned that your child is not getting the calcium she requires, consult your doctor or a registered dietitian who can assess your child's food intake to help meet the requirements through either food alternatives or supplements.

In addition to serving milk and milk products such as yogurt and cheese, you can increase your family's calcium intake when preparing meals. Here's how.

Big days outside mean big appetites.

- Make oatmeal with milk, not water.
- Dilute condensed soups with milk, not water.
- Top casseroles with a cheese topping.
- Grate cheese over salads.
- Dip fresh fruit into yogurt dips.
- Pour cheese sauce over broccoli and cauliflower.
- Serve quiche, cheese soufflé, and cheese pasta dishes often.
- Add skim-milk powder to meat loaf, mashed potatoes, casseroles, and baked goods. Just 15 mL (1 tbsp.) of skim-milk powder contains 70 mg of calcium.
- Make milk desserts—pudding, tapioca, rice pudding, and baked custard.
- Use evaporated skim milk in baking—it has double the calcium of fresh milk.

Boosting iron

In a country with ample food supplies, it is alarming that there are many children with nutritional deficiencies. About 5 per cent of Canadian children from middle-income homes do not receive enough iron in their diet, but as many as 50 per cent of children from disadvantaged homes are iron-deficient. If your child's intake of iron is low, he may develop iron-deficiency anemia, which is characterized by a pale complexion and listlessness.

The iron available in meat, fish, and poultry (called heme iron) is more easily absorbed and used by the body than the iron available in vegetables and grains. However, foods containing vitamin C enhance the body's ability to absorb the iron in grains and vegetables. To increase your family's iron intake:

- Serve meat, fish, and poultry often.
- Bake bran muffins chock full of raisins and dried apricots.
- Add red kidney beans to casseroles.
- Choose whole-wheat breads and whole-grain cereals.
- Pick iron-fortified dry cereals. A cereal fortified with iron may list iron or ferrous sulfate in the ingredients.

Boosting fibre

Constipation is a common childhood problem. Exercise helps us maintain regular bodily functions. But we need dietary fibre to keep the bowels moving. Other forms of fibre also lower the risk of acquiring some diseases in adulthood. Developing the habit of eating soluble fibre such

She made it all by herself.

as oat bran, oatmeal, legumes, and pectin-rich fruit may reduce your child's risk of developing diseases of the bowel, diabetes, obesity, and high blood cholesterol later in life.

How much fibre does your child need? She needs to eat her age in grams (g) plus 5 grams. So a six-year-old needs 11 g (6 + 5) of fibre daily, a twelve-year-old needs 17 g (12 + 5). Chances are your child's tallies are nowhere near the target. Calculate your child's daily grams of fibre intake.

- Score 3 g of fibre for every apple, banana, or orange eaten.
- Score 2.5 g for half a baked potato (with the skin), 125 mL (½ cup) of broccoli, or carrot.
- Count 1.5 g per slice of whole-wheat bread.
- Score a whopping 5 g for 125 mL (½ cup) of legumes, such as chickpeas or lentils.

The Heart and Stroke Foundation estimates that most Canadians need to consume twice as much fibre as they do now. To increase your family's fibre intake:

- Choose whole-grain breads and cereals. Read cereal box labels and choose one with at least 3 g of fibre per serving.
- Top cereal with raisins, sliced bananas, or berries.
- Pop blueberries into pancake batter.
- Slip slices of tomato, cucumber, and zucchini into sandwiches.
- Serve hummus (chickpea spread) with whole-wheat pita bread.
- Prepare hearty soups like split pea or minestrone.
- Thicken soup with puréed cooked vegetables.
- Toss legumes or vegetables into pasta or rice dishes.
- When baking, replace white flour with a mixture of one part whole wheat flour, one part white flour.

- Snack on fruits—pears, raspberries, apples, oranges, nectarines, and bananas.
- Mix a handful of oat or wheat bran into casseroles.

Kids Need Fat

Childhood is a step-down time between the higher-fat diets of infants and toddlers and the lower-fat diets of adults. Reduce fats gradually so that by the time your child finishes puberty, her fat intake is that of an adult. Kids can eat both the lower-fat foods enjoyed by the adults in the family, as well as nutritious higher-fat foods such as peanut butter and cheese. As a concentrated source of calories, higher-fat foods are particularly important to kids with limited food preferences, children with small appetites, vegetarians, and kids involved in sports.

The Canadian Paediatric Society (CPS) concludes that nutritious food choices should not be eliminated or restricted because of their fat content. Its message differs from that of the Committee on Nutrition of the American Academy of Pediatrics (AAP), which states that the best time to start cutting back on fat, saturated fat, and cholesterol is after age two. The CPS argues that children are not mini-adults. They point to cases of Canadian parents, overzealous in their reduction of fat intake, whose children have suffered delayed growth and delayed puberty because of the misapplication of dietary advice that the CPS believes is meant for adults, not children.

Vitamin and Mineral Supplements

Although you may be tempted to give your child a multiple vitamin as insurance that he's getting all the nutrients he needs, children seldom need supplements if they are eating well. Your body requires over fifty nutrients every day, and you can only get these nutrients through a balanced diet. Vitamin and mineral supplements won't make up for not eating well.

However, Health Canada advises that children may need a supplement if:

- they don't include enough milk or milk products in their diet.
- they don't eat animal products (meat, milk or milk products, or eggs).
- food choices are limited by food intolerances or allergies, personal dislikes, cultural preferences, or religious beliefs.
- their drinking water is not fluoridated.

It's preferable to have your family doctor or a dietitian assess your child's diet rather than prescribe supplements yourself. A child can easily overdose on vitamins. Across Canada, accidental poisonings have occurred when children, lured by the bright packaging and sweet flavours of children's vitamins, popped handfuls of vitamin pills as if they were candy. If you use supplements, store them in a locked cabinet away from children.

The fluoride question

Health Canada, the Canadian Paediatric Society (CPS), and the Canadian Dental Association (CDA) all agree that a fluoridated water supply is the most effective, cost-efficient means of preventing dental caries. The CPS recommends that children be given fluoride supplements if they live in an area where there is little or no fluoride in the water supply.

If you're unsure whether your tap water is fluoridated, contact your municipal office. The level of fluoride will be identified in parts per million (ppm). Bottled water generally has very low fluoride content. If you use bottled water, read the labels. Also take into account the proportion of tap water to bottled water that your child uses. The chart below shows the CPS's recommended dosages.

Canadian Paediatric Society
Fluoride Guide for Children 6 to 16 Years

Fluoride concentration in principal source of drinking water	<0.3 ppm	0.3–0.6 ppm	>0.6 ppm
Amount of fluoride supplement needed, per day.	1.0 mg/day	0.5 mg/day	0 mg/day

In contrast, the CDA recommends fluoride supplements for children aged six to thirteen only when the fluoride in the water supply is less than 0.3 ppm. For them, it recommends 1.0 mg a day, as does the CPS. But the CDA is wary of recommending fluoride supplements when the fluoride concentration in drinking water is at the higher levels. Too much fluoride causes dental fluorosis, which in its mildest form causes white flecking on the teeth. In its severest form, fluorosis causes pitting and brown staining of the teeth. The CDA believes that children may be getting more fluoridated water from other sources than home, such as at school or at daycare.

The CPS recommends that parents supervise tooth brushing to ensure that children limit the amount of toothpaste with fluoride per brushing to the size of a pea; that they spit it out, not swallow it; and that they rinse thoroughly after brushing.

The fluoride supplements are available in drops, chewable tablets, and lozenges. Chewable tablets or lozenges are recommended because the primary action of fluoride is topical. Be sure to keep fluoride supplements in a locked cabinet away from children, because swallowing 230 to 500 mg of fluoride can be fatal.

Snacking

Contrary to what your mother told you, there's nothing wrong with between-meal snacks. The Dietitians of Canada insists that "snacking between meals is great for your kids!" Nutritionists agree that children are more likely to meet their dietary needs if they have two or three scheduled snacks a day, in addition to three meals. Most children don't eat enough at meals to provide them with the nutrients they need. If you satisfy nutrition requirements across the day, it eases the pressure on kids and parents during family meals. Besides, kids love to snack.

The key is to plan snacks as you plan meals. If you haven't prepared a wholesome snack, your child will grab a stack of chocolate cookies to fend off his hunger. No need to plan snacks for school recesses; once children hit grade one, they need recess for physical activity. But you will need to plan an after-school and bedtime snack. When your kids are active on days off, a morning snack may also be needed.

Maintain control. You probably don't ask your child what he wants for dinner. Don't ask your child what he wants for a snack. Offer something from the food groups whose recommendations aren't being met through the three meals of the day. Older kids will want to help themselves. Keep nutritious snacks where your older child can see them. If the taco chips are at eye level and the carrots are in a bag in the back of the crisper, guess what she'll snack on?

Most kids need two or three snacks a day.

To quench thirst, serve:

- water.
- plain or flavoured milk.
- yogurt beverages.
- hot cocoa.
- juicy fruits (watermelon, plums, peaches, oranges, cantaloupe).
- succulent vegetables like cucumber and cherry tomatoes.
- vegetable juices.

To satisfy hunger, serve:

- popcorn.
- applesauce.
- bread sticks.
- a half-sandwich (cheese, egg, tuna, or peanut butter).
- cottage cheese.
- yogurt.
- devilled or hard-cooked eggs.
- peanuts, pumpkin seeds, or sunflower seeds.
- whole-grain muffins and cereals.
- toast with honey.
- fig bars and other fruit bars.
- leftover pizza.
- half a bagel spread with cheese or peanut butter.
- raw vegetables (snow peas, celery, and sweet peppers).

Snacking and Dental Decay

Frequent snacking on sweets increases your child's risk of cavities. The Canadian Dental Association recommends that if you serve sweets, you serve them with meals. Increased saliva flow during meals helps neutralize the effects of sugar. Our saliva contains several cavity-protecting factors, including fluoride, calcium buffers, and antimicrobial agents.

Soft, sticky sweets such as raisins, fruit leathers, and granola bars may be nutritious, but they stick to the teeth. Fruit juices, even if unsweetened, also contain sugar. Since fruit juice pools around your child's teeth, it may also pose a risk for cavities. The CDA suggests limiting, or even eliminating, juice between meals.

If your child has a sweet snack, have him try a slice of Cheddar or mozzarella cheese to counteract some of the negative effects of sugar. Or give him a celery stick or apple. Because they help clean your teeth, these foods are sometimes called "detergent foods." And as your child has probably already pointed out, sugarless gum can help reduce dental decay. Of course, children can always rinse their mouths with water if there's nothing else available. Or you might try to accustom your children to brushing after snacks as well as after meals.

Selective Eaters

Your most well-balanced meals and wholesome snacks won't nourish your child if she turns up her nose at them. All children—and most adults—snub at least a few foods. But some children keep ever-lengthening lists of foods they detest. Or they decide to become vegetarian, eliminating meat from their diets.

Sometimes an unpleasant experience with a food causes an aversion to that food. Maybe your child accidentally drank sour milk and began to gag at the taste, smell, and even the sight of milk. To counteract such a food aversion, let time heal. Until she's ready to drink milk again, keep up her calcium intake with other milk products—yogurt, cheese, or milk pudding. Reintroduce milk in a relaxed situation in which she can control the amount. She may want to try just a few sips at first.

The best thing you can do for such a child is to relax about his eating style. No matter how selective your child is about food, don't call him a "picky eater"—he may feel he has to live up to the label. If you give your child a lot of attention, positive or negative, over his food choices, a small problem might grow into a big problem.

Don't worry if he rejects all sandwiches except peanut butter, and don't comment on the fact that he's had a peanut butter sandwich for lunch six months straight. You may think his peanut butter sandwich jag is a challenge to your authority. It's not. He's just exercising his right to choose. He wants peanut butter.

"I hate green beans. I don't like asparagus, hotdogs, celery, or cucumbers. And I hate tomatoes and squash. I don't like milk, I only like chocolate milk. I don't like cooked carrots, just carrot sticks. I don't like homemade fries, just McDonald's fries. What I really like is Kraft Dinner."

MAIA, AGE 7

It may be useful to take a look at the eating behaviours of the rest of the family—your child may be imitating you. Do you or does your spouse pick out all the peas in a serving of shepherd's pie and roll them to the side of the plate? Do you berate yourself for eating "too much" and being "too fat," then ponder why your child eats such minuscule quantities?

Your concern from preschool on should be that your child receives adequate nutrition and develops a healthy attitude to food and eating. Try inviting him into the kitchen. Helping prepare meals can accustom your child to a wider variety of foods. This is also a more opportune time to talk about Canada's Food Guide to Healthy Eating, the four different food groups, and the advantages of a variety of foods.

SEE PAGE 42

As long as your child continues to grow well, and your doctor agrees, don't worry about the lack of variety. Your six-year-old or eight-year-old may reject your food choices, but the protests won't last. When they begin the final growth spurts of puberty, they'll be too hungry to reject any foods.

Nutrition Check

If you're concerned that your child's selective eating is leaving him malnourished, keep a food diary over a few weeks. Once you have the facts, solving the problem may be as simple as one, two, three.

1. If your child doesn't like a certain food, replace it with a food from the same food group. If your child despises vegetables, serve fruit to her. If your son won't drink milk, maybe he'll go for cheese, yogurt, yogurt beverages, or flavoured milk and homemade milkshakes.
2. If your child eats little from any one food group, increase her intake by disguising the despised foods in dishes that she does like. If she rejects most fruits and vegetables, try mixing grated zucchini and carrots into spaghetti sauce, muffins, meat loaf, and lasagna. If your child shuns dairy products, serve milk-based soups, toss skim-milk powder into meat loaf, and make milk puddings.
3. If your child refuses all foods from an entire food group and all dishes containing those foods, consult your physician or a dietitian as to whether she needs a vitamin or mineral supplement.

SEE PAGE 228
For a referral to a dietitian, ask your child's doctor or contact the Dietitians of Canada for the name and number of a dietitian working in your area. In some provinces, if your doctor refers you to a dietitian, there may be no charge. Otherwise, the typical fee for consultation is $60 an hour. Check whether your health plan covers this service.

Vegetarian Kids

Overnight, your child became a vegetarian. She says she just can't stomach the idea of eating an animal. About 7 per cent of North Americans are vegetarians, and the numbers are increasing all the time as more and more preteen and teenage girls turn vegetarian.

If your child has turned vegetarian, respect her choice. If she's only a vegetarian until dinner, refrain from remarking on her lack of willpower. If she's a vegetarian except for fast-food burgers, it's her choice. If she gives up meat for good, ensure that she receives sufficient nourishment from other sources.

If you are a family of carnivores, how will your daughter achieve adequate nutrition? Becoming a vegetarian means more than just not eating meat. It means replacing the nutrients we obtain through eating meat with the nutrients available in legumes, seeds, nuts, eggs, and dairy products.

When you make a stir-fry, before adding the chicken take out some vegetables for your daughter and mix a portion of tofu into her serving. When you're barbecuing burgers for the rest of the family, include a veggie burger for your daughter. Add chickpeas to the rice dish instead of ham once in a while, so the whole family can enjoy a vegetarian meal.

"I was looking at some pictures of animals in a book, and I thought it would be a good idea not to kill them. I don't like the idea of killing animals for meat. You have to kill pigs for meat, and pigs are my favourite animals.

That was last year, and except for a month, I've been a vegetarian ever since. I have a friend at my school who is a vegetarian.

When I became a vegetarian, at lunch time kids began chasing me around with their meat sandwiches saying, 'Ooooh, oooooh! Meat! Meat!' I said, 'Stop! Stop! Stop!' I ran to my friend who is a vegetarian and they stopped teasing me because, to make fun of me, they would also have to make fun of her. Her whole family are vegetarians.

I think that, if we had a lot more vegetarians in this world, we would have a lot more animals in this world."

KATIE, AGE 9

Vegetarian food usually has less fat and more fibre, and it's more economical. Compared with meat-eaters, vegetarians reduce their risk of heart disease, osteoporosis, hypertension, and some types of cancer in their adult years, and are less likely to die from Type II diabetes.

Nourishing the vegetarian child

If your child is a *lacto-ovo vegetarian* (she eats eggs, milk, and dairy products), getting enough protein is not a problem. However, you must take care she obtains adequate energy, iron, and zinc.

Energy Vegetarian diets tend to be high in fibre, so a child can feel full before her calorie needs are met. Higher-fat foods, which are a concentrated source of energy, can help your child receive adequate calories. Serve energy-dense foods such as nuts, cheese, peanut butter, dried fruits, and tahini.

Iron Vegetarians get sufficient iron if their meals include iron-rich foods such as seeds, legumes, eggs, blackstrap molasses, dried fruits, iron-enriched breakfast cereals, broccoli, and wheat germ. To double or triple the iron intake from vegetables:

- Eat them with a source of vitamin C such as fruit juice, broccoli, potatoes, tomatoes, or citrus fruits. Vitamin C helps the body absorb iron.
- Cook in a cast-iron pot. Some of the iron in the pot will transfer to the food, especially if the dish contains acidic foods such as tomatoes or lemon juice.

Many breakfast cereals are a good source of iron for kids.

Zinc Good sources of zinc for the vegetarian child include nuts, sprouts, legumes, eggs, wheat germ, and milk.

If your child has turned *vegan* (that is, he eats no eggs or milk products), you not only have to be careful that he receives adequate energy, iron, and zinc, but also sufficient calcium, protein, and vitamins D and B_{12}. To plan a vegan diet for a growing child, it's best to consult a dietitian.

The Allergic Child

If your child has food allergies, paying attention to food restrictions may have become a way of life for him by the age of six. Your child is probably sophisticated way beyond his years in what ingredients are hidden in foods. As you gradually give your child more and more responsibility for avoiding the foods to which he's allergic, be aware that with the responsibility comes the risk of his making mistakes. If your child's food sensitivity is not severe—for example, he gets diarrhea if he eats a forbidden food—then the transition to self-monitoring is simpler. But if your child has a life-threatening allergy, it's difficult for parents to just be supportive rather than overprotective.

When your child is six or seven, you still control his diet. But as he approaches his teens, he'll want to eat out with friends in restaurants or go on overnight school trips. At the same time, he may begin to hide his food allergies because they're not cool, and you may find his medical alert bracelet tossed in a drawer. If your child has a severe allergy but is slipping into denial, it's time to step in. It's just too dangerous to let him learn from experience. Through his doctor, arrange for counselling. For information on childhood allergies, consult the Allergy/Asthma Information Association.

High-Energy Eating for Athletes

Your child eats breakfast in the back seat of the car on the way to her 7:00 a.m. practice. You suspect she skips lunch at school to get in some extra time shooting baskets. She rushes through dinner to make it to the basketball game on time. Parents of sports enthusiasts need a nutrition game plan for their children. Not only must a young athlete meet his or her body's high demands of nutrients for growth, she must also recognize the extra requirements of energy (calories) and fluids that a training program imposes. Three meals a day won't do it. She'll also need snacks.

Appetite is the best guide to amounts, but six- to twelve-year-old children still look to parents for guidance on what and when to eat. Every day, choose at least the minimum number of servings in each food group in the Food Guide. Select more servings from these two groups: grain products, and vegetables and fruit. Especially important are starchy vegetables like potatoes, peas, and corn, fruit, and lots of bread, pasta, rice, and cereals.

SEE PAGE 42

These foods provide carbohydrates, the main source of energy for all exercise. Carbohydrates in the form of blood glucose and muscle glycogen offer the body's primary sources of fuel during intense training. Once glycogen stores are depleted, athletes suffer fatigue. The National Institute of Nutrition recommends a diet providing about 60 per cent of total energy intake from carbohydrates for children participating in high-intensity training for long periods of time.

SEE PAGE 230

Give your young athlete extra fluids to avoid dehydration.

Some adults load up on carbohydrates for high-demand athletic events such as marathons. This strict regime, which involves consuming a very high-carbohydrate diet and the tapering off of activity for two or three days before competition, may be harmful to children.

There is room in the athletic child's diet for higher-fat foods such as peanut butter, cheese, and ice cream. High-fat foods provide a concentrated source of calories for the child on the run.

If your child is involved in activities such as diving, dancing, gymnastics, or figure skating, she may balk at eating even the minimum requirements of the Food Guide. Weight control may be part of training for the Olympics, but it's not required if your child participates in sports simply because he enjoys them. If your child's coach suggests that your daughter or son go on a diet, it's time to change clubs. Your child has the wrong coach, not the wrong body size or shape. Limiting a growing child's food can jeopardize her health by delaying maturation and stunting growth. Possibly more serious, it can lead to an eating disorder.

"The hungriest our son ever got was when he went to a football training camp when he was 11. I don't think I ever filled him up. He was hungry again right after he ate. He craved pasta, and ate huge portions of spaghetti and lasagna for supper. I used my biggest pots. Before supper he'd have a large-sized bowl filled to overflowing with cereal and milk. Then he'd have another large-sized bowl of cereal before bed. He was training hard, and what I learned is that appetite is directly proportionate to exercise."

LISA, MOTHER OF TWO

Drinking enough fluids

Drinking several glasses of water each day should be part of every person's healthy diet. Additional water, however, is necessary during times of intense training or competition. The active child needs to drink extra fluids to regulate his body temperature. Active muscles generate heat, and fluids help remove that heat. Without adequate fluid, your child may become dehydrated, which causes fatigue and increases the risk of cramps and heat exhaustion.

To prevent dehydration, your child should drink water before, during, and after exercise. You or your child's coach may need to insist he drink. Thirst may not be an adequate indicator of the body's need for water, especially during exercise, which blunts one's thirst.

Exercising in the heat poses unique problems for the child athlete. Because children sweat less than adolescents and adults, they have a greater heat gain in hot weather. When it's hot, children should drink every 10 to 15 minutes, approximately 30 mL (1 oz.) for every 15 kg (33 lb.), and pour water over themselves to cool down.

Fill your child's water bottle with plain water. Avoid iced tea and colas. The caffeine in these drinks acts as a diuretic and may increase urine output and fluid loss. Since children sweat so little, they don't lose as much sodium, potassium, and other minerals while exercising. Unless it's extremely hot and humid or the exercise is extremely strenuous, sport drinks are not likely to benefit children, but they won't harm your child.

Body Image

As they approach puberty, children become aware of, and sometimes concerned about, their appearance. Your son may ask you to feel his biceps. Your daughter will gaze at herself in the mirror, checking out her changing shape.

Preteens, particularly girls, begin to compare their looks with those of the people they see in movies, on TV, and in magazines. It's an unfair comparison. Early adolescence is a time of voracious eating and rapid growth. It's common for girls and boys approaching puberty to look chubby. Then after a growth spurt, they may not be used to their new height, so they will slouch awkwardly for a while.

Girls as young as six can fret about their figures. But typically they begin to worry about their weight between the ages of nine and eleven. By age eleven, 47 per cent of Canadian girls say they would change how they look if they could, and 37 per cent say they need to lose weight.

Along with adults, children at this age may buy into the myth that you can have any body you want—if only you exercise and control your eating. But body size is not a choice. Increasing evidence suggests that weight is genetic.

Size Is Inherited

Some children are naturally small, others naturally large. Large kids do not necessarily eat more than their smaller counterparts. There's increasing evidence that we have an inherited set-point, a certain weight that is genetically determined. Like hair colour and height, size is part of our inheritance.

If your child is excessively overweight, of course you should consult your family doctor. With the help of a dietitian, you need to examine if his diet is too high in fats or calories. Also worth looking at is whether he takes opportunities to exercise. If you're secure that your child is physically active and that his diet is good, relax. There is no evidence that being plump is unhealthy, although being too skinny does have definite health risks.

"I'm obsessed with weight. I do aerobics. I lift weights. I weigh myself every week. So when I had a child on the big side, I was caught off-guard. But he has a really good attitude about himself. He always feels good about himself. He doesn't look in the mirror in the critical way that I do. He just wants to be healthy. Together we take our bikes down to the bike trails and ride in the sun."

TERESE, MOTHER OF TWO

Problems for the larger-than-average child originate in how he is treated by our fat-phobic society. Studies show that children consider a "fat" child the least desirable playmate. Children describe heavy people as dirty, lazy, ugly, and stupid.

To try to spare your child this ridicule, you may become critical of your child's weight or eating. You may even be repulsed by the extra roll around your son's middle. But if you don't feel comfortable with your child's body shape, it could be time to look at your own thinking about body shape.

In a society that equates *fat* with *bad* and *skinny* with *good*, we need to remind ourselves that thin children are no more lovable than large kids. In fact, your love and acceptance may be even more essential for the overweight child, who may be taunted at school. If you overhear your child being called "fatty" or "porker," you may want to act out of anger. But a more constructive approach is to state simply, "We don't make fun of the way people look."

Say No to Dieting

Don't put your child on a diet. You risk her developing an eating disorder, since many begin with seesaw dieting. The majority of people who lose weight through dieting regain the weight they lost plus a few pounds.

Celebrating as a family is the glue that keeps us together.

Putting a child on a diet could set him up to fail. When you restrict his food, he may feel deprived and experience an increased interest in having those foods that are considered taboo. Then he may seek to satisfy his hunger by sneaking a bag of chips or, more likely, half the contents of your fridge. With that, he may feel ashamed and out of control, although this scenario is not always inevitable.

As a parent or caregiver, your job is to prepare nutritious snacks and meals. It's your child's job to choose what and how much she wants to eat. Fighting about food usually leads to eating more. Denying particular foods only makes them more appealing. If your child isn't allowed ice cream, she may crave it!

Can we change our weight? Dieting may adjust our metabolic requirements in the wrong direction. It pushes them down. The only way we can increase our energy requirements is through regular aerobic exercise.

Aerobic exercise refers to the continuous movement that makes the heart beat faster, but not to the point where you're puffing. During aerobic exercise, you should still be able to speak comfortably. To reap the most benefit from aerobic exercise, maintain the activity for at least twenty continuous minutes. It's best not to single out your overweight child by insisting, "You need to exercise." Chances are that your whole family needs to exercise. Make fitness a family goal.

The beginnings of anorexia nervosa

Eating disorders tend to appear when a person is facing several changes at once. One such time is early adolescence, when a child faces a changing body, emerging sexual feelings, and is likely graduating to a senior school. Life may seem out of control. Food may seem like the one thing your child can control.

Anorexia nervosa, a drastic weight loss from dieting, is a predominantly female disorder. It doesn't usually develop until between ages thirteen and twenty-five. However, symptoms of anorexia can begin as young as age nine.

Anorexia may start with the child establishing a strict rule of no desserts. Then she may also exclude bread from her diet. She could go on to deny herself more and more foods until she's existing on only celery sticks and water, or just water.

Maybe your child has turned vegetarian. If she is unwilling to eat higher-fat vegetarian foods such as nuts, seeds, tofu, and legumes, her preference may be masking the beginnings of an eating disorder, especially if her new way of eating is accompanied by weight fluctuations and a preoccupation with her weight or shape.

Behind this potentially fatal illness is a strong desire to be thin, even though the child may be thin to begin with. However, some children who become anorexic were heavy, were ostracized because of their weight, were encouraged to diet and praised when they lost pounds.

Seeing a child struggle with an eating disorder might make you feel helpless. You can best help her by keeping communication flowing, but do talk about things other than food and weight. Avoid power struggles over food. What your child needs most is to know that you care about her. As a family member, not a therapist, express concern about her health and seek help from your family doctor or an eating-disorder clinic. Don't wait until you can persuade her to seek help. Anorexics believe their only problem is being too fat.

SEE PAGE 230

Ten Ways to Promote a Healthy Body Image

Are you unknowingly telling your child there's something wrong with her body? Follow these guidelines to help your child feel radiant about who she is—inside and out.

1. Accept your own body weight and shape. If you stand in front of the mirror poking at what you perceive as imperfections, your child will follow suit.
2. Toss out your bathroom scales. There's no need to weigh yourself or your child.
3. Check that your child's clothing fits. Waistbands that pinch and shirts so tight that they inhibit arm movements tell your child he's the wrong size.
4. Celebrate the diversity of human shapes by plastering your fridge door with pictures of people of all shapes and sizes. Point out unrealistic media images. Question whether the hero and heroine must always be thin.
5. Discuss dieting. If your child hears that 95 per cent of diets fail, he's less likely to start one.
6. Educate your child on the genetic basis of weight.
7. Avoid food fights. Don't limit a child's portions or ban foods. Your job is to prepare and serve nutritious foods—that's all.
8. Hug your child, shake her hand when she gets an A, massage her shoulders after a tense day. Your comfort with your child's body sends a strong message that her body is lovable.
9. Don't comment on a child's weight. Instead, comment on his skateboarding skills, his ability to make new friends, and his wacky sense of humour. Your child can't have both good self-esteem and a poor body image.
10. Don't allow others to comment in a hurtful way on your child's appearance. Stand up for your child, especially with other adults.

Make Meals Family Time

If your children are eager to help prepare meals, their childhood is an ideal time to teach cooking skills and pass on family recipes. Encourage your child's interest in cooking by setting aside a kitchen shelf or drawer for his cooking supplies. Find him an apron and oven mitts that fit, a recipe box, and a cookbook that illustrates cooking techniques. Don't buy a cookbook he'll grow into. Instead, find one that's a bit below his current reading level. He'll feel more capable in the kitchen if he can easily follow the recipes and stir at the same time. What's most important is that children learn to enjoy preparing and cooking foods. Praise their efforts, even the simplest.

Before you can relax while your kids whip up dinner, you will have to spend time teaching them. Establish and enforce the rule: Leave the kitchen the way you found it. And make sure they know safe kitchen habits.

Make playfulness and being together the focus of the family meal.

Safety First

Don't assume that children know about safety in the kitchen. Before you let your kids loose among the appliances, sit down together and review these basic safety rules.

1. Before any cooking adventure, ask an adult to be on hand. Always ask for help when you need it.
2. Begin by washing your hands. If you have long hair, tie it back. If you have sleeves that could drape onto a hot burner, secure them with elastic bands.
3. Make sure that oven mitts are within reach. Pots and microwave containers may not look hot even when they are.
4. Chop and peel safely. Direct the sharp edge of the knife or peeler away from your hand. Always cut downward, never up toward yourself.

"I like to cook spaghetti, pizza, burgers, hot dogs, and steak. There's a good recipe for porterhouse steak with a South American sauce that I like. But most of the time I just cook with a dash of this, a dash of that. I really, really like cooking. I'd like to become a chef."

DASHIELL, AGE 11

---

5. To avoid the possibility of contracting salmonella poisoning, set aside the cutting board, plate, knife, and any other utensils you may have used to prepare meat and poultry. Don't use them to prepare other foods until they have been washed. Note to parents: To eliminate salmonella, wash in hot, soapy water, then scrub with a mixture of 15 mL (1 tbsp.) chlorine bleach to 1L (4 cups) water, leaving the solution on for at least 45 seconds before rinsing.
6. Resist licking the spoons or the bowls. The raw eggs in cake and cookie batter could cause diarrhea (food poisoning), as could any half-cooked hamburger or chicken dishes.
7. Never lay your recipe or cookbook on the stove; don't pile up ingredients there, either.
8. Turn pot handles toward the back of the stove in order to avoid knocking over pots of scalding food.
9. If fire breaks out in the microwave, leave the door closed and unplug it. If a fire breaks out on the stove, use a fire extinguisher. Don't use water to put out an oil fire—use baking soda. If you can't put out the fire quickly, phone 911 or your local fire department.

10. Ask for help or instructions on how to use the blender or the food processor, or other kitchen equipment. The rule for microwave use is: If you're too young to read or follow the directions, then you're too young to use a microwave without an adult.

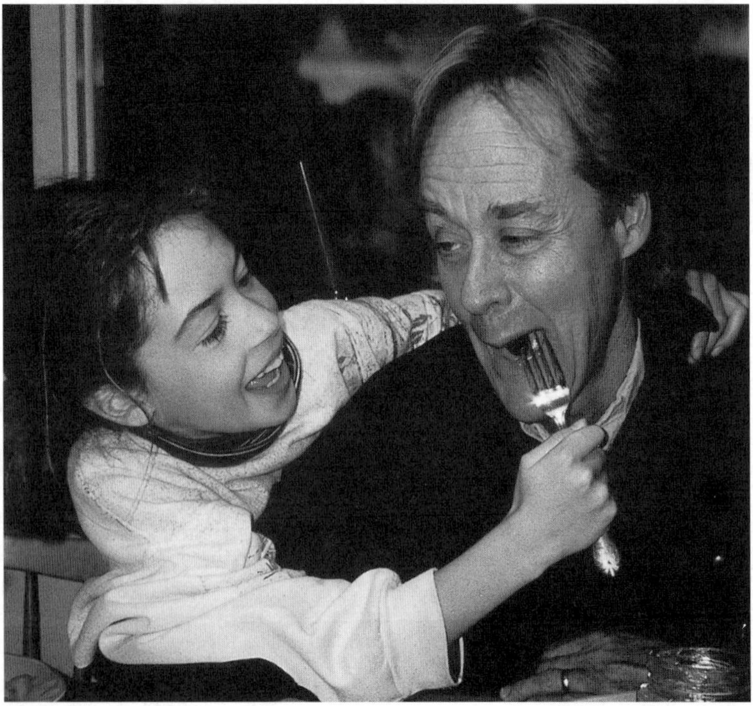

Children learn table manners by imitating their parents. Whoops!

Dinner Conversation

Make the focus of the family meal conversation rather than the act of refuelling the body. Children need to know that at dinner the family matters most. By spending uninterrupted relaxed time with your kids, you convey that you're emotionally available to them which, in turn, encourages your child to open up to you.

Except during the Stanley Cup or the Olympics, perhaps, you'll be wasting precious family time if you eat in front of the TV. So turn the TV off and take the phone off the hook. Some kids get so wrapped up in a show that they don't even know if they've eaten. And your child will miss his body's cues of hunger or satiation if he's mesmerized by a TV show.

Children learn manners by imitating their parents. So remember: no elbows on the table; no dunking your cookie in your coffee; bring your food up to your mouth, not your mouth down to your plate; compliment the cook. The kids are watching and listening.

Make dinners special. Celebrate the first snowfall or the last day of school. Ask a family member to contribute a centrepiece or make a special dessert. Eat together at the dining-room table occasionally. Light candles or dim the lights, and the conversation will soften, too.

Talk, Talk, Talk

Jan Kindred of White City, Saskatchewan, craved meaningful conversation around the dinner table with her husband and their nine-year-old twin daughters. Kindred developed questions to draw families into more meaningful dialogue. For dinner conversation tonight, try one of Kindred's openers.

- If you were given $10,000 tomorrow, how would you spend it?
- If you could travel in a time machine, would you go into the past or into the future?
- If you could be invisible for one day, what would you do?
- If you could run away with the circus, what performer would you like to be?
- Tell one fond memory that you have of each family member.
- If you met someone who knew nothing about you, what interesting things could you tell them about yourself?
- Name some things that make you happy that do not cost money.
- How long do you think a couple should be engaged before they marry?
- Do you believe in miracles?

A Child's Point of View: My Body

My coordination is improving and my body will do most of what I want it to do. Soon I will begin puberty. You may notice the first signs of change by the time I'm nine.

Age Six

6

- I'm in perpetual motion. I test my new physical skills by doing tricks on climbing bars or balancing on one foot on a fence. I'm not as well coordinated as I think, though, and I sometimes fall.
- Physically, I'm extra-sensitive. I can wail over the tiniest cut. When you brush my hair, it can really hurt my head.
- I can be loud, boisterous, and physical. I may still have the occasional tantrum.
- When I'm forced to sit still—like in school—I get fidgety and restless. I wriggle, kick, and jump out of my seat.
- I'll have gaps in my smile as my baby teeth begin to fall out. My six-year molars start to appear.
- I'm a good eater, but messy. I stuff my face, eat with my fingers, spill my juice, reach across the table. I might try to stand up on my chair to tell a story.
- I'm curious about bodies. My friend and I might pull our pants down and take a quick peek at each other. I'll need you to set limits around this behaviour.
- When I'm excited or tired, I can have bathroom mishaps.

Age Seven

7

- I'm more coordinated than I used to be. I might be ready for organized sports, gymnastics, or dance lessons.
- My body is sensitive to certain clothing and textures. I might complain that the waistband is too tight (even if it's my size) or the neckline is too loose or the whole outfit "just doesn't feel right."
- I'm becoming more modest about showing my body, even to the same sex. I might prefer to undress behind closed doors.
- My appetite is not as big as it used to be. I get tired quickly.

- I like handling objects such as odd-shaped stones, pencil stubs, colourful shells. When you do the laundry, you'll have to empty my pockets of my various collections. Please don't throw anything out without checking with me—I might have a strong attachment to my lucky stick or magic stone.
- Sometimes I wear a worried or sad expression. I pout.
- With so much to think about and worry about, I may have a hard time going to sleep at night.

Age Eight

- I'm fast. I tear around the house, talk quickly, bolt my dinner. I'm likely to burst in through the door shouting "Guess what!"
- I enjoy physical sports and games, such as wrestling, hide-and-seek, and tobogganing. I like testing my limits. In the playground I might try setting up my own race courses or obstacle courses and timing myself against the clock.
- My actions are looking more coordinated, graceful, or rhythmical, but I can still be accident-prone.
- I'm a bit of a risk taker. I might want to ski down the "black diamond" hill before having a single lesson. Falling won't stop me from trying again.
- My stamina is increasing, so I can run farther and swim longer before I get tired.
- My appetite has come back. I'm starting to use a knife to cut my food.
- I make funny faces and clown around.
- My hand-eye coordination and fine muscle control are developing rapidly. My artwork becomes more detailed.
- My peripheral vision is increasing, but it won't be fully developed for several years. I may be temporarily distracted by movement in my side vision.
- As my permanent front teeth grow in, they'll look too big for my face.

Age Nine

- I do an activity over and over, to the point of exhaustion.
- I'm busy all day with school, sports, and lessons, and yet I want to sign up for even more activities. I'm anxious to try everything.
- I'm good with my hands. I can build intricate structures with small building blocks, learn to use a needle and thread, and do cursive handwriting.
- I become better coordinated physically, but at the same time I'm more self-conscious about my body. If I don't know yet about the physical changes of puberty, I'm ready to learn—both about my sex and the opposite sex.

- I may complain that I can't write because my hand hurts or I can't walk to school because my legs hurt. These "growing pains" are real, but rarely serious.
- I'm more interested than before in competitive team sports, such as hockey or soccer.
- I resist bedtime because I feel compelled to finish whatever I'm working on.
- I tend to stare at people and things without blinking. My friends and I have staring contests.
- I look at you without really seeing you. When you call me, I honestly may not hear you.

Age Ten

10

All Kids

- Most of the time I'm busy and active. I'm willing to try almost any new activity.
- Just as when I was much younger, I can get physical when I'm angry. I might stamp around the house or throw things.
- I don't cry as much as I used to (or as much as I might next year), but I yell.

Girls Only

- My body gets a little softer and rounder, especially around my hips and chest. I could have a rapid weight increase. I might need some reassurance that I'm not getting fat.
- My nipples may start to stick out a bit or become tingly and sore—or there might not be any obvious changes yet.
- The contours of my face fill out a little. I'm starting to lose my elfin appearance.
- I may start to grow some downy pubic hair.

Boys Only

- I start looking a bit more solid and sturdy. My face, neck, and chest begin to fill out.

Age Eleven

All Kids

- I'm always in motion. Even when I'm sitting, I'm restless and jumpy.
- I eat a lot, sometimes of one food—for example, three apples at one sitting or a whole pizza.
- I get tired easily and I need more sleep, but I often have insomnia.
- I'm becoming more conscious of my appearance, especially my clothes and hair.
- When I'm upset I'm like a tornado—I might kick, hit, yell, swear, slam doors, then, just as quickly, dissolve into a puddle of tears.

Girls Only

- I'm starting to grow taller than some of the boys.
- My breasts may be growing. Even if my chest is still flat, it may be getting a fuller and softer look. My nipples can be very sensitive and sometimes painful.
- I sweat more. I may need deodorant.
- Gradually, my waist is looking more like a waist. I might even be able to wear a belt comfortably, without having it slide down my hips.
- My pelvis continues to get wider. I probably have at least the beginnings of pubic hair.
- For months before my periods start, I might have cyclical moodiness, headaches, and vaginal discharge.

Boys Only

- I won't have many noticeable signs of sexual maturing. I may be shorter than a lot of the girls my age, and my weight is barely half what it will be as an adult.
- My muscles are getting stronger and my endurance continues to increase.
- I might have a "fat period" as fatty tissue develops around my chest and hips. I'll grow into it over the next year or so.
- I may start to have erections.

Age Twelve

All Kids

- I'm a bottomless pit. I can have a huge snack after school, eat all my dinner, and still not feel full.
- I have bursts of high energy alternating with very low-energy times.
- My sleep can be restless.
- I may start showering regularly without being reminded.
- I have most or all of my 28 permanent teeth.

Girls Only

- My periods will most likely start this year, although I can get my first period at any age from nine to sixteen.
- By the end of this year, I'll be at least 90 per cent of my adult height.
- My breasts fill out, or I may not have much breast development yet.
- I have pubic hair and maybe some underarm hair.
- I might start to get pimples.
- I may or may not masturbate regularly.

Boys Only

- I probably haven't had my growth spurt yet.
- My testicles may start to enlarge. One testicle may hang lower than the other.
- I may have some pubic hair.
- I probably get frequent erections and masturbate regularly.

Mind

2

Between six and twelve, kids' brain activity is extremely rapid, and they are primed to absorb information in many different ways. Children each have their own learning style and unique intelligence. Your child's mental development is nurtured by every kind of stimulation, including his experiences in school. Some kids need individualized attention because of a special need or disability. All kids need parental support in negotiating the world of homework and school-yard controversies, and in developing their special talents.

Scientists speculating how babies acquire different skills and levels of intelligence used to debate the relative importance of genetics (what a child is born with) and the environment (what a child experiences in life) in influencing the child's progress in growth and development. The debate has gradually ceased to be relevant in the past two decades as scientists have discovered that an individual's genetic endowments interact continuously with his or her environment.

A child is genetically designed to feast on environmental experiences. Every sort of stimulation that a child is frequently exposed to—from cuddling before bed to watching robins in flight to sorting baseball cards—is part of the feast, and it's parents who contribute most to the banquet.

What's Going On in That Head of Yours?

Until about the age of ten, a child's brain is a fireworks display of electrical activity. Your child comes equipped with about one hundred billion brain nerve cells, called neurons. Shortly after birth, these nerve cells are busy emitting electrical pulses to construct connections to other neurons. The brain makes trillions more of these connections than your child will ultimately keep. The connections that endure are strengthened as they are used or stimulated by sensory experience. If the connection isn't used, the pathway withers and that particular connection can be lost. Myelinization is the process that occurs to neural connections as they become more stable. Specialized cells form a fatty, protective, insulating sheath around the nerve fibres.

Using Positron Emission Tomography (PET), a method of scanning the brain's activity by measuring its glucose consumption, researchers have found that by the age of three, a child's brain is more than twice as active as an adult's brain, and continues so until the age of ten. The PET scan also shows that the brain does not activate just one area when responding to stimuli, but retrieves knowledge or information from a complex web of neural connections.

Educators and neurobiologists believe that the activation of the web of connections explains why kids learn most effectively when they are given information about a particular topic in several different forms. A teacher of a grade two class, for example, with the goal of having her students learn to identify robins, might read with them a story about robins, have them count the robins at a bird feeder, and then suggest they draw pictures of robins. The more places in their brains that they store information about robins, the greater the number of access routes they have to retrieve that information, and the more firmly the child retains that knowledge.

The creation of the neural connections follows a developmental schedule, and there are critical ages or periods for a growing child to best understand particular concepts or to begin acquiring particular skills. The neural pathways that enable your child to see or to walk or to talk, for example, are already well established by the age of six.

The window of opportunity to become fluent in another language is also open widest between birth and the age of six. This doesn't mean that an older child or adult cannot learn a second or third language, just that she will never learn one as easily as when she was a young child. But rest assured that wiring the brain for language continues throughout childhood. Wiring the brain for music also has a critical period. The opportune time to begin learning to play an instrument is between the ages of three and seven.

Around puberty, the complex and explosive neural activity in a child's brain begins to slow down, and by the age of sixteen, the adolescent's brain development of neural connections levels off. New connections are made throughout life, but at a slower pace, and our capacity to learn continues. However skills and knowledge, once acquired, are maintained only through use and grow rusty or are lost through lack of use. The opportunities for learning and acquiring the associated neural connections are endless during childhood when the learning appears to be the most effortless.

Multiple Intelligences

In the past decade, many educators have incorporated Howard Gardner's observations about multiple intelligences. Gardner is a professor at Harvard Graduate School of Education and the author of *Frames of Mind: The Theory of Multiple Intelligences* (Basic Books, 10th anniversary edition, 1993). Gardner describes a set of definable areas of intelligence that are common to all human beings, but which exist in different strengths in each person. However, our society in general and our education system in particular have valued most highly the intelligences that demonstrate

"When our son Adam became interested in music a few years ago, we bought him a guitar. That interest, which has grown, has spawned other interests. He reads biographies of his musical heroes, writes poetry—before then, reading and writing were certainly not on his list of favourite activities!"

LOUISE, MOTHER OF THREE

Some kids learn best by following written instructions.

linguistic, logical-mathematical, and spatial abilities. But, as Gardner points out, we all respond in different ways to information presented by different means—in written language, in oral tales, or in music, for example. The most effective way of accommodating these different intelligences is to gear teaching to the different learning styles of the individual kids in a group. A kid who is good at spatial representation and who can draw an understandable map for a treasure hunt should have that skill recognized just as readily as the kid who writes out—with perfect spelling, usage, and grammar—the instructions for other students to hunt the treasure.

The Eight Intelligences

Linguistic intelligence The capacity to use language to express and understand.

Logical-mathematical intelligence The capacity to understand underlying principles as a scientist would, or to manipulate numbers and operations and test possible solutions to problems the way a mathematician does.

Spatial intelligence The ability to represent the spatial world internally in your mind, like a navigator or pilot, a chess player or sculptor.

Bodily kinesthetic intelligence The ability to use the body, in whole or part, to solve problems or to create.

Musical intelligence The ability to think in music; to hear, recognize, remember, and manipulate musical patterns.

Interpersonal intelligence The ability to empathize with and understand other people.

Intrapersonal intelligence The understanding of self, of who you are, your own strengths and limitations.

Naturalist intelligence The ability to discriminate between and classify objects in nature and living things.

How Kids Learn

All young children learn naturally by playing, by observing, and by association. Having unstructured time to play alone never loses its importance for kids to learn through experiences. The child who claims the floor of the family room for a dinosaur village may appear to be playing with no particular goal. But his journey is his destination—his carnivores are chasing herbivores; the feeding station near the waterfall is littered with bones; he is creating a rich mural in his mind that makes connections with his burgeoning network of knowledge.

"Adults have all the terminology to explain things to a child, yet sometimes one child using vague language can get a concept or an idea, like borrowing in subtraction, across to another child more easily. Maybe it's because they explain the simple mechanics without worrying about all the background."

JOYCE, MOTHER OF FOUR

But by the time a child is six, the adults in his world impose a formal structure on his learning that we call school, or our education system. There are dozens of theories about what is the best learning environment or educational structure for children at different ages. However, in most elementary schools in Canada, kids are grouped by age with one or more classroom teachers who are responsible for presenting the common curriculum devised by each province's ministry of education.

In developing curriculum and learning resources, educators follow the basic progression of how all children learn.

From simple to complex A child must understand the simpler idea of the number 2 standing for two objects before she can add 2 + 2.

From known to unknown A child can take in new information if it connects to what she already knows. A child has to understand what a noun is before he can understand how adjectives modify nouns.

From self to other Young children learn best about themselves and their own world. As a child matures, she can connect to what's outside her world.

From whole to part Children begin drawing figures that have little detail. As they mature, they add hands and feet and curly hair.

From inaccurate (approximation) to more accurate A child learns to spell by writing letters that approximate the sounds of the words, then gradually becomes more aware of different spelling patterns for words.

From concrete to abstract A child needs to understand how to cut an apple into two equal halves before she can understand the abstraction of dividing by 2.

From exploratory to goal-directed A child begins learning about money by holding and playing with coins before he develops the goal of saving some of those coins to buy a treat.

From impulsive to self-controlled A child learning to get along with others has to learn that she can't be the only one to play with the blocks in the classroom; she gradually learns to be less impulsive or self-indulgent as a way of getting along with others.

Learning to Read

Long before your child begins school or learns her letters, she is on her way to reading. Educators tell us that reading is not a separate skill that a child acquires but rather part of her general language development, which includes listening, speaking, and writing. So your child's opportunities to tell stories, hear stories, have conversations, ask questions, answer questions are all part of helping her learn to read. Reading aloud to your child, even up to about twelve years of age, not only helps her to become a successful reader, but helps you maintain close connections.

Reading aloud to your child is the best way to help her become a successful reader.

Once your child begins to receive instruction in reading and writing in grade one, she will learn that both activities have a purpose: to inform (instructions), to entertain (stories), to direct (traffic signs). At the same time as she learns the letters and the sounds each letter or combination makes, she learns to use those letters to communicate. Her spelling will be inventive at first; she'll begin by approximating a word, perhaps with one letter—*c* for *cat*, then some months later *ct* may become *cat*, and finally she writes *cat* as *c a t*. The more opportunities she has to write, without feeling constrained by having to get the spelling right, the more opportunities she has to expand her knowledge of how letters and their sounds correspond. This comprehension supports her development of reading skills. To be a skillful reader, your child must learn to identify words quickly and accurately. To do this, she needs regular opportunities to read. She also needs to learn phonics, the relationship between letters and their sounds, so that she can decode new words. After much debate about the emphasis on phonics in reading instruction, most educators agree that inclusion of phonics instruction helps children develop skills in word recognition.

As your child begins reading picture books and simple stories, she brings her background knowledge into play to help her comprehend the characters, the setting, and the action. For example, in a story about a boy walking his dog, a child needs to know that dogs must be walked regularly in order to understand the story. Teachers may supply this background information during class discussion, but parents attuned to their child's needs can help provide the experiences and discussions about those experiences that give their child a context for reading and comprehending what they read.

Your child also needs many opportunities to read aloud to demonstrate her new abilities. It gives you a chance to evaluate her progress and to assess what reading errors she continues to make and why. When you're listening to your child read, ignore mistakes unless they prevent her from comprehending the text. Correcting every small error breaks her train of thought and will make her feel frustrated and unsure. When she makes a mistake that does affect the meaning, wait a second to see if she goes back and finds the right word. If she doesn't, help her to decode the word and pronounce it properly, and then have her reread the sentence to comprehend the meaning.

Your child also needs opportunities for silent reading. If you talk conversationally about the story after she has read it silently, she can demonstrate her comprehension of the material. Even after your child begins to read comfortably on her own, continue to read aloud to her. This gives you the opportunity to introduce books that she may enjoy but not yet have the ability to read herself. It is also a wonderful way to continue to share the joy of reading with your child.

SEE PAGE 214

Learning Styles

Imagine your child making popcorn in a microwave for the first time. Would he: a) read the directions on the package? b) holler "How long do I zap it for?" at you? c) toss the packet into the microwave, hit a few buttons, and then watch to see what happened? Your answer will give you a clue to your child's learning style.

Most kids follow a favoured path when processing new information. This path becomes more apparent in the early years of school; by grade two or three, parents and teachers can often detect which children are visual learners, who learn by observing and seeing; which are auditory learners, who learn most easily by listening; and which are kinesthetic learners, who soak up knowledge through hands-on experience.

Most children, though, don't show a complete preference for one learning style over the others. Many draw on two of the three different styles, and those students who excel in school usually show facility with all three styles. You may have already identified your child's preferred way of learning, whether or not you use one of these labels. If so, you can probably help her both to take advantage of her strongest style of learning and to work on improving her ability to use the other styles. There are hot debates among psychologists over classification issues, and expert opinions do vary, but the labels and descriptions that follow offer a starting point for parents interested in exploring the topic further.

Learning Styles

Visual learners:

- learn by seeing; for example, by watching others, by reading.
- have a preference for the "look-say" approach to learning to read.
- have creative imaginations; daydream, draw detailed and/or colourful pictures.
- remember faces better than names.
- have good handwriting.
- tend to check out a new situation carefully before joining in.
- prefer art to music.
- often see a detail first rather than the whole.
- are often meticulous about their work.

Visual learners represent about 65 per cent of the population.

Auditory learners:

- learn most easily by listening to explanations.
- have a preference for phonics instruction as part of learning to read.
- love to chatter and socialize.
- often talk to themselves while working.
- have strong vocabularies.
- are easily distracted by noise.
- may have a strange sense of fashion, mixing unmatchable colours and patterns.
- prefer music to art.

Auditory learners make up about 15 per cent of the population.

Kinesthetic or tactile learners:

- learn best through direct involvement in the action: modelling, building, producing.
- are adept at taking things apart and putting them back together.
- excel at some sports.
- are good dancers.
- fidget and touch things constantly.
- touch you to get your attention.
- respond well to touch.
- are poor spellers.
- have poor handwriting.
- have difficulty with verbal or written direction.
- read with difficulty and often don't enjoy being read to.

This group comprises about 10 per cent of the population.

Note that about 10 per cent of learners use two or three styles of learning.

Current teaching methods focus on helping kids learn in a variety of ways that accommodate different learning styles and expose kids to the other modes of learning that will be useful to them in acquiring some skills and disciplines. When you talk to your child's teacher, inquire how he accommodates the different learning styles when preparing lessons in each of the major strands of the curriculum–the language arts, mathematics, the sciences, the social studies, and the arts:

- slides, films, written work, and demonstrations for the visual learners.
- tapes, verbal instruction, periods of quiet time for the auditory learners.
- experiments, opportunities to build or to move around the whole classroom and school for the kinesthetic learners.

Educators in the primary grades usually create rich learning environments that respond to the different intelligences and learning styles of all students. By grades four or five, when the curriculum is more demanding of nine- to eleven-year-olds, teachers may tend not to balance their style of presentation and involvement of the students. Their classes may become weighted toward learning by reading and writing.

"Andrew is so much a visual learner that he has a problem with spoken instruction. If you give him directions that include several parts, he seems to panic and lose track of everything after the first part of the directions. So, if the teacher stands at the front of the class and tells everyone, 'Take your textbooks out, read chapter 3, do questions 10 through 20, and then hand your notebooks in to me,' he'll get lost after 'Take your textbook out.' If the instructions are written down, he's OK, and if he gets one-on-one direction, he's fine.

This difficulty became apparent in grade four, when he started getting more of these complicated instructions. We spoke to his two teachers who seemed to be aware of the problem, but they had the whole class to cope with. Luckily for us that year, there was an extra teacher in the class who was working with a learning disabled child who happened to sit very close to Andrew. She was able to give him that little bit of extra help he needed. Since then, we've made a point of making his teachers aware of the problem at the start of the year."

CINDY, MOTHER OF TWO

If you're concerned that your child isn't learning as well as she might, discuss with her classroom teacher what you know of your child's learning strengths to see how together you might meet your child's needs. Parents can help their child become more adept at incorporating all learning styles and techniques.

To improve visual learning skills:

- practise with flash cards and fill-in-the-blank worksheets.
- ask your child to choose a passage from a favourite book to copy out in his best handwriting.
- send notes in his lunch box and ask him for a written reply.

To exercise auditory skills:

- ask your child to describe the plot development of a TV show.
- have her write down on a grocery list the items that you dictate.
- read stories and poems aloud to one another.
- have her describe a piece of art, a map, or a design aloud as she looks at it.

Practise the kinesthetic style of learning by doing activities together, with your verbal explanations and instructions. Try:

- cooking or baking from simple recipes.
- washing the car.
- cleaning the bathroom.
- sorting the laundry.
- spelling words in sand.
- working out math problems using coins, toothpicks, beads, buttons.

Observe your child to understand how she learns best.

Learning Exceptionalities

Most children start school with an optimistic outlook on the first day. Your son may head off with a scrubbed face and a brand-new school bag, eager to learn. Then, somewhere between kindergarten and grade two, his enthusiasm starts to wane. He may seem reluctant to go to school, or his self-esteem may be suddenly in decline. If this happens, you might consider either behavioural change a sign that he has a learning problem at school.

Trust your instincts

Research shows that a parent usually has a gut feeling that something isn't quite right in the way her child's skills are developing. Similarly, if you notice at a later age that there's a discrepancy between what you believe your child is capable of and what he's accomplishing in language or mathematics, consider whether this signals an exceptionality. Of course, the parents of a child coping with a physical or developmental challenge will usually have been involved for several months or even years in attending to and advocating for their child's special needs. But some children cope quite well with less visible disabilities through early childhood and even through the primary grades. In the classroom environment, where children of the same age are expected to progress at a similar rate, the gap begins to widen in grade three at the ages of eight to nine. The challenges of the curriculum begin to overwhelm their coping strategies and make their difficulties more obvious to either parents or teachers.

At eight or nine, a child's special talents or learning difficulties become more apparent.

At this time, special talents as well as learning disabilities become more apparent. Both the students with special talents or academic gifts and the students with less visible learning disabilities are often grouped as students who require "special education." Some provinces group under this term all children with exceptionalities—the developmentally challenged, the physically challenged, the gifted and talented. It's education policy in most provinces now to include students with exceptionalities in regular classrooms. Classroom teachers must attempt to respond to the learning needs and learning styles of all students. The right to specialized training or an individualized program of study depends on a formal assessment by an educational psychologist and the recommendations that evolve from that. You might investigate what the specific guidelines and requirements are within your province or board.

What Is an Assessment?

Ideally, the assessment begins with your child's classroom teacher reviewing with you your child's schoolwork, report cards, and the results of any general tests administered in the school. If there is reason to think SEE PAGE 86 that your child has Attention Deficit Hyperactivity Disorder (ADHD), the teacher might also suggest a medical assessment by a pediatrician. Medical assessments within the public health system can be arranged through your family doctor. Academic assessments by an educational psychologist employed by the school board are also publicly funded. However, there may be a long wait, anywhere from five months to two years.

Parents may decide to arrange and pay for a private assessment (fees range from $800 to $1,500). The faculty of education at a nearby university or the child development clinic at a hospital may offer subsi- SEE PAGE 230 dized assessments. The Learning Disabilities Association of Canada, with 140 local chapters, can provide a list of recommended psychologists. If you choose this route, ensure that the school agrees to recognize the private psychologist's findings.

An action plan

The psychologist who does the assessment prepares a report outlining the specific ways that teachers and parents can help the child. Be sure you receive your copy of the report before the meeting arranged for you, your child's classroom teacher, and other staff who may become involved in helping your child. The psychologist should present the report at the meeting, at which the goal is to develop a specific plan to help your child and to ensure that the resources, including human resources, are available to put the details of the plan into action.

Parents will be responsible for some of the subsequent work with their child. But once the action plan is in process, continue to monitor the school situation to ensure your child is receiving the help outlined in the plan. You may be dealing with several different members of the school's staff. Have regular telephone chats or meetings with them and keep your own notes on meetings and conversations.

If you find that some aspect of your child's remedial help is not being addressed, speak first to your child's classroom teacher. If she's unable to help, follow up with the principal. Some parents of children with special needs find they must advocate for the programs their kids need with their board's superintendent and local trustees. To be an effective advocate, find out all you can about your child's learning problems by talking to experts and other parents. A good place to start is your local chapter of the Learning Disabilities Association of Canada, one of the most active advocacy groups in the country. If you encounter delays in receiving either the assessment or the remedial help at your child's school, you might consider hiring an experienced tutor.

So much is still unknown about why some kids have trouble learning to read or to add and subtract. Parents of children with learning disabilities often find themselves on a difficult path through assessments by different experts and a range of recommended treatments. If you're one of those parents, you may be relieved to know that your child can reach the same educational goal as other kids his age—the journey may just take a little longer.

Most learning disabilities are identified within the first three years of school, although the problem and its symptoms may have been present earlier. Often the children who prove to have a learning disability had difficulty in developing language skills in their preschool years.

Speech Difficulties

If, for example, your child stutters or can't articulate particular sounds, you have probably been working with him to overcome the speech difficulty since you noticed it. However, some parents and their doctor believe that a child will grow out of an oral idiosyncrasy, as many kids do. But if he hasn't grown out of it by the time he starts school, it's important to act quickly.

First, approach your child's classroom teacher and possibly the principal. Some school boards require an assessment by a speech language pathologist whose diagnosis is used by the board's speech therapists. You may have to wait a month or up to a year for the assessment, which has no separate fee if handled by the school or a hospital. If the wait seems too long, you might ask your family doctor for a referral. Speech language pathologists charge about $100 an hour, but some health plans cover up to 85 per cent of that cost.

SEE PAGE 224

"From the time he began talking, it was apparent Matt had a speech problem. It turned out he was tongue-tied—the membrane that attaches the underside of the tongue to the mouth was too tight.

Not too long after he began kindergarten, about seven years ago, the school had him assessed and he started going to special speech classes within the school. The other kids teased him so much—for the way he talked as well as for going to these special classes—that I would leave work early so that I could pick him up at school so he wouldn't have to take the bus. He had exercises that he did regularly and after a year his speech had improved so much he was no longer teased. It meant a lot to me that the school picked up on the problem right away and scheduled an assessment. This year, Matt won a public speaking contest."

LAURIE, MOTHER OF FOUR

Supporting your child's extracurricular interests will encourage her, especially if she's frustrated by some other aspect of school.

Once your child has been diagnosed and is working with a speech therapist, you can usually supplement the therapy with work at home. Ask the therapist how you can help. Lynn Barnhardt is the only speech language pathologist for the fifteen schools in the Nipissing–Parry Sound Catholic District School Board in Ontario. Once a week she holds an after-school clinic for her student clients and their parents to help them understand how to do the required exercises properly at home. According to Barnhardt, the kids whose parents participate in the free clinics show a better rate of improvement over the kids whose parents don't attend.

The Talented or Gifted Child

To a loving parent, every child is special. We marvel at our baby's first words, applaud a first step, and beam with pride when she learns to print her name. School accomplishments, athletic prowess, or artistic talent fill us with joy. Some children are more talented than others in a particular skill or in one of the multiple intelligences. Unfortunately, standing apart from their peers can sometimes make them miserable.

Many intellectually gifted children become bored in traditional classrooms or in playing with kids their own age. Story time in grade one may not appeal to a six-year-old who can pick up her father's university textbook, read it, and understand it. As her classmates learn to add 2 plus 2, this child may be ready to work out square roots.

"He was a bright, sunny, happy little kid who, within a year of being in school, became a sad little boy. He was totally bored and frustrated. Teachers described him as rude and defiant, and some people actually suggested he was a sociopath."

JOE, FATHER OF TWO

Given the number of students a classroom teacher deals with, it may take some time for her to detect a child's extraordinary ability, to involve the child's parents, and to suggest assessment using the school board's resources. There is tremendous debate about how to measure intelligence and what measures to use. One way intellectually endowed students are identified is through intelligence tests, such as the *Wechsler Intelligence Scale for Children* or the *Stanford-Binet* test, on which the children score 130 or higher. A child's performance in the regular school program and on the classroom teacher's tests may or may not reveal individual gifts.

An estimated 2 to 4 per cent of Canadian children are exceptional in their intellectual gifts. If you think your child is really bright, talk with his classroom teacher and, if she agrees, request an individual assessment by an educational psychologist, if the school has not yet undertaken broad-based IQ testing of all students. Some school boards do such testing only toward the end of the primary grades. Most students in grade three are eight to nine years old, an age at which they have gained enough knowledge and skill to participate in standardized tests.

"I always thought bright children did better in school, that they would thrive on their own, but that's not the case."

JOE, FATHER OF TWO

If you want to arrange for individual testing of your child at an earlier age, explore the possibilities with developmental psychologists at the nearest children's hospital. You might also look for a parent support group, such as the Association for Bright Children (ABC). However, not every province has an ABC chapter. Each province has its own guidelines and legislation for assessing students, recognizing exceptionalities, devising programs, and providing resources to respond to their needs.

SEE PAGE 222

The Ministry of Education and Training in Ontario, for example, recognizes intellectual giftedness as one of the exceptionalities, and special education legislation ensures that resources are available. The support ranges from that provided by classroom teachers in a regular classroom to one hour per week of special studies to having the children attend full-time separate enriched classes, sometimes at another school.

Educators are divided on the benefits of separate classes. Research indicates, however, that intellectual giftedness is the only exceptionality from which kids benefit by being grouped together to study apart from the regular classroom. Some parent organizations like ABC support this solution, among other school-based programs that satisfy the child's needs. Teachers who work with intellectually gifted children grouped in a separate classroom say that the students establish the pace of learning for the class and probe the material on the curriculum much more deeply.

Language Disabilities

Over the years, learning disabilities have been given many labels. But the definitions of the various disabilities overlap and not all experts use the same labels for the same problems. Dyslexia, which describes a complex of reading and writing comprehension problems, is the term that covers the most common learning disability.

In the past, dyslexia was considered a problem of perception. The core symptom of this difficulty is the inability to sound out words or to read individual words quickly or automatically. But it is now believed that there isn't a problem with how the child perceives the letters and words, but there is a problem with her "working memory." Working memory is the term for holding something in your memory in the way that you've just seen or heard it, while simultaneously manipulating or working with it. It appears that kids with a reading disability don't remember the orientation of the letters in a word they've just seen.

Reading disabilities and phonics

Children who have difficulty associating the sounds of language (phonemes) with the letters that represent those sounds have another type of dyslexia. A difficulty translating sounds into letters or letters into sounds may be seen in youngsters who have trouble sounding out words like *caterpillar* as *cat-er-pil-lar*, or in the child who can't string rhyming words together like *mummy, tummy, yummy.*

Most kids learn to read at their own speed within the first year of school, so grade one may be too early to do any formal assessment. But if you become concerned during the first term of grade one that your child has made very little progress in language skills, discuss your concerns with his teacher. Inquire whether her language arts program for the class includes specific instruction and practice in phonics and spelling. Many children learn to read and write without problems, but some children, especially those with learning disabilities, benefit from the slow and steady process of linking the sounds they hear to the printed letters that represent these sounds. Emphasis on phonics instruction has gone in and out of favour over the years in Canadian schools. The pendulum has swung back, and phonics again has a prominent role in the language arts curriculum for kindergarten and the primary grades.

Phonics again has a prominent role in the primary language arts curriculum.

Although all kids have to learn about the shapes and forms of letters and how they're grouped to form words, most kids grasp these basics by the age of seven. If your child still has difficulty and hasn't progressed in his language skills by the end of grade two, it may be because of a learning disability. You might ask the classroom teacher and the principal to arrange for an assessment by an educational psychologist. If the psychologist's report describes a particular disability, your school or neighbourhood of schools should provide the help your child needs. A resource teacher may work with him and others in his regular class, or he may attend a separate resource class part-time or full-time.

SEE PAGE 80

At home, parents can supplement their child's language experiences by playing games with language, by a daily session of reading, by taking turns reading and being read to, and by talking together about what you've read or about any activity you've been doing together. In these ways, you help him explore written materials that match his intellectual level or interests, and he picks up new vocabulary, increases his comprehension skills, and maintains a love of books.

Writing disability in language and mathematics

Children who have problems with the number operations in mathematics often also have difficulties with printing and spelling. They have difficulty putting words down on paper, whether copying written work from the chalkboard or writing a story. Composing the story is not the problem; the stumbling block arises when they try to transfer the ideas from their imagination to the paper. These kids may sometimes read slowly, but their comprehension skills are solid, and they seldom have difficulty talking and answering questions.

To be a skillful reader, your child must learn to identify words quickly and accurately.

The difficulties become apparent during grade three, when the amount of mathematics and written work in all subjects increases. Share your concerns with your child's teacher and principal. If they agree that the child's difficulty is serious, there may be reason to request a formal assessment. But sometimes just acknowledging the difficulty and undertaking remedial work is the best help. The help should focus on teaching the child strategies for coping with his disability and practising techniques to improve in the areas affected.

SEE PAGE 80

These strategies include, for young kids, the concrete manipulation of numbers (as on an abacus), doing math problems on graph paper to keep the digits in columns, highlighting the mathematical symbols for operations like addition and subtraction, or, for older kids, using a calculator and an electronic dictionary for spelling. These kids do much better on assignments with fill-in-the-blanks answer sheets and multiple choice tests, than on projects that require more writing. Some schools also permit them to have extended time to complete essays and exams in later years.

Attention Deficit Hyperactivity Disorder

SEE PAGE 223

Attention Deficit Hyperactivity Disorder (ADHD) is the expanded term that encompasses what was first called only "attention deficit disorder," but one of whose characteristics was hyperactivity. ADHD comprises two distinct clusters of problems that can interfere with learning. A child with ADHD may be hyperactive and impulsive. Sometimes he has an inability to pay attention or focus on work, even for a short period of time. The two problems are often combined, and sometimes ADHD can occur with other learning disabilities.

Not all kids who show signs of ADHD actually have the condition. Some of them respond to a change in environment—a more structured classroom, less ambient noise. Even an extra hour of sleep each night has improved the behaviour of some children showing signs of ADHD. If you suspect your child has ADHD, discuss his behaviour with your family doctor. You may decide to ask for a referral to a psychologist or psychiatrist. The diagnosis of ADHD requires an assessment by a professional with experience in the disorder. For an accurate diagnosis, your child's behaviour should be assessed in every context—at school, at home, and during other activities. If your child's behaviour is consistent in all contexts, then he may be diagnosed with ADHD.

ADHD is a neurobiological disorder thought to be caused by an imbalance in the brain's neurotransmitters, and it may require chemical treatment. Currently, the main medication for the disorder is the stimulant drug Ritalin. However, most parents are loath to put young children on a powerful drug that might have side effects. Also, Ritalin may not work for every child. Before agreeing to Ritalin as a treatment for ADHD,

---

> "Matthew was a handful from the time he was born. I couldn't take him anywhere—he would go wild in a store or anywhere there was a crowd. The doctor told me he was just a typical boy. By the time he was in grade two but working at a kindergarten level, my sister who's a social worker advised me to get him tested for ADHD. At that point, the school board didn't even consider ADD/ADHD to be a learning disability. We had him tested privately by a psychiatrist who prescribed Ritalin and taught all of us coping strategies. She would re-examine him every month before writing a new prescription, checking for any side effects and also how he was doing in school.
>
> It took another three years for the school to recognize ADHD. We have an annual meeting with them to sign papers that say what subjects he needs extra help with. He's supposed to get extra help, but it's not happening much this year. We've been told that they don't have the funding and that other kids need help more than Matthew. We've hired a tutor, though, and that's working well. Each fall we talk to his teachers and tell them he's on Ritalin—some of them can't believe it. For Matthew, it helps him to focus in situations where he otherwise wouldn't be able to."
>
> JOANNE, MOTHER OF TWO

---

ask your doctor to administer a double-blind test to ensure the drug will be effective for your child. In such a test, the child receives the Ritalin for a number of weeks and then a placebo for the same period. The child, his parents, his teacher, and his doctor don't know when he's on the drug and when he's on the placebo, but they assess the child's behaviour during both periods to see whether there is any change. This process establishes whether the child's behaviour improved or not during the period he was on Ritalin.

Alternative therapies to treat ADHD include adjusting the child's diet and environment. The Canadian Naturopathic Association can provide you with information on licensed naturopathic doctors in your area. However, there is no scientific data currently available on the effectiveness of dietary treatments or other such alternative treatments.

SEE PAGE 225

Coping with ADHD

You want to help your child learn coping skills that he will eventually apply himself without your prompting.

- Help your child to maintain order in his day by establishing clear routines. When he gets off track, remind him gently, "What's the first thing you need to do? What comes after that?"
- Be firm about his staying on track. "When you have brushed your teeth, then you may watch TV."
- Monitor his schedule. A child with ADHD is especially sensitive to being overloaded with too many activities. He needs to break up his activities into smaller chunks and focus on each one at a time.
- State directions clearly and simply. Avoid long explanations, however well-intentioned.
- Catch your child in good behaviour and comment on it frequently. Sometimes it's so easy to be overwhelmed by his inappropriate behaviour that that's all you focus on.
- Catch your child paying attention, and give him positive feedback. Some children with ADHD don't really understand what "paying attention" means. They need clear feedback when they are displaying appropriate skills.
- Talk to your child about his experience with ADHD. Tell him that the condition is not his fault. It's just a part of his life and he needs to learn coping strategies to deal with it. Let him know that he can achieve as well as his unaffected peers, but that it might take him a little longer. Many adults with ADHD have learned to manage their condition and are creative and productive.

Evaluating Student Progress

Most elementary schools in Canada issue report cards on student progress three times a year. Your child's report card is meant to give you a good understanding of your child's achievements. If the report card doesn't enlighten you about how your child is doing in each subject evaluated, it may be because of an overdose of educational terminology: outcomes, benchmarks, indicators, standards, and pat phrases may be confusing. Here's how to "assess" the report and interview your child's teacher so that you have a clear picture of your child's progress.

Teachers have a variety of techniques to evaluate student progress at different ages. They may include the following:

Ages five and six: kindergarten and grade one

- *Observation* The primary means of evaluation at this age. The classroom teacher notes her observations daily or weekly on your child's work and contribution in class.
- *Performance* Students perform a task to show how well they can apply the knowledge and skills they've developed during each term.

Ages seven to nine: grades two and three

- Both observation and performance.
- *Portfolios* The teacher and the student put a selection of the student's best work in a folder. Its contents may include book reports, tests, drawings, or videotapes. Students help choose the samples of work collected in the portfolio over the school year. The range makes the student's progress over the year more obvious for the student, the teacher, and the parents. At parent-teacher meetings, parents can discuss with the classroom teacher how their child's level of ability and understanding is demonstrated in the work.
- *Tests or quizzes* Teachers usually develop tests or quizzes to assess what students have learned in each unit of study throughout the school year.

Large-scale assessments

- *Curriculum-based tests* These tests are based on the provincial or board curriculum and measure the students' mastery of the curriculum. These tests usually are undertaken during grade three (nine-year-olds), grade six, grade nine, and grade twelve.
- *Standardized tests* In some boards or provinces, students may participate in a board-wide or province-wide test, like the Canadian Test of Basic Skills (CTBS), which measures their general skills and knowledge. The results are analyzed (often by computer)

and reported in different printouts that allow educators and parents to compare each student's achievement with other students of the same age and grade.

Ages ten to twelve: grades four, five, and six

- *Projects* These take on greater significance. Students are assessed on their ability to work independently or in a group on a project with a specific deadline for completion.
- *Journals* Students are encouraged to express their ideas and feelings, ask questions, and respond to open-ended questions in their own journal of learning. Their classroom teacher gains insight into the students' learning processes, as well as their social and personal growth and intellectual development.
- *Tests and quizzes* Teacher-developed quizzes and tests assess what students have learned throughout each unit of study in the curriculum. The results in each subject area contribute to the year-end marks.
- *Observation, performance and portfolios* These continue to be important parts of the teacher's evaluation.

Reading a Report Card

The results of these varied evaluations appear on a report card issued at the end of each term. Recent trends in report cards indicate that ministries of education are listening to and acting on parent complaints that report cards had become difficult to understand and were filled with education jargon. Most boards issue report cards that use levels of grading: A, B, C, and D or 1, 2, 3, and 4. Be sure you understand what the levels mean.

What's in a child's report card shouldn't come as a surprise to her parents. If she had been having serious difficulty with mathematics or the language arts, the teacher should have contacted you as soon as she became aware of the problem. However, on a report card, teachers do avoid being blunt in what they write, and tend to use general comments. A teacher might write "Greater attention in class would bring improved results," which probably means that your child is easily distracted, spends too much time talking to other kids, or doesn't listen. Teachers are careful to use standard phrases since all comments appear on a child's Student Record Card (SRC) which

Her teacher will observe on her report card how well your child listens.

follows her throughout her school years in any province or from province to province. Also, teachers do not want to arouse emotional responses from parents that will not help the child improve her performance.

To get a fuller picture of your child's performance, use the report card commentary in subsequent discussions with the classroom teacher. Ask what "good work" means. Does it mean that it's a personal best for your child or that she's at the top of the class? Can she improve her personal best academic performance, or is there another avenue like music, art, or sports that can help her become a well-rounded student. When you read "Michael is working to his greatest potential," ask what the teacher thinks Michael's potential is relative to that of his peers. Ask if you can see samples of the work of other students that reflect three or four different levels of achievement. If the teacher believes that your child can improve her skills or her performance, ask what you or your child can do or what the school can provide to achieve that improvement. Here are good questions to ask your child's teacher.

Ask your child's teacher how your child gets along with others.

Ages six to nine

- What will my child learn in language arts and mathematics?
- How will she learn it?
- Has she learned it?

Then ask questions that reveal work and study habits, such as:

- Does my child stay on task?
- Can she work independently?
- Will she work with others?

Ages ten to twelve

In addition to the above questions, ask about her attitude and willingness to actively pursue learning.

- Does my child have a positive attitude toward learning?
- Is my child keen to learn?

Parent-Teacher-Child Dynamics

First impressions count, so don't wait for problems to occur before you make yourself known to your child's teacher. A friendly first meeting can go a long way to setting the groundwork for a positive partnership.

By Week Two the class has settled into a routine and the organizational chaos of opening week is over. This is a perfect time to drop by for a quick introduction. The best time to visit is at the end of the school day as the last student walks out the door. Keep the conversation friendly and the meeting brief. Chances are the teacher will have a staff meeting to attend or another appointment to keep. Find out what the best time of day is for you to contact her in the future. If you're able to volunteer in the classroom, let her know.

A friendly first meeting with your child's teacher can set the groundwork for a positive partnership.

Make it a habit to talk to the teacher regularly. There will be several opportunities to visit your child's classroom during the school year, but if you want the teacher's undivided attention, schedule an individual meeting. At open houses and parent nights, the teacher has to make herself available to many parents. It's not an appropriate time for you to have a serious individual discussion with her about your son's learning difficulties. You might contact your child's teacher when:

- *good things happen.* Your daughter comes home from school excited because she got an A on her book report and she was asked to read it to the class. Call her teacher to say how happy your child was to be rewarded for her efforts.
- *a child is disciplined.* Your daughter complains that she was unfairly sent to the principal's office for bad behaviour. Call her teacher to get the full account.
- *a child is unhappy or fearful in school.* Your son says the teacher is picking on him and doesn't like him. Does the teacher know your child feels this way?
- *there's a crisis in the family,* such as the death of a family member, or your separation or divorce. Things that disrupt family life at home may affect your child's schoolwork. Let the teacher know so that she can help your child cope.

If you would like more information about what's happening in your child's classroom and how he's handling his schoolwork, don't wait for a problem to occur or for the first scheduled parent-teacher interview. Do wait, however, until the second month of school. By that time, the teacher will know more about your child and how he's managing. Request a 30-minute interview. Let her know you would like to find out more about the curriculum and the learning resources being used and how your child participates in class activities.

Parent-Teacher Interview Etiquette

After you receive your child's report card for the first term, you will be invited to a formal parent-teacher interview. Even if your child loves school and is getting straight A's, don't miss this opportunity to get to know his teacher better. Attending Home and School night shows your child as well as the school staff that you care about what happens in his classroom.

"I always try to use the back door. It gets more done. Go to council meetings early so you can speak directly to department heads. Call school trustees at home and share confidences, and attend locally advertised political speakers' conferences."

TANYA, MOTHER OF THREE

At this meeting, the classroom teacher will likely have a portfolio of your child's work to discuss with you. The teacher may also have displayed around the classroom samples of work by other children in the class. Don't be shy about asking to see other work samples by your child's peers; they might provide you with valuable insights into your own child's school performance. Sometimes the board or the provincial ministry of education produce guidelines with samples of the levels of achievement.

Talk to your child, too, before the meeting to remind yourself of what subjects or topics he likes and dislikes and what skills he's working to improve. Kids are concerned with more than grades, so talk about how they feel they're getting along with their classmates. If you have specific concerns, take a prepared list of questions and a copy of your child's report card to the meeting.

Let the teacher take the lead in your discussion. Listen carefully to what she says, and if she uses unfamiliar educational terms, ask her to clarify. If at the end of her comments you're still not clear about your child's progress, ask more specific questions.

SEE PAGE 90

If you still have questions after your 15-minute interview is over, request another meeting. Don't try to extend this interview into someone else's time slot. The teacher won't be able to give you her full attention if she's thinking about the parents waiting their turn outside the door.

Advocating for Your Child

Becoming an advocate for your child means learning to deal with conflict. To help parents improve their conflict resolution skills, the British Columbia Confederation of Parent Advisory Councils put together this guide to effective advocacy.

- **Listen to your child.** Carefully consider her views. Challenge your own attitudes and question your feelings. Can you listen even when you don't like what you hear?
- **Know the facts.** Ask questions in a way that gathers information.
- **Identify the issue.** Work to clarify and pinpoint issues. Decide on a key issue even if there are several. Make sure it's also an issue for your child.
- **Decide** if your child needs your support. Self-advocacy is an important life skill. Help your child build communication and conflict-resolution skills.
- **Document.** It's easy to get confused or forget. Jot down notes, record the dates of meetings and phone calls, and keep copies of all correspondence.
- **Identify appropriate support.** Talk over the issue with your spouse or a trusted friend. Seek the assistance of an advocate, if necessary.
- **Commit to resolution.** Don't give up and don't let others discourage you or divert you from representing your child's best interests.
- **Plan.** Think of the effect your plan will have on your child. Be flexible and open-minded.
- **Communicate.** Share your ideas with the people who can make change happen. Work to be assertive, not aggressive. Don't indulge in hearsay.
- **Stay involved.** Confirm action plans and arrange for follow-up. Help define reasonable deadlines for each goal and make sure you and your child are part of the resolution.

"Parents always seem to be worried that, if they criticize a teacher, she'll end up getting back at them through their children. In over twenty years of teaching, I've rarely seen it happen."

GREG, SCHOOL PRINCIPAL AND FATHER OF TWO

When Your Child Hates School

When your child is very unhappy about going to school, he feels the same way that you do when you're very unhappy about going to work. He opens his eyes in the morning and thinks, "Oh no, I have to go back there." His stomach churns and he tries to think of ways to avoid doing what he'd really rather not do. Unhappiness about school grinds down a child's spirit and has the same effect on his parents. You need to find out what's making your child unhappy and help him to solve his problems so that you can all start your days with a smile on your face.

Ages Six to Eight

During these ages, when a child says he hates school, his relationship with his teacher is rarely the source of discomfort. He may be unhappy about something that's happening outside the classroom. Perhaps he hates the bus ride to school: The noise, the roughhousing, and the threat of being pushed around by the bigger boys and girls can be scary. Remember that recess and lunch hour may also be a daily ordeal for shy, quiet children who don't have like-minded friends to play with. Try to determine what part of the school day your child doesn't like and why. Then discuss her worries with her classroom teacher, who should be able to help ease her distress. Here are some solutions for typical problems.

On the bus

Start a "bus buddy" program in which you pair older, responsible kids with younger kids for the ride to and from school. You might also have adult volunteers hop aboard to ensure that all the kids feel safe and secure.

Find out what part of your child's school day is making her unhappy.

At recess and lunch hour

Include more organized games or activities that give all the kids something to do. This will lessen the time that a shy child may be left standing alone.

On the way home

The walk home can be scary for a child if other children tease or bully her. If bullying is the issue, talk to the principal—bullying should never be tolerated. Also talk the situation over with her teacher. The teacher may know of another child who travels the same route home and could suggest that the two travel together.

Ages Nine to Eleven

By the age of nine, your child's relationship with his teacher or bullying by other kids are the two most likely sources of the I-hate-school blues.

Teacher-child relationships

If your child complains about her teacher, take her concerns seriously. Teacher-child conflicts are real and shouldn't be dismissed as trivial or part of the growing-up process. Try to find out what exactly is affecting your child's relationship with her teacher. Does he have a loud voice that she finds frightening? Is she in a big class and her teacher has to be very strict to maintain order? Or do the two of them just not like each other?

When the relationship with the teacher is the problem, it becomes personal and it's difficult for a parent to deal with. But you need to talk honestly with the teacher about how she feels so that you can work together to resolve the problem. If your child spends five-and-a-half hours a day in a small room with a person she dislikes and who may dislike her, very little learning can occur.

At the meeting with the teacher, be prepared to listen to a different version of the situation—your child may have neglected to tell you that she's been disruptive in class. Ask the teacher what he can do to help your child feel more comfortable. Follow up the meeting with a friendly note outlining the discussion and conclude with a suggested date for talking again in a couple of weeks.

"My teacher was always yelling, even if you didn't do anything bad. Like, she'd yell at you if you didn't get an answer right. Right before school I always felt kinda sick. Sometimes I'd get a stomachache. I think it was an excuse to stay home."

MIKE, AGE 10

Over the next week or two, watch for signs of change. If your child appears happier, let the teacher know at your next meeting. If not, discuss what other strategies the teacher and the child might pursue to improve their relationship. If there is no improvement over the next week or two and your child still complains about school, contact the principal. You may need to request that he arrange to transfer your child to another classroom.

Bullying

If your child arrives home with unexplained mud- or grass-stained clothing, if he's frequently "losing" toys or he's often ravenous as if he hasn't eaten all day (his lunch was stolen), you may well suspect that your child is being harassed by another student or students.

"I stayed home a lot and got so sick about how another boy was treating me at school that I would throw up before I had to leave my house. I'm not the target anymore, but things are not the same at school. I still don't feel comfortable."

MARK, AGE 12

Talk to him about what goes on at school. Ask what he does at recess or lunch hour. Whom does he play with? Is anyone nice to him? Is anyone mean to him? Try not to show anger in your child's defence. Put your energy into comforting and helping him. Talk to the parents of other children in the class or at the school. Find out if other students have had a similar problem. You need to know how widespread the problem is, and it may take some discussion to get the full story.

Kids are not always keen to have their parents involved in their problems with other kids. Your child may be afraid of retaliation if he tells you what's happening. But if your child doesn't want to go to school because other children call him names, threaten him, kick him, or steal his lunch, you need to inform the principal immediately. Being victimized by other kids can have a devastating effect on your child's self-esteem and make it impossible for him to learn at school.

Tell the principal what you understand is happening and ask if she has any insight into the situation. Ask her to investigate and let you know how she'll deal with the situation. In most provinces, the education legislation gives the principal the authority to maintain order and discipline in the school, so she has somewhat broad powers. The school might opt to arrange counselling for the aggressors, or to punish them by cancelling privileges, or to suspend them. If the problem continues during the first two steps, discuss the situation with the principal immediately. The school officials must deal even more seriously with any further aggressive act.

Some schools have programs for conflict resolution run by students themselves with the help of their teachers or consultants who have developed expertise in this area. Encourage your child's principal to start a conflict-resolution program. It can be as simple as discussing it regularly at Home and School meetings, creating a peer-mediation program, or involving students in role-playing games that teach them appropriate social behaviours.

Teach your child to speak out against bullying. Assure him that he is not a tattletale if he reports when someone is getting hurt by another person. If you discover that your child is the bully, teach her to talk out problems instead of resorting to aggression. Teaching her to take a time-out from a situation or to count to ten to calm down could make a big difference.

SEE PAGE 125

Age Twelve

The social scene

For senior elementary students, friendship or the lack of it is the Number One cause of problems. Being left out of or dropped by a group can upset your child and make her anxious or depressed.

SEE PAGE 158

- Contact your kid's classroom teacher or a guidance counsellor if the school has one, and let him know how your child feels. Ask for his advice and insight into the situation. He may be able to help just by talking with your child and steering her into a school activity with other like-minded kids.

For senior elementary students, friendship or the lack of it is the Number One cause of problems at school.

- Help your child find a sport, hobby, or club outside of school that will introduce her to other young people with similar interests.
- Go shopping. No, you don't want your child to think that making friends means wearing the "in" labels. But having the right hairstyle, the right clothes, the right look is very important to twelve-year-olds. Let your preteen choose some cool-looking clothes that fit the family budget.
- If friendship and the lack of it continues to be a problem, talk to your child about choosing a different high school from the one in the neighbourhood, a high school where she'll be able to get a fresh start.

Going to a new school

Before your child's first day at a new school, you can make the transition go a little smoother.

- Visit the school as often as you can before the first day of classes. Attend school plays, band concerts, or fun fairs that offer your child a sneak peek at what's to come. The grade eight play may not look polished to you, but a six-year-old will be dazzled by the stars on stage.
- Let an older brother or sister give a personal tour of the school hot spots outside of the classroom. The tour should include such things as water fountains, washrooms, and the school yard.
- One week before classes begin, drop by the school and introduce yourself and your child to the principal, the school office staff, and his new teacher.

Teach your child to speak out about bullying. It's not tattling if she reports when someone is getting hurt.

Homework

Views differ widely on the value of homework. For kids in the primary grades, some parents and teachers see homework as just busy work. Others value it as a bridge between home and school and a way to teach children to take responsibility for their own learning. By the time a student is in grades four to six, however, there is more consensus among educators and parents that applying what they've learned in class by doing assignments as homework is a good way for kids to learn to work independently.

Will doing homework improve your child's performance? Research indicates that high school students who spend 60 to 90 minutes a night on homework can improve their grades. But for elementary school students, especially those in the primary grades, there are no answers about the effectiveness of homework to improve grades.

Just as teaching methods have changed over the years as we've learned more about human intellectual development, so has the concept of homework changed. A trip to the zoo, or an afternoon in the park collecting leaves to mount and label, or tallying the number and length of commercials in a few television programs are all different forms of homework, that is, schoolwork outside the classroom.

By the time they're nine years old, many children consider homework something of a chore, something to fit in between time spent with friends, or watching favourite TV programs, or playing. Teachers recognize that many children aged six to twelve have busy schedules of lessons, group activities, and team sports, so some elementary schools make it a policy never to assign homework on weekends. Adding major homework assignments for Monday just means adding more stress to family life.

The amount of time that your child spends on homework should relate to his age, somewhat like this:

Ages six and seven Up to grade two, five minutes of reading or other language activity with Mom or Dad constitutes homework.

Ages eight and nine By grade three, a child's homework may consist of a page of mathematics that wasn't completed in class or a special project that requires some research. Kids may spend about 20 minutes a night on such homework. For this age group, most teachers give outside class assignments for the weekend only if the child has been absent and needs to catch up to his peers.

"It only takes two to five minutes to do a sheet of questions. It's not hard work and it's pretty fun."

JOE, AGE 7

Ages ten to twelve By grade five, the number of homework assignments and special projects increases. Depending on their classroom teacher, students may have to spend up to 45 minutes a night on their schoolwork. By this age, managing his time to handle short-term (next day) and long-term (individual or group projects) homework assignments becomes a learning activity in itself. These skills are essential for success in senior elementary school and in high school—and even as a life skill.

Be positive about the necessity of doing homework assignments and planning personal study time. The catch phrase "lifelong learning" is more than just a phrase; it stresses the most important part of education—"learning how to learn." A parent's negative comment, such as "I wouldn't do this assignment either" or "Does your teacher think we have nothing else to do at night?" removes the responsibility for learning from the individual child and turns it back to something imposed from "outside," by the teacher and the school system.

But homework is of little value at any age if every school night turns into a "fight night" at home. Many children argue with their parents from time to time about whether they're doing enough homework or independent study, but when the fights become routine, it's time to take action.

- Schedule daily time for homework. During that scheduled time, your child must stop all other activities and concentrate on the assignments. If your child rushes through so that her homework is often messy or incomplete, set a specific number of minutes for the homework. If she gets her math done in five minutes but it's sloppy, let your child know you expect her to spend the rest of the allotted 20-minute homework time reading or writing.
- If your child dawdles over his homework so that he never seems to finish in the time frame, suggest an activity he enjoys for you and him to do after he's finished the homework so that he'll work more quickly.
- Set up a study area for him that's free of distractions. The kitchen table is fine, as long as other family members respect his "quiet" time.
- Create a homework survival kit, and put an end to the time-wasting search for school supplies. In a shoe box or other container, place the supplies she needs to do assignments: pencils, sharpener,

"Kids should start getting into the habit of doing a little extra work at night in the early grades. Sometimes I wonder, though, if too much homework isn't a sign that not enough is being done during class time. If that's the case..., why?"

CATHY, MOTHER OF TWO

eraser, pens, ruler, tape, scissors, markers, and perhaps a dictionary appropriate to her age. Have available a supply of different kinds of paper: loose-leaf paper, graph paper, unlined paper, Bristol board, construction paper.

- Avoid over-scheduling your child with outside activities on school nights. If your child finds it difficult to fit homework in between bagpipe lessons and soccer, perhaps it's time to cut back.
- Teach your child time management skills along with research skills. Show her how to tackle major projects by listing the main stages and individual steps necessary to complete them. She'll get a sense of accomplishment from checking off each step as she completes it:
  Monday: Get books from the library.
  Tuesday: Read and make notes.
  Wednesday: Write a first-draft copy.
  Thursday: Revise the writing and do the illustrations.
- Show your interest in your child's progress by reading his homework when he's finished, and give him a pat on the back for a job well done.

"After much thought on the homework issue (and, believe me, I've been one of those parents who encouraged, helped, and occasionally cajoled, her children into getting their homework done), I have decided that homework is a non-issue. It just should not exist."

DEB, MOTHER OF THREE

Too much homework

Kids do need time to be kids, so if you think your child has too much homework, contact his classroom teacher. Ask if she gives out homework every night and how much time she expects students to spend on the homework. Try to evaluate how the teacher's goals fit yours for your child at a particular age. Perhaps your child spends more time than average on the homework assignments because he's struggling to understand the concepts and requires extra time and attention in class.

A teacher will sometimes misjudge her students and assign too much homework to a class. If you feel this is the case, express your concern. Let her know that your child finds the amount of work stressful and ask that it be reduced. Monitor the situation and, if there's no change, speak to the principal.

Not enough homework

Not enough homework or no homework is just as common a complaint from parents. If your child tells you frequently, "I don't have any homework" or "I already did it in school," double-check with his teacher.

You're probably getting the straight goods. Some children are able to complete all their assignments in class; others choose to stay in at recess or use some of their lunch hour to do the assignments.

If you discover that your child isn't bringing her homework home, ask her teacher whether your daughter needs to record her assignments in a homework book that she brings home with her. A teacher usually writes assignments on the chalkboard for students to copy into their homework books. In the primary grades, teachers usually check planners or homework books to make sure students have copied all the information they need. By grade four, nine-year-olds are given much less assistance to list homework assignments, upcoming tests, projects, and unfinished work in a planner. By grade six, or ages eleven and twelve, the student should be solely responsible for the planner contents. The teacher might spot-check the books from time to time and initial them to verify that the work has been completed.

Tackling the BIG Project

If your child is overwhelmed by a major project assignment, help him understand that "big" can become "small" by following these steps:

1. Read the assignment together and discuss his ideas about the project. Make sure he has chosen a topic that's focused and manageable. No youngster can do justice to "Ancient Greece." But a grade five student can do a good job on "Chariots of Ancient Greece."
2. Help him describe verbally first, then write down the steps necessary to complete the project: gathering research materials; reading and taking notes; producing an outline; writing a rough copy; and doing a final draft.
3. Make a schedule. Estimate how long each step will take on a calendar. When each step is complete, your child can cross it off and see the end in sight!
4. Talk about the project as her work progresses to help her think it through and crystallize her ideas.
5. Review the rough draft, but resist any temptation to red-pencil any mistakes. Find something good to say. Be gentle in your comments. If the project is a total disaster, the first thing you say should still be positive, even if it's only "Oh good, you underlined the title."
6. Resist the temptation to do the project yourself. Your job is to show an interest, to be there as a resource, and to cheer him on.

Family Games for Fun and Learning

Playing Scrabble on a rainy Sunday and Twenty Questions on a car trip are wonderful family times. Games are, by their nature, fun, invigorating, and even exciting. Board games and card games also offer a wealth of learning opportunities. They can enhance our memory, teach spelling and mathematics, build cooperative learning skills, and provide lessons in strategy and logic.

Sometimes families get caught up in the win-lose aspect of the games and miss out on the fun. Parents should guide a young child through a game with words of encouragement. Ensure that she wins often by changing the rules of the game to fit both her level of skill and her level of comfort at losing. For example, play a game so that there's more than one winner, or take the focus off individual scores by adding up joint scores and seeing how high a score the team can achieve. By the time they are ten, most children understand that they can't always be winners and they'll want to play the game just for the fun of it.

Word games for reading

By the time your child is six, you've probably found that riddles and rhymes have helped her talk her way to improved language skills. Encourage her to continue repeating these rhymes for you or playing other silly rhyming games at home.

Language games Children aged seven and eight can practise reading skills in the junior versions of games like Monopoly or Trivial Pursuit. With help from family members, a ten-year-old can follow the instructions. Their spelling skills get a workout in Scrabble, Yahtzee, and Boggle.

Everyone Is a Winner!

You can't lose with an investment in these classic board games:

Age 6	Ages 7 and 8	Ages 9 and up
Parcheesi	Sorry	Battleship
Checkers	Boggle	Risk
Pop-o-Matic	Scrabble	Monopoly
(also called Trouble	Bingo	Clue
or Frustration)	Clue	Trivial Pursuit
Snakes and Ladders	Pictionary Jr.	
Memory	Monopoly Jr.	
	Top Story	

Games that add up

Number songs and number rhymes also help young children learning to manipulate numbers. A six-year-old probably already knows half a dozen rhymes like One, Two, Buckle My Shoe and This Old Man that teach counting forward and backward.

Other games offer practice in the skills of adding and subtracting. Think of a Number is a good game to play in the car, in the grocery store lineup, or while waiting in the doctor's office. Say "I'm thinking of a number that is 4 more than 5. Do you know what it is?" Getting the right answer gives your child a chance to think up the next question for you.

Simple question-and-answer games like I Spy or Twenty Questions are time-tested games for helping children develop problem solving skills. Number cubes and dominoes help them practise counting as they throw a pair of dice, add up the dot patterns, and move their piece around the board in a game of chance. Any game in which a score must be kept provides practice with mental addition.

Card games offer another fun way to play with number recognition and memory. Use simple card games to introduce younger children to the 52 cards in a deck, to the four suits of cards, to the values assigned to the face cards, and to the number cards. You might begin by playing Snap! Remove from a deck of cards the 10s, jacks, queens, and kings. Shuffle the remaining 36 cards and deal them out. Each player turns over one card, either in turn or at the same time. If the numbers on the two cards turned over add up to 10, the first player to shout "Snap!" wins those two cards. Play the game through until all the cards are won and lost. When children are older and more familiar with mathematical operations and with card values, they may be ready to play cribbage with Grandpa.

These young card sharks don't realize they're improving their math skills.

The Television Dilemma

Most Canadian kids spend, on average, 18 hours a week watching television, or the equivalent of three and a half school days a week. If, as parents, we feel strongly about how our children learn and develop in school, then we should be equally concerned about how these hours of watching television affect their development—socially, emotionally, physically, and intellectually.

There's one thing we can be certain of: The child who spends 2 or 3 hours a day watching television is not spending time in other activities. He's not reading, not collecting baseball cards, not talking with friends, not setting the table, not doing his math homework, and not arguing with his brother, all of which are just as important, if not more important, activities for his development.

It's true, however, that when he's watching television he's taking in massive amounts of information. Whether he's learning how duck eggs hatch on the Discovery channel or how Bart talks to Homer on *The Simpsons*, your child's brain is processing information, forming impressions, and having vicarious experiences. The better the quality of the TV programming, the higher the quality of the information.

"From the time I was six until I was twelve, we didn't have a TV. Usually I didn't mind at all—I loved to read and I figured I had it better than my friends because I could read under the covers with a little light after I was supposed to be sleeping—which they couldn't do with a TV. When I was twelve, I bought a set with my own money and became addicted to TV. I stopped reading for years. I will definitely monitor my own children's TV-watching—but I will have a TV in the house. Maybe if my parents had gone that route, I wouldn't have gone overboard when I was a teenager."

DAVE, FATHER OF INFANT TWINS

There have been many studies to assess how TV programs affect what kids think and how they behave. The most-often-asked question is how watching violence on TV affects kids' behaviour. Are they more likely to be violent? Are they less sensitive to seeing violence in real life? No one has proved direct cause and effect, but the cumulative result of many studies is that watching violence on TV skews the attitudes of some kids. These kids may feel that the potential for violence in their community is higher than it actually is, and become fearful. Or they may see violence as a valid way of solving problems (if someone makes you really, really mad, it's OK to punch him), and may act on this view.

The furor a few years ago over the Mighty Morphin Power Rangers came about because parents and teachers noticed that kids had become more aggressive with each other and were imitating the behaviour of these very popular TV characters. There is no question that kids incorporate what they see on television programs into their play in various ways. Whether the programs make children less imaginative in their play is another topic often debated.

Kids can learn an incredible amount of information about their world both from the TV programs and from the commercials developed by their sponsors, but sometimes that information is inaccurate or deliberately skewed to make a dramatic point or to sell a product. If children were to learn how to make their food choices from food commercials only, they might choose mostly foods that are high in fat, salt, and sweets. There are very few commercials for fresh fruits and vegetables on TV.

Children may also develop inaccurate impressions about what people should look like. The actors in dramas and the announcers in other programs are most often physically attractive, white, thin, and well-dressed. If kids perceive that they don't fit this physical ideal, they may become unhappy with their own appearance.

Television is a powerful force in your home, and can be used both for good and for ill. Recognizing that, you may want to devise means of controlling and "channelling" that power. The Alliance for Children and Television created a quiz to help parents assess whether television is interfering with their family life. It appears in their booklet *Minding the Set: Making Television Work for You and Your Family* (1994, 24 pages), produced by The Alliance with Rogers Cablesystems.

SEE PAGE 222

Sometimes agreeing on which TV shows to watch can cause friction among siblings.

Ask yourself:

- Does your child play outside?
- Does she play with friends?
- Does he use his imagination?
- Does she do her homework and chores?
- Does he have a hobby?
- Does she enjoy sports, music, reading?

If you answered No to three or more questions, then ask the following questions:

- When friends come over, do their children sit with yours in front of the television for the entire visit?
- When it snows, would your child rather keep watching TV than go outside to build a snowman or go sledding?
- Does she watch first thing in the morning, after school, before bed, and all weekend?
- Do you have trouble getting him to come to the dinner table or go to bed because he's watching TV?

Give yourself 1 point for every Sometimes and 2 points for every Always. Never scores 0 points. If you scored 4 or more, then television is probably interfering with your lives. Negotiate some rules with your kids about what programs they may watch.

Television keeps kids from playing freely, which is vital for their development.

There are several ways to manage TV watching in your household. Once you decide how much is enough, tell your kids, and then stick to your decision. You might settle on one hour per day or give your child a number of hours per week and let her spend them as she likes. You might limit her to programs on certain days of the week, say from Thursday through Sunday, or restrict her viewing choices to only certain channels.

Use the remote control to scan the programs available at regular times. Read the weekly TV listings together to select special programs. If there are movies or programs that your child wants to watch but that cause you some concern, watch them together and discuss the issues involved. If you have a VCR, don't let your child's favourite program prevent her from participating in another activity. Videotape the program and play it at a more convenient time. One way to curtail kids' viewing—and your own—is to keep your TV set in the least comfortable room in the house.

Computer Literacy

Computer literacy has become an essential part of your child's life. But parents, educators, and kids have been frustrated by the inconsistent integration of computer literacy training in schools. Equipping classrooms with hardware and software and giving teachers computer training is so expensive that there never seems to be enough of anything to go around. If there's only one computer for the thirty students in a class, individual students can't use the programs long enough to develop their skills.

Not all teachers have learned how to incorporate the software programs into the curriculum, or even to operate the equipment to its capacity, so it may sit in the classroom unused. But over the last two decades, many educators and involved parents have been successful at incorporating a variety of software programs into the different disciplines of the curriculum. In most provinces there are associations, like the SEE PAGE 228 Educational Computing Organization of Ontario (ECOO), that provide a forum for educators, parents, and students interested in the effective use of technology and computer software in education. Many school boards have designated one or two schools to serve as models in the "how to" of learning and teaching using the converging technologies of television, telecommunications, and computers.

"We have two computers in our classroom, and on Fridays we go to the library and work in the computer lab. My favourite is writing stories with Storybook Weaver and playing the games in Math Workshop. When the teachers went on strike, I did a project at home on Canadian horses and found really good information on the Internet. I found lots of stuff about the Spice Girls, too."

CHRISTIE, AGE 9

There are several exciting initiatives in some boards that "twin" schools SEE PAGE 223 internationally via E-mail and the Internet. When working with the language curriculum, classroom teachers often incorporate features of a word processing program into the children's individual work. The successes and failures of these demonstration schools guide the acquisition of networks, equipment, and programs for educators at the board's other schools.

Although ministries of education try to ensure that schools receive current equipment and software and that teachers are trained to guide our children into the high-tech future, they face the difficulty that choosing to spend education dollars on computer technology and software may mean less money for other programs. Not all parents are happy with the tradeoffs.

What computer skills does my child need and when?

- Your child certainly needs keyboarding skills, which are best learned as early as grade three—most eight-year-olds have the manual dexterity necessary. An older child can still pick up keyboarding almost as quickly as the younger child—many parents currently using computer keyboards learned to type in high school.
- Your child needs to understand what a computer and different software programs can do for her. Probably most important to students at the elementary level are the word-processing programs.
- Children find that writing moves along more quickly when they can change and polish their work using editing functions, including a spell checker for proofreading. Writing is the most advanced of the language skills, and on a computer, kids have more opportunities to write and refine their work in a shorter space of time than they do when they work with pencil or pen on paper. Preparing their writing for the printer also gives them the opportunity to learn about type size and formatting, including graphics.
- Also important to understand is that the modems connecting computers to the World Wide Web through the Internet can put your child in touch both with other students around the world and with a wide range of sources of information. If she wants information about dinosaur digs in Alberta or what kids in Japan think

Kids can start learning keyboarding by grade three.

Kids need confidence on the computer, but they don't need to learn every new program upgrade.

about hockey, she can learn how to ask the questions and hone her research skills—and she'll have her answer back sometimes in seconds. Canada's Media Awareness Network <http://www.media-awareness.ca> is an excellent resource on the Internet, and provides guidance to parents on "safe surfing" for their children.

SEE PAGE 230

➢ Your child may not have the opportunity to do all her writing on computer or do all her research through the Internet, but she needs some computer time to understand what a computer's capabilities are and become familiar with the constantly evolving nature of technology. Computer developers and software producers respond so rapidly to customer feedback that they are constantly upgrading and improving their products. Whatever hardware and software your child learns today in school or at home, she may use in a different version a year or two from now. It's more important that she develop confidence in her ability to learn and refine her skills at the programs she needs than that she know all the intricacies of what's in her classroom today.

Do you need a computer at home?

With access to a computer at home, your child may become more proficient faster. But it may not be until she enters high school that the technology and the programs offer her significant educational advantages. If, however, your child has a certain type of learning disability, you may find some computer programs very helpful. Kids who have difficulty with handwriting, for example, may find it easier to keyboard or to manipulate a computer mouse and the cursor. This might help reduce their level of frustration at communicating or doing school assignments, although they should continue to develop fine motor skills using writing or drawing instruments on paper.

If you don't have a computer at home but want to give your child more opportunity to work on one, consider hiring a high-school student with her own computer as a tutor. Also, many libraries have computers available to the public, and some libraries offer free classes on accessing the Internet or learning basic computer skills. If you have access to a computer at work and your employer is willing, you might take your child into the office on a weekend for some computer time.

Internet safety

- Protect your kids from unsuitable material on the Internet by keeping the password to your Internet master account to yourself. Then your children will have to ask you before they do any surfing of Web sites.
- Keep tabs on where your kids have ventured on-line using your browser. (Simply go to Location, type in "about:global" and you will see a list of the Web sites most recently used.) Let the kids know you use this feature.

Keep tabs on where your kids are visiting on-line.

- There are Internet filters that block out offensive sites.
- Set up the computer in a common area (the kitchen or family room), rather than in your child's bedroom, so that you can monitor what appears on the screen.
- Have an action plan for dealing with any uncomfortable or threatening Internet contact.
- Finally, tape to the family computer a list of basic cautions about E-mail messages and chat groups.
  - Never reveal any personal information.
  - Never arrange to meet any on-line friend in person.

Fostering Talents and Hobbies

Your child may develop an absorbing passion, like collecting baseball cards, that he'll enjoy for many years. Or he may flit from hobby to hobby—one year it's making models, the next year he's interested only in building kites. Or your child may fit her interests into whatever the family does together. If you love to garden, she may happily join you in transplanting the annuals in the spring.

Encourage your child in her choice of activities, whatever form they take. Kids gain confidence and a sense of self-esteem from the activities they choose themselves. They may have had a bad day at school, or their best friend might be mad at them, but they can forget their frustrations, at least temporarily, when they focus on their current interest. Some children develop hobbies that accompany them through adolescence and perhaps into a career.

Leave enough time in your child's schedule for him to just be a kid.

Kids need a smorgasbord of activities to choose from, but their weekly schedule should be appropriate for their age. Between the ages of six and twelve, children still need opportunities to explore, undirected, in order to develop their individual imagination and build confidence in themselves. A weekly schedule that contains too many classes or organized activities might stifle that inner development. Let them choose from the variety of activities available in your community, but limit the number in any season to what you both can handle while still allowing time for their homework, friends, and family time or chores. Older children can soon catch up to a peer who started at an earlier age in an activity that interests him, so your child's potential for success is not sacrificed if you don't enroll him for a year or two.

Suggest a trial period

Expect some of their hobbies to be short-lived—it's just as important for them to discover what they don't like as what they do like. But when the interest may involve a family investment in years of lessons, be sure your child is ready to commit to attending classes and practising regularly. Agree on a reasonable trial period before she can drop the activity. Tell your seven-year-old daughter who wants to be a ballet dancer, for example, that you will pay for three months of ballet lessons. Once the three months are over, she will have to decide whether she likes it enough to continue or wants to quit or change to tap-dance or jazz dance lessons. With a twelve-year-old, you might want to draw up a contract outlining your expectations and her commitments.

"It was difficult to watch my eldest son, Matthew, grow frustrated when his younger brother could come along and quickly master activities that Matthew had taken much longer to adequately execute. Then at age 11, Matthew discovered horses. For the last three years, it's been like watching a flower bloom. It's his own niche, an area that he excels in and gets complimented on. He rides, cares for horses, feasts on the knowledge that his grandfather, a saddle-maker, shares with him. He has learned a tremendous amount all on his own—and this is a kid who expends far more energy making excuses for why his homework isn't done than doing it."

CINDY, MOTHER OF TWO

One of the best ways for your child to explore a variety of hobbies and interests is to join an organization such as the Boy Scouts or Girl Guides. Many youngsters are ready for such group activities by the age of six or seven. Both organizations offer different programs, based on age: Girl Guides begin with Sparks (age six) and Brownies (ages seven to eight); Boy Scouts start with Beavers (ages five to seven) and Cubs (ages eight to ten). The 4H program, another inexpensive group for kids to explore new

Camps and clubs such as Girl Guides let your child try a smorgasbord of activities.

interests, has an enrollment age of ten in some provinces. Such groups offer both camaraderie and a chance to explore a variety of hobbies as your child accumulates badges. Boys and Girls Clubs offer activities for a wide range of ages, as do municipal recreation programs. Some municipalities offer subsidized activities for children throughout the seasons. Watch for the seasonal announcements in the paper or in newsletters.

Developing a child's love of music, whether she has a special talent or not, is a gift that will enrich the rest of her life. An additional benefit, as the research shows, is that early exposure to music helps children develop spatial awareness. Research also suggests that a knowledge of music, musical chords, and music notation helps kids understand the relationship between numbers and the reasoning involved in mathematics.

SEE PAGE 71

Like learning a second language, learning to play music comes most easily to children during a defined window of opportunity—the ideal time to begin is between the ages of three and seven. The piano is the instrument of choice for many budding musicians, but if you don't already have one it can be a major investment. Until you're sure of your child's interest, you might start with an electronic keyboard for practice. On this keyboard, a child can still learn the notes and hear the pitches and connect musical notation to the sounds. And once a child learns to read music, he can apply that knowledge in learning any other instrument.

SEE PAGE 230

Whether or not your child shows any interest in playing an instrument, take every opportunity to expose her to a wide range of music styles and the sounds of different instruments. Encourage her to sing with the "instrument" she was born with. Fill your home with music. It's as simple as turning on the radio.

A Child's Point of View: My Mind

My ability to think abstractly and to reason grows. Soon I'll begin to develop a conscience. Learning to read continues to expand my world.

Age Six

- I'm becoming more creative in my thinking. I get excited about new games, new ideas. I spend more time in fantasy play.
- I often daydream.
- I start having performance fears. I worry that I might make an embarrassing mistake in class.
- I'm interested in where babies come from. I like hearing stories about my own birth and what I was like as a baby.
- I love to talk. I ask endless questions.
- I can't make decisions. I'm interested in all possibilities, so I want to order the spaghetti and the chicken fingers. Sometimes I'll need you to choose for me.
- I can print my name and maybe several other words, but I often reverse letters and numbers. I'm learning to read. Even if I can read easy books on my own, I still love to be read to.
- I'm developing my sense of humour. I find your jokes hilarious.
- I tattle to get my brother or sister in trouble.
- I have scary thoughts that my favourite people might get sick and die.

Age Seven

- I'm often lost in my own thoughts. I'm forgetful, absent-minded, and easily distracted.
- I criticize myself a lot. I hate it when I make even the tiniest mistake. I'll need a supply of erasers.
- I'm fascinated by thoughts of death, graveyards, and violent endings. I may talk about my own future death, or a pet's, or yours. My interest may seem morbid, but it's mostly clinical. I might ask, "What would Grandpa look like if we dug him up?"
- I'm starting to think abstractly. I realize that a problem may have more than one solution. I enjoy the challenge of open-ended questions.

- I like riddles and knock-knock jokes but I'm also starting to appreciate puns, as I realize that one word might have two meanings.
- I'm interested in magic, fantasy, wishes.
- I'm learning to tell time, and I like to plan my day. I would enjoy a watch of my own.
- I can count to 100 and do simple adding and subtracting. I'm starting to understand that there are 4 quarters (or 10 dimes or 100 pennies) in a loonie.
- My figure drawing becomes more detailed. I include hair, hands, and feet, and maybe fingers.

Age Eight

- I'm fascinated by language, including secret passwords, nicknames, silly made-up words and, unfortunately, swearing.
- I can tell fantasy from reality, although I don't always tell the truth.
- You can usually reason with me.
- I'm beginning to understand that what people say is sometimes different from what they feel.
- I enjoy the humour in stories, especially when self-important characters get outwitted by smaller, less powerful ones.
- I notice not only my mistakes but yours and everyone else's, and I'll be the first to point them out. I love to argue.
- I can play board games or card games for hours. I love card tricks and magic tricks.
- I'm taking more interest in sorting, arranging, and displaying my collections.
- When you ask me to do something, more often than not I'll forget what you said.
- I'm learning quickly how money works and what it can do for me.
- I lean toward dramatics. I'll say, "This was the worst day of my life," or "I fell off my bike. I'll probably die."
- I repeat dirty jokes, even if I don't get them.

Age Nine

- I'm developing a conscience. When I apologize, I can feel genuine regret.
- I'm obsessed with fairness. I'll be extremely upset if you blame me for something I didn't do.

- I'm starting to plan for the future. I might be interested in your job and how much money you make. I may tell you how many children I'll have and what their genders will be.
- I'm less interested in magical concepts like the Tooth Fairy and more concerned with the real and the concrete.
- I'm very conscious of clocks, calendars, and numbers. I'll want to know exactly how old you are.
- I realize more and more that you aren't perfect.
- Once I start something, I have to finish it.
- I'm very critical of myself but ultra-sensitive to criticism from others. I'll say, "Look at this drawing. Isn't it terrible?" But if you agree, I'll be crushed.
- I argue less, except over the issue of bedtime. I still might put up a verbal struggle.
- I'm able to take things that I learn in school and apply them to real life, like using math while shopping.

Age Ten

- I love to talk. It's hard for me to keep quiet even while I'm doing homework or being read to.
- I can carry on several interests at the same time. I can flit from topic to topic.
- My world view is broadening. I'm able to join in simple discussions of social issues, such as homelessness or drug addiction.
- I tend toward hero-worship. I might want to plaster my bedroom walls with posters of my favourite athletes, actors, or musicians.
- My memory continues to improve. I can memorize poetry, recite TV commercials word for word, and remember all the lyrics to a long song.
- I have strange dreams and vivid nightmares.
- I'm getting better at telling jokes.
- I'm very concerned with justice for all. I can't stand cheating, and I often say, "That's not fair!"
- Instead of describing teachers as either "nice" or "mean," I can critically analyze their teaching skills.
- I'm always acutely aware of the potential for embarrassment. I take great pains to ensure that I won't do anything to embarrass myself in front of my friends.

Age Eleven

11

- I become more excited about learning. I might try to sneak in some extra nighttime reading after you've told me to turn out the light.
- I demand that schoolwork be relevant and meaningful to my life.
- I argue for the sake of argument. I watch you like a hawk, ready to pounce on the smallest error. It's important for me to win every intellectual argument with you as I constantly test my intellect.
- I have impossibly high standards for other people. If you beg off a social obligation by saying that you're not feeling well, I'll grill you mercilessly about whether you were telling the exact truth. If I uncover any inconsistencies, I may call you a liar or a hypocrite.
- I understand very well the difference between right and wrong, although I don't always do what is right.
- I hold a grudge. I can pout and sulk much longer than the circumstances warrant.
- I'm much more aware of my shortcomings than of my good points.
- I have lofty ambitions. I may want to be an Olympic athlete, a movie star, or anything else that guarantees fortune and fame.
- I'm still very enthusiastic about my collections.

Age Twelve

12

- My intellectual growth slows down for the next couple of years. I can't learn as quickly as I used to or as I will again.
- I'm not as concerned with winning as I was only last year. I don't mind giving others a chance.
- I'm not as argumentative as I was. When I do argue, it's not so much to win as to make a valid point.
- I'm becoming more reasonable. I'm willing to listen to other people's arguments.
- The opinions of my friends are much more important than the opinions of my parents. What my friends say about me shapes the way I feel about myself.
- My interest in sexuality is growing.
- My biggest worry is schoolwork.
- I understand dirty jokes and sexual innuendoes, and I enjoy repeating them if only to show other people that I'm sophisticated enough to get them.
- I might want to redo my bedroom, clearing out all the old toys and pictures that remind me of my younger self.

Heart and Soul

3

Your child is born with a unique personality, which becomes more multifaceted as he gains experience in the world and takes on more roles. Your child's self-esteem begins with your unconditional love. As he grows, his school experiences, his ability to make friends, and his assessment of his own talents all affect his view of himself. Your time, attention, guidance, and encouragement help your child to build strong relationships, to manage stress and anger, to learn self-discipline, and to be tolerant and kind.

A child with self-esteem feels good about herself. She feels loved, valued, and respected for who she is with all her strengths and limitations, her personality and physical traits, her ideas and opinions. A child's self-esteem comes from being accepted, respected, and valued just for being the person she is. When parents give their baby unconditional love, they lay a firm foundation for the child's developing sense of her self. The child must feel that she is accepted by her parents, whether she conforms to their expectations or not, and must feel sure they neither give nor withdraw their love based on her performance.

Affection and approval that come with conditions imposed do not make a child feel good. Acceptance and approval that come and go confuse her; she never knows what to expect, never feels certain that her parents love her and accept her as she is. Love that's given only with conditions based on the parents' expectations about the child's behaviour can contribute to the child's creation of a false self. The child may try to please her parents, to satisfy their expectations and respond to their needs, which delays the development of her true self and her own voice from her temperament, personality, instincts, capabilities, and needs.

What Is Self-Esteem?

Your child's self-esteem begins with your unconditional love and builds as you encourage him to develop all aspects of his self. His self-esteem becomes a secure foundation for his healthy growth and development in all domains—social, emotional, physical, intellectual, and spiritual.

Children with solid self-esteem feel confident about themselves and their ability to learn. They are comfortable taking risks and are eager to master new challenges. Most children develop more confidence in some areas than in others. A six-year-old who has experienced his parents' uncon-

"So many social ills would not be there if every kid had that loving secure zone where children are valued for what they are, their strengths encouraged, and their weaknesses shored up or dealt with in loving words."

JAMES, FATHER OF ONE

ditional love will feel secure. However, as he moves out into the world of school and playmates, he encounters experiences that may shake his self-esteem. At ages seven and eight, your child's self-image begins to be defined by his group, and by the pecking order in school and on the playground. Children do rank themselves against each other. If your child struggles to learn in school, has trouble making friends, or is behind his peers in athletic ability, his self-esteem may be shaken.

By the time a child is nine or ten, individual relationships with friends may have become more complex. Your son's best buddy one day may become his bitter rival the next, which can be very upsetting to him. The transition to puberty triggers surging hormones and turbulent emotions. A twelve-year-old may find it unsettling if he develops physically at a rate that's faster or slower than that of his peers. Part of doing a good job of parenting is to remain aware of everything that's going on in your child's life. Listen for clues; you can't assume that everything's OK outside just because it's great at home.

You may find it painful when something jolts your child's self-confidence. Take heart that your unconditional love provides a secure foundation for him. A child with poor self-esteem may need more patience and encouragement from his parents in order to help him grow and

"I think Kathleen has good self-esteem because, if she doesn't have something other people have, she doesn't feel the world will come to an end. There's more going on inside. She has internal resources. She doesn't really need platform shoes yet.

Self-esteem comes from being treated well. But it's not enough. Self-confidence also comes from doing things well. It's hard to have good self-esteem if you can't do anything well but others around you do."

MARGARET, MOTHER OF TWO

develop. When your child's self-esteem is low, you can help by giving him time, attention, encouragement, and guidance to develop in areas of strength, as well as in areas in which he's less confident. Don't focus only on the problems; focus on all the good things in his life and on his abilities.

Be a mirror for your child to appreciate his own emerging unique self by giving positive feedback on his personal qualities as well as on his accomplishments. Both are important. Saying "I like your silly sense of humour" is often as helpful as saying "That's a great report card." A child's self-esteem reflects who he is, as well as what he achieves. Encourage your child to pursue his goals and dreams. Be clear about your expectations for his behaviour and values, but love and respect him for who he is, what he wants, and what he does.

What Is Personality?

You've been aware of your child's personality since she was born. Our personality is our own human signature, encompassing all the distinguishing personal and social traits that make each of us unique. No two personalities are exactly alike—even those of identical twins.

You would probably come up with very different words to describe the personality of each of your children. Although psychologists have devised dozens of systems and tests to analyze, categorize, and measure personality types, there is no universally accepted system. That's because people are simply too complex to be fully and accurately described by one system.

Nature or Nurture

SEE PAGE 70

Is personality a product of nature or nurture? In recent years researchers have found that both genes and temperamental tendencies influence the development of personality. Children are born with different temperamental traits or predispositions. Some are bold and aggressive and actively seek stimulation. Others are more reactive, inhibited, and highly sensitive to stress, so they tend to avoid too much stimulation. Each child is born with a characteristic mood, activity level, and style of responding to stimuli. Some children are calm and have a relaxed, sunny disposition; others are more difficult to appease, anxious, and sensitive.

"It's good to try to develop all sides of yourself. I like to push the limits a lot. My children know about personal growth. I want them to go out and taste life. I don't fear losing them to the world."

PATTY, MOTHER OF FOUR

These temperamental traits are only part of the story. A child's personality develops from the interplay between inborn traits and life experiences. The child's parents, peers, and social environment affect that development from birth on, but so do the phases of physical growth. For example, the moodiness of your nine-year-old may have more to do with early puberty than with personality, so keep in mind that it is only part of a phase, and refrain from feeling hurt or angry.

Personality is both stable and dynamic. The child has a bedrock core of traits, but her personality is enriched and expanded as she develops and grows. Her personality becomes more multifaceted as she gains more experience and assumes more roles—sister, daughter, friend, student, musician, athlete, team player, or group leader. Just as an actor can play many different roles well, a child's personality becomes more fully developed as she fulfills different roles through new experiences and

Your child's personality is multifaceted as she assumes new roles–she is daughter, sister, friend, student.

relationships. By the time your child is twelve, she has a fuller sense of her own core traits. She develops an inner picture of herself based on her emerging values and attitudes, which help her shape her own goals. And she has a clearer sense of where she fits into her peer group.

A shy child who learns how to make friends may become socially adept, well liked, and comfortable with people, although she is unlikely to seek the limelight. A hellion may grow into a more responsible person with a bold personality. Your role as a parent is to respect and respond to the personality of each of your children and help them flourish through their life experiences.

Parents do have a major influence on their child's personality. The values that you instill and model will influence the kind of person your child becomes. How do you treat him? And how does he treat you? Through your example and guidance, you can shape your child's tendencies to be kind and sociable, proud and compassionate; similarly, you can discourage any tendency to be mean and selfish, snobbish and cold. It's true that we're influenced by the company we keep, so you can expect that your child's friends will also help shape his personality and reflect his sense of himself.

"Alex, who is eight, is artistic, creative, temperamental, a good mixer. I'd put him on a team, but I wouldn't make him captain. He's not reliable enough yet. His sister, Kathleen, has always been reliable, dependable, cool under pressure. She's kind and practical. If I could hire her for a job, I'd put her in management. She handles pressure well."

MARGARET, MOTHER OF TWO

Accentuate the Positive

What tapes do your children play in their heads? How do they talk to themselves? Does your son give himself credit and take pride in his accomplishments? Or does he downplay his successes and dismiss them by saying that he was just lucky? Does your daughter get totally discouraged when she receives low marks on a test or is rejected by a friend? Or does she quickly bounce back and tell herself that she can do better next time? How does she talk to herself when she's facing a new challenge?

The messages that children repeat to themselves influence how they feel and how they perform in school, in social situations, or in sports—in all aspects of life. These messages reflect the child's self-image, whether positive or negative, and her outlook on life. As they turn eleven or twelve years old, many young girls begin to feel the limits that social patterning imposes on their expectations. Parents need to counter this feeling by ensuring their daughter knows they want her to set goals for herself that reflect her own interests, goals she feels she can achieve in spite of external limitations.

The way that your son talks to himself is influenced by many factors: his self-image, his self-esteem, his temperament, his ability to meet challenges and do things well in life, and the way that you praise and criticize him or his behaviour. You have an important effect, too, on how your daughter talks to herself by the way you respond to her views about herself. If your six-year-old has difficulty with steps in her ballet class and says, "I'll never be a good dancer," don't tell her she's the best dancer in the whole class, but don't just say to try harder. Instead, practise with her to encourage her. Praise her when she improves. She may soon say that she's having fun and has become so good at practice that she wants to take a more advanced class.

One child who, by objective standards, does several things well but whose parents constantly criticize him and tell him to do even better may become highly self-critical, riddled with doubts, and constantly put himself down. Another child who has less natural ability but whose parents praise his successes and encourage him to learn from his mistakes might continue to try hard, and he may enjoy lots of successes and learn from his failures. That child is likely to create an internal audiotape on which he talks to himself as a coach and cheerleader, repeating the comments of his parents.

"When Abby's worried on Sunday night about school the next day, she'll psych herself up. She has become pretty self-motivated. We don't have to prod her. We just suggest a path."

JAMES, FATHER OF ONE

Teaching positive self-talk doesn't mean that you teach your child to ignore reality. No child believes praise that isn't genuine; nor does false praise help your child develop the problem-solving skills or achieve the positive successes that serve as touchstones for pep talks to himself.

What do you say to your twelve-year-old when he complains that he's "a loser" because he received only an honourable mention at the Science Fair when he had his heart set on winning a first place? Congratulate him on his honourable mention and praise him for his hard work. Remind him that his project was ranked better than those of many other students. Ask him if he knows why the first place entry won. Encourage him to talk about how he might do better next time.

Look for those qualities, strengths, and accomplishments that you can encourage, and praise them in such a way that your child understands. Help him to verbalize and value his own strengths. Your positive feedback and constructive guidance for improvement, lightened with humour, are what helps your child learn to assess his own performance realistically and develop a strong, positive sense of self that is grounded in reality. The key is to make room for feelings. You don't have to solve all problems, but your empathy for what your child is experiencing is worth a lot to him.

Venting Anger without Hurt

Some kids are so hot-tempered that you wonder whether they will ever learn to express their anger without an explosion. Other kids rarely express their anger, but they may cry or say that they're sad or that they have a sore stomach.

Anger is a normal, healthy, natural emotion that we all need to learn how to handle. Experts suggest that parents must look at how they deal with their own anger, for that's the behaviour that their children will learn first. Do you suppress your anger? The classic definition of depression is "anger turned inward." Or do you explode in a destructive way? Or do you find healthier outlets?

A parent who is afraid to express his or her own anger but who lets it seep out in other ways teaches a child to fear and avoid expressing anger. A hot-tempered parent who has frequent, explosive outbursts teaches her child that anger is frightening. Some children react by becoming passive peacemakers who try at all costs to avoid anger, while other children model their behaviour on their angry parent's and throw temper tantrums. The parent and child keep pushing each other's buttons, and outbursts from one will trigger more intense outbursts from the other.

It's important for all of us is to learn to acknowledge the anger we feel and to act out our angry feelings in a constructive way. We must help children understand that it's OK to feel anger, and we also need to show them how to make good choices about what to do about their angry feelings and the person or situation that aroused the feelings.

What's OK and What's Not

All feelings are normal, but it's how we react to and express those feelings that makes the difference between what's acceptable and what's unacceptable, what's healthy and what's unhealthy, what's constructive and what's destructive. Your child needs to know which behaviours are acceptable and which behaviours are not.

Physical violence and verbal abuse (whether directed at parents, siblings, friends, or animals) are not acceptable ways of expressing anger. Kicking, hitting or spitting, breaking things, and calling others nasty names are not OK. When deciding how to respond to inappropriate behaviour, make the distinction between your child's getting wound up and his actually fighting with another child. Before an angry situation spins out of control into violence, give your child several alternatives to find out what best helps him calm down when he's angry. Distractions are a good strategy, as are energy-burning activities. But quieter games and creative activities may be helpful with some children.

Once the child has calmed down, encourage him to talk about his feelings. What makes him angry and why? Can he take steps to deal with the situation so that he will feel better? Help the child identify and acknowledge the feelings. When he says, "I hate Johnny," help him understand that he may mean he's angry with Johnny for taking his bike, but that's not the same as hate. You can also give the child an example of how you cope with similar situations. Teach a young child to name his feelings. By the time a child is six years old, he should be able to say, "I'm scared" or "I'm mad." If a situation is more serious and your child has lashed out physically or verbally at another person, send him for a time-out (one minute for each year of age) to cool down. You can forewarn children by saying, "If everyone doesn't calm down, we'll have to take a time-out."

An older child of eleven or twelve begins to feel a more generalized anger at the wrongs he perceives in the world. At this age, kids become more idealistic, and their anger may be about the destruction of the environment, about cruelty to animals, or the plight of the homeless. Help your child find her own outlet for this kind of anger. She might get involved with a social or environmental group, or write a letter to the local newspaper that expresses her angry feelings in a constructive or creative way.

Both parents should talk about their own family experiences and share stories about what makes them angry and how they deal with it. Be a mirror for your child so that he can see the effects of his behaviour on others, both positive and negative. Teach him that anger, when constructively channelled, can be a powerful motivator and a source of energy. It can make him more determined to solve a problem, to overcome obstacles, and to accomplish a goal. That way your child learns to control his anger rather than let the anger control him.

"To me, a major problem is that people don't know how to deal with anger. If they keep it in as children, they see me twenty years later."

LINDA, A PSYCHIATRIST AND MOTHER OF ONE

Reward him for handling his anger in a constructive way, for talking out his feelings, and for coming up with solutions to the problems that make him angry or unhappy. Sports or any vigorous physical activity can also be a terrific outlet for channelling and releasing feelings of anger and frustration.

The way you discipline children also models how you handle anger. If you go out of control when you're upset by your child's behaviour or actions, that's the adult behaviour they'll remember. But going to the extreme of not expressing what you're feeling is equally misleading. Instead, communicate your feeling in a firm tone to show that you mean business, and follow up with clear consequences for their misbehaviour. Your children will learn from this an effective way to modify how they express anger. Helping your children learn how to vent anger in a healthy way teaches them that all their feelings are important.

Teach your young child to name her feelings of pleasure and of sadness.

Heart and Soul

Kids Feel Stress, Too

All kids feel stress, but they show it in different ways. Your child might complain of aches and pains or lack of sleep, be clingy or whiny, erupt with temper tantrums or pick fights. She might try to avoid school or other situations, she might have trouble concentrating and appear lazy, or she may lack motivation and withdraw into a shell. Or she may fall ill frequently with colds, the flu, or other infections.

Each child has her own characteristic way of showing her stress, which parents have to learn how to read. If she's acting stressed, assume there's a reason that she's uptight or upset. A seven-year-old may refuse to do an activity that she previously enjoyed. Take that as a signal that she's worried about something related to that activity. Don't blame her for how she feels; it will only make her feel worse. Talk to and listen to your child to find out what's really going on.

A twelve-year-old may tell you angrily what an idiot his teacher is when he's really worried that he hasn't understood fractions and is getting low marks in mathematics. Get your child to express his fears by asking, in a nonjudgmental way, about the teacher. Why does he dislike the teacher? How does the teacher treat him? How does the teacher explain things? Once your son starts talking to you, his underlying problem or fear will emerge.

"You don't ignore a child who's upset. Don't say, 'Get over it.' You want to bring down her anxiety level. We find that it works to comfort her and calm her down. Tell her how you felt in a similar situation. Make her a cup of tea.

Abby's had to deal with many difficult things, including some family health problems. When times are tough, I'll take her out of school for an afternoon. She's an honours student, so there's no reason not to. We'll go downtown and see a movie. You keep things fun. I try to surprise her. I get her lots of small presents."

WANDA, MOTHER OF ONE

Parents sometimes forget that their children feel just as many pressures as they do. Today both parents and kids feel that they have too much to do and too little time in which to do it all, which puts pressure on everyone. Experts remind us that just like your day job, school is work for a child. Your child feels pressure from you, from his teachers, and from his friends to perform, to deal with problems you aren't even aware of—fights with friends, bullying on the bus, an offer of cigarettes. When a child shows signs of more severe stress, it may signal problems in the family, too.

SEE PAGE 184

Like adults, kids have their own way of expressing stress, which parents can learn to read.

Talk with your child about the stress he feels—identifying the problem may relieve some of her anxiety. Your child will feel better when she has a sympathetic ear. Then you can start working together on solutions to her dilemma. Lots of kids clam up during a face-to-face conversation but are more relaxed when talking in the car or while doing activities. You need to find the time and the place that your child is most comfortable talking with you. Look for your opportunity.

"Molly is a challenging child. She feels great stress over clothing, school, and friendships. She finds her self-image reflected by her peers."

HUGH, FATHER OF TWO

Encourage your child to talk about any stressful situation whenever he wants. And when he does start to talk, respond calmly but with interest. Don't get upset, and don't be too quick to offer solutions or lay blame, even if you support his position. If you increase your child's anxiety, he'll be less inclined to talk to you. Often the best way you can help your child handle his stress is to play with him and have fun together. Lots of vigorous physical activity works well, too. So if your eight-year-old is anxious and whiny because his best friend is moving away, encourage him to talk about his feelings and help him to plan how he will stay in touch with his friend. Then head outside together to play catch or to run with the dog.

A Kid's Fears and Worries

Kids are afraid of many things. Their fears are often very specific. They may be afraid of the dark, of fire alarms, of bugs or dogs, and of any and all strangers, or they may be afraid that you will die. Sometimes a child's fear and anxiety are so intense that she develops a real phobia, perhaps following a frightening experience like being bitten by a dog.

After the age of eight, most children have worries about how they fit in. They worry about being popular, about how they dress or how they look. They worry about succeeding or failing in school subjects or at sports.

All kids have everyday worries, but some kids have more serious fears. They may be afraid that their parents will divorce, or they might worry because of alcohol or drug abuse, or because of emotional or physical abuse in their family. Perhaps their fears originate in situations at school. They may be afraid of a teacher or of another student who bullies them, or they may have encountered a dangerous situation with drugs.

Make your home a place where your child feels comfortable talking about her fears and worries, without giving up her privacy or feeling invaded. Home should be the place where your child feels safe to put into words what's bothering her, and she'll need your help to identify her

Even Santa Claus can be a little scary for some kids.

feelings. Your child may also feel embarrassed about having the fear, so it helps if you can find a way to broach the subject that allows her to confide but at the same time to save face. Your role is to guide and support your child, to help her solve problems on her own, when possible, but also to intervene in the situation, when necessary.

To help your child deal with a specific fear or worry, you need to know what's really going on. Don't dismiss or downplay his concerns. This shuts down the lines of communication and discourages your child from sharing his fears with you. When you're familiar with what's going on in your child's life, he is more likely to talk to you. Be ready to listen whenever he decides to talk. He's more likely to open up when you're doing dishes together than to respond when you ask him a direct question at the dinner table. Face-to-face discussions about a fear or worry can seem confrontational and may increase your child's anxiety level. Children can often express what's on their mind better when they are engaged in doing something else.

Children often express better what's on their mind when they're engaged in an activity rather than talking face to face.

When your child talks about his worry, it may help to talk about your feelings in a similar situation and how you solved the problem. Your child may be glad to know that you, too, failed a math test but then went to the teacher for extra help and managed to pass the next one. She won't feel so alone, and she'll be glad to hear about a possible solution.

The fearful child needs compassion and support from her parents. But you also need to help her learn how to take risks at her own pace. If being fearful is a basic part of her personality, it's important to help her learn to calm herself, so she can become less anxious and more confident. The ten-year-old who is afraid of dogs might try putting her hand down for a friendly dog to sniff after one of you has asked the owner if that's OK. She can decide to give dogs without owners nearby a wide berth.

"My son finally said, 'I need my father to do things with me.' He felt a lack when he saw what others had. The attention of my husband makes him feel good. Alex responds to it."

MARGARET, MOTHER OF TWO

You don't want to coddle a fearful child, but you do need to find appropriate challenges that he can handle. Help him take small, manageable steps in resolving fears or problems that loom large in his mind. Kids often find it calming to face their fears with older, supportive kids. An eight-year-old who's afraid of spiders might look at one with interest if her older cousin is examining the spider's web with her.

Draw your child gradually into challenging situations rather than force him to sink or swim. Fearful children need to get comfortable with new situations by putting one toe in the water at a time. Sometimes his progress may appear painfully slow to you. But allow him to take his own time; work with him at the level he's at. He needs to feel competent in order to participate in a new activity.

If your child wants to play soccer but is afraid of the ball hitting him, practise with him by kicking the ball toward him gently until he gets used to a light kick before you kick the ball harder. As he gets more skillful at stopping the ball and more comfortable with the feel of the ball when it hits him, his confidence will grow.

If his fears prevent him from functioning day to day, you may want to seek professional counselling. Although the fearful child may go into counselling as "the patient," in most cases the whole family needs to become involved to find a solution. Parents need to look at all the layers of the child's environment: the immediate family, the extended family, neighbourhood, community, and school. The child's fears may be based in realities that the family is not aware of. His experiences in life, either at home or outside the home, may reinforce his natural tendency to be fearful.

Helping your child solve problems increases his confidence.

Addressing the real issues, especially if they are family issues, will help to solve the problems for the child so that he can become more comfortable, secure, and connected to his world. When you help your child solve problems, he learns how to cope and to deal with his worries and fears. You can help him learn the kind of optimism that makes him calmer, more confident, and resilient.

"What doesn't work is to deny the fear, to talk them out of it and say everything's fine, there's nothing to be afraid of. To say it's just a TV program doesn't work. It doesn't take away the fear. Children need the security of people they trust. Make him feel better. Hold him."

MARGARET, MOTHER OF TWO

The Fearless Child

Cameron is a fun-loving, boisterous eleven-year-old who knows no fear. When he was little, he would ride his fire engine right off the porch. He was usually covered with Band-Aids and bruises, and he was a well-known regular at the emergency room of the nearest hospital. He was also the child who scurried off into the crowd and got lost on any outing. His parents would be scared out of their wits, but that wouldn't faze him a bit.

Cameron is one of those fearless children who are born risk takers. Genetic research has shown that some children are born bold. They seek out novel stimuli from their earliest weeks. The fearless child lives in the fast lane. These boys and girls dive into new experiences, jumping first and looking later. The fearless child presents one of the greatest opportunities and challenges for parents.

The fearless child is assertive, aggressive, impulsive, and exhausting. Parents need lots of support to keep up with him. Don't hesitate to enlist the aid of aunts, uncles, siblings, friends, teachers, and coaches to play with him. Organized sports are natural outlets for the active, aggressive child to learn how to master his raw energy within the team setting and the rules of the game.

"Cameron learned to walk at three. Up to that point, he ran. I had recurring nightmares of leaning over a cliff with Cameron. He has a hard time connecting actions with consequences. The thought of Cameron driving.... I don't like to think of that."

ALLAN, FATHER OF TWO

The fearless child is potentially the hero we would all like to be. But without proper guidance, direction, and discipline, he can also be reckless enough to endanger himself and others. The fearless person, who worries little about consequences, may become a great leader or a hero, but in some instances, he might become a sociopath.

Guide that bold spirit

The fearless child is willing to try different things and feels comfortable even when he heads into new and different situations. Don't stifle that spirit. Healthy risk taking and courage when handling new challenges promote a child's growth and development. Respect and encourage her bold spirit within certain parameters, and expect your child to push those limits. Be a mentor in guiding that risk-taking spirit into growth-enhancing areas.

The fearless child needs to learn from her parents, by your setting limits and consequences and describing what's appropriate and acceptable behaviour. You can't be as permissive as you would be with a shy child who doesn't always push the boundaries and test the limits. Instill a healthy respect for the dangers of particular sports or activities. Help the risk taking child to visualize and think about consequences, and to see the impact his actions might have on himself and others. Start early. It's important to be firm and consistent with a six-year-old who is constantly testing limits. If you apply limits appropriate to his age when he's young, he will have internalized the need for caution and preparedness in new situations by the age of twelve, when you may be more willing to let him demonstrate his self-control.

Once this child develops a clear sense of right and wrong and the consequences of unsafe risk taking, he may become a friend and support or guide to more timid friends rather than become a bully. Be clear about your family rules for behaviour, language, treatment of other siblings, friends, and parents. As your child grows older, discuss and negotiate new rules and discipline appropriate to his age. When he has input into the rules and the consequences for breaking them, he's more willing to be guided by them, but be firm on the follow-through. If you've agreed that he is to let you know when and where he goes on his bike and that the consequence of not letting you know is that he loses the use of the bike for a week, then lock it up if he breaks the rule. Also, find ways to reward your child when he acts less impulsively.

It's important to be firm and consistent with a six-year-old who is always testing limits.

If you discover that your eleven-year-old daughter performs daredevil routines for friends by walking along the top of a high wall at a nearby construction site, take her through what would happen if she fell, what her injuries might be, what the impact would be on her, on you, and on the rest of the family. Discipline her for her behaviour, perhaps not letting her play outside after dinner for a couple of nights. Then talk with her to find out why she needs or wants to get the adrenaline rush from danger. Sometimes a depressed child acts out self-destructive tendencies through recklessness, or perhaps she's trying to prove herself to other kids. On some level, a reckless child doesn't care about consequences. The adrenaline rush may be her only high in an otherwise low-spirited existence. Try to get to the bottom of the problem.

The Shy Child

Shy children are cautious and slow to warm up to new situations and people. To people who don't know them, they may appear standoffish and cool. Research suggests that 10 to 15 per cent of children are born with a tendency to be shy. Shy children seem to have different physiological reactions to stress. Their nervous systems are more sensitive, and they are more easily startled than other children. A shy child, when exposed to new situations, will likely produce more stress hormones and have a higher heart rate for a longer period of time.

Just because a child tends to be shy doesn't mean that he or she is destined to be lonely or unhappy. But, as with a personality trait like recklessness when taken to extremes, shyness can be a serious problem if it becomes an obstacle to the child's social and emotional development. As a parent, you shouldn't expect a shy child to suddenly become a social butterfly and seek out the spotlight. But you don't want your child to be a recluse either.

It's important to respect your child's temperament and to use a parenting style that helps her develop confidence and social skills. Not all parenting styles are helpful. A firm insistence that the child be more adventurous may cause her to withdraw even further into a shell. Pushing a child into an intimidating social situation with the instructions "Don't be shy" won't help her. She will simply become more anxious when what she needs is to become less anxious in order to gain confidence.

Give your child the time she needs to warm up to a new situation.

But too much protection is not a solution either. If you protect your child from every new situation that might cause her to become anxious, she'll have no opportunity to show initiative or to take risks and develop confidence in her own abilities. She may also sense your lack of confidence in her, which will further weaken her self-esteem.

What works best is a middle path that respects your child's sensitivity but encourages her to meet challenges, take risks, and develop social skills at her own pace. Shy children generally need time to warm up to

Making Friends: The Best Antidote

Friendships are critical to the social and emotional development of any child, but shyness may sometimes make it more difficult for a friendship to develop. Shyness is a potentially serious problem if a child is unable to make or keep friends. It's important to address the problem when your child is young by helping him to make friends, and then encouraging and supporting the development of those friendships. Shy children may need more contact with their parents; when you take your child to an event, don't just drop her off. Stay awhile and talk to help your child warm up a bit to the others.

The shy six-year-old may be hesitant and reluctant to meet other kids in the neighbourhood. Encourage him to befriend another quiet child who doesn't threaten your son in any way. As they become comfortable with each other, encourage the two of them to visit and get to know other kids in the neighbourhood, which should be easier together than on their own.

Take an active role in arranging activities that your child will enjoy, but be selective. Make your home a secure and inviting place for your child to play with friends. Keep games, puzzles, and refreshments on hand. Get the child involved in nonthreatening activities like swimming, painting, music, summer day camp, or a team sport in which he has some ability. If the child enjoys the activity, then social interaction may be a natural byproduct.

Some shy children are just slow to warm up to people, but they may be very observant and sensitive to nuances. They may develop friendships with fewer children, but these friendships may be closer. Many shy children are more comfortable one on one or in small groups, rather than in a large crowd. Show your child that you value and respect his friends. Treat them with good humour, and make them feel like members of your family. Good friends, who like and are comfortable with each other, help one another to grow and develop.

new experiences and people. Once they feel comfortable with a person or situation and know what's expected, they can surprise you with their warmth.

Don't label your child by saying "She's shy" in front of other people, or by acting embarrassed when she is tentative or holds back in social situations. Let grandparents, relatives, or friends know in private that she simply needs time to warm up to people. Tell them in private about her likes and interests, that she reads to her little brother or that she's taking gymnastics, so that they can ask her something specific to help break the ice.

If a shy child enjoys a new activity, then new friends may be a byproduct.

A perceptive, sensitive teacher can also bring out the best in a timid child and help him to flourish. But if the teacher is overbearing or indifferent, your shy child may not get recognized. She may be ignored or intimidated and do poorly in her schoolwork. It's important for you to be your child's advocate and to intervene, if necessary, in problem situations. If the school environment doesn't let a kid feel secure and comfortable, discuss the situation with the classroom teacher first and then the principal, if necessary.

Teachers, parents, aunts, uncles, and supportive friends can help turn a child's shyness around. They can model appropriate behaviour at social functions, giving the shy child practice in socializing, and, most importantly, encourage and reward all the child's attempts to interact with people and become a more social person.

Before you visit family or friends, prepare your ten-year-old for the visit by telling him casually what to expect. Talk about who will be there and what activities will be going on, and repeat some nice things that some of the other visitors have said about him so that he realizes they like him and find him interesting. Say, "Uncle John will want to hear more about your woodworking class. He was impressed last time you saw him when you told him about the shelf you made." Afterward, talk with him about what went on, focusing on events that were interesting and fun.

The Out-of-Control Child

Temper tantrums, kicking, hitting, bullying, yelling, spitting, throwing things—it's frustrating, annoying, infuriating, and upsetting when your child acts out. If he does it in front of other people, it's embarrassing, too. When your child's behaviour seems a strain for you, you will also fret about what an innocent bystander thinks.

All children act out occasionally, as do adults. That's part of being human. But when the difficult behaviour becomes the rule rather than the exception, your child and your family have a real problem and you need to take action and find appropriate solutions.

The difficult behaviour is almost always a symptom of an underlying problem—it doesn't happen in a vacuum. You need to identify what's going on in the life of your child and your family and understand how it is contributing to the child's behaviour. There are, of course, a great many possibilities. Your child may be experiencing a stressful situation at school or having problems with peers. If you, his parents, are having marital problems, substance abuse problems, or problems at work, you may not have enough time to pay close attention to your kids.

SEE PAGE 184

A child who acts out may be uttering a cry for help or for attention. Usually, he doesn't feel very good about himself and lacks self-esteem. Ask yourself if his behaviour is restricted to home or if he behaves the same way in every situation. It's not surprising for a young boy to act out if

Accept Negative Feelings

The out-of-control child presents a major challenge for parents. When the child is difficult or demanding and doesn't respond to reason, he wreaks havoc on your mind and your feelings. At times, you may feel anger, resentment, and disappointment toward your child, and may even feel that you dislike him. Then, because you also deeply love your child, you feel guilty about having such negative feelings.

Experts advise that some negative feelings are a perfectly normal, natural response to the child's behaviour. Parents need to accept that it's OK to feel that way sometimes. By denying your feelings, you may think that you hide them from him, but your child will probably sense them anyway.

Accepting your negative feelings helps you to recognize that there is a problem, which could be the first of many steps toward a solution. By paying attention and listening to those feelings, you can get some valuable clues about what's causing the problem for your child.

his father spends most of his time working and has no time or energy for his son. But if the father responds to this wake-up call and sets a time to do activities with his son, remarkable changes in the child's behaviour and personality can occur.

"Parents are afraid to have their kids mad at them. We see a lot of unbelievable acceptance of bad behaviour. If our children are being ungrateful, we'll call a day off. They remember those things. They're family memories."

ALLAN, FATHER OF TWO

Once the problem is identified, parents should take steps to improve their relationship with their child, to build his self-confidence enough to alter his behaviour. There are no instant miracles, but the right moves can make a big difference over time. Children need some family structure and effective discipline. Parents need to set out their expectations about behaviour and apply consistently the consequences they've established for misbehaviour. Discipline is a difficult issue for new parents who may have felt oppressed by their own strict, authoritarian parents with rigid rules. Faced with difficult behaviour from a demanding child, they may go to the opposite extreme, becoming so permissive that their children believe anything goes. Unfortunately, when parents fail to set clear, meaningful limits, the logical consequence of their behaviour is a child who develops no self-control or self-discipline.

To turn things around and give the child positive alternatives, see that he receives positive reinforcement and feedback from his family and peers when he does behave in a more socially acceptable way. He also needs lots of love, attention, connection, and support from you—something much more positive to build on. The more time you spend together doing things that are fun, playing and learning from each other, the bigger the boost to your child's self-esteem and to your relationship.

Children need to understand how their behaviour affects others. In a constructive way, you want them to see how negative behaviour affects other people and turns them off. Talk with your child about his feelings and help him develop empathy about the feelings of others. You want to help him grow beyond his narcissistic way of looking at the world. Show him how to get a response from people in an OK way. Show him how positive social behaviours get positive feedback from both his family and his peers. Encourage and reward him for acting in ways that lead others to respond positively to him. As you do more things together and communicate better, your child may start to feel better about himself and behave in ways that make you feel better. Gradually, the better qualities of his true personality will emerge and develop.

Learning Self-Discipline

One of the most essential skills parents can help a child develop is self-discipline. That inner sense of discipline will guide your child long after your influence wanes. It will give him the drive, the dependability, and the sense of responsibility that increase his chances of finding satisfying work and enjoying his life.

The goal of all discipline is to instill self-discipline, not to punish. When we use discipline and a child behaves a certain way to avoid that discipline, he's not really controlling his own behaviour. When no one is watching or if he no longer fears the discipline when he's a teenager, he may no longer feel the need to control his behaviour.

Instilling self-discipline also differs from talking about self-discipline. Many parents talk to their kids or warn them repeatedly about their behaviour and talk about the consequences, but they end up putting away the coat or picking up the toys themselves, often grumbling that they won't be so nice about it next time. Their kids learn that they don't have to take personal responsibility because, sooner or later, Mom or Dad will step in and do it for them.

The Importance of Consequences

Most experts believe that children have to see the relationship between what they choose to do and the consequences of that choice before they learn self-discipline. That means giving children choices, even though their choices may turn out to make them unhappy. By the age of six or seven, your child is old enough to live with the consequences of his choices.

Suppose your son left his baseball glove on the ground in the back yard again. He has done it often before, and your reminders have had no effect. It's obvious to you that it's going to rain and the glove will be ruined or at least very soggy. It's your son's responsibility to bring in the glove; it's your responsibility to point out the impending bad weather. However, he must make the decision to act. Give him a simple, clear reminder: "It looks as if it's going to rain. Your baseball glove could be ruined outside in the rain." He can either take responsibility and get the glove, or he can choose to ignore it. If he hasn't picked up the glove when the rain comes, don't rescue it. Although your son will have a ruined glove, he will also have learned an important lesson: He has to look after his own belongings if he wants to be able to enjoy them. He may have to save money for many weeks to buy a new glove. But there's a clear link between the choice he made and the consequences of that choice.

You might want to modify this approach for more expensive items—for example, a new bike—by not letting your daughter's bike be stolen after she left it unlocked in the driveway. You can instead create a logical consequence: "You have a choice. The rule around here is that you have to have your bike locked up properly by 8:00 p.m. or I'll put it away for you. But if I have to put it away, you won't be able to use it for the rest of the week." Again, your child has a choice, one you've explained ahead of time. If she chooses not to look after the bike, she has to deal with the consequence of that choice.

The key to making this work is to be clear in your own mind that you're not punishing your children; you're allowing them to face the consequences of their actions. Explain what you're doing ahead of time and make it clear why you're doing it. If it's a logical consequence, it must be a fair one. Never offer a choice you can't live with yourself. There's no need for anger, and you can even be sympathetic. After all, you really don't want to see your son's favourite glove ruined or have your daughter unable to go biking with her friends. In both cases, they made bad choices. Odds are they'll make better ones next time.

"It got to the point where I was yelling at the kids and giving them a smack on the bottom, and I didn't feel right about it. So we sat down and talked about what we could do. Now when the kids misbehave, they get one discipline point written down on a piece of paper. They can get the slate wiped clean by losing a privilege, or by being helpful around the house. The kids think that's fair."

SUSAN, MOTHER OF TWO

Don't be too ambitious in your efforts to instill self-discipline. Concentrate on one or two chronic problems at a time until you see some improvement. Don't demand perfection. If a child shows responsibility by putting away nine toys, don't dwell on the one toy that was left out. Be sure to praise your children when they make responsible choices or show self-discipline. Tell them how pleased it makes you feel. Attention and recognition from their parents can be powerful motivators for all children.

Be prepared to be flexible. Many children don't have the attention span at the age of six to remember everything you ask them to do every time. Just be sure that, when you let him know he has a choice, you follow through with the consequence. By the time they've reached the age of ten or eleven, most kids should be able to look after their own things—with just a few reminders.

Logical consequences for small infractions can even have an element of fun. Do you have a problem getting your kids to hang up their coats? When everyone is in a good mood, tell them that they create clutter and a cleaning problem for you when they just drop their coats on the furniture or the floor. Then tell them the new rule: Anyone who finds the coat of another family member—even an adult—off its hanger can fine that person five cents. Children suddenly become keenly aware of the coat problem, because they stand a chance of making a little money and look forward to the delicious possibility of catching their parents off-guard.

There are other kinds of reward systems that can result in positive consequences. For younger children, use a chart on which you record the points or the stars they earn for doing regular chores like making their beds. Let them accumulate stars for a special reward, such as an extra story at bedtime. Again you lay out the rules, but the children experience the positive consequences of developing enough self-discipline to follow them. Just be careful not to offer a reward for every positive behaviour or you will end up bribing your children with money and treats rather than instilling self-discipline. Used judiciously, a simple reward system can motivate your kids.

Sometimes it's possible to offer choices even in matters like homework that can't be negotiated. For example, you have a house rule that the homework must be done every school day, but you could offer the children a choice about whether they do their homework before or after dinner. Choosing the time gives the kids one small measure of control over what they're doing, which increases their motivation to actually do it.

Sometimes self-discipline means learning to make wise decisions such as in handling money. Don't be afraid to let kids make mistakes. Suppose your eleven-year-old has saved money to buy a new T-shirt. You may voice your concern that his choice is one he won't be happy with for long. You can even suggest he think about it again. But allow him to make the mistake, and if he's upset later with his choice, be sympathetic. The unwanted T-shirt is a relatively small price to pay in return for his learning how to make better choices.

Finally, be a role model for your children. Think about your own choices and, when it's appropriate, explain your reasons for behaving the way you do. The more you allow your children to make their own choices and deal with increased responsibility, the more power you give them, and they internalize and accept the lessons learned from their own choices. Although you set guidelines and rules, your children experience the positive consequences of developing enough self-discipline to follow them.

Taking on Chores

All children should have age-appropriate chores that involve them in the daily care and feeding of the family. But often, busy parents find it easier to do chores themselves than to take the time to show a child how to do it or wait for a child to complete it. Your child may not set the table or make his bed to your standards. Resist the urge to let him off the hook or to do the chore yourself. He needs to learn how to do the jobs and to feel capable of contributing his fair share.

When deciding which chores would be appropriate for your children, think about what they like to do. A six-year-old who is just learning to

Some chores can be fun. Oooh! Squishy!

read may be happy to help clean and sort the pantry by reading labels and expiry dates. A twelve-year-old who is particular about his wardrobe may be ready to help with the laundry.

Most kids resist chores, so don't be deterred by the grumbling. Some kids do better with daily chores and get into the routine of clearing the table every night or walking the dog after school. Many kids work better when you work along with them and when you make the time together fun. On a Saturday morning, put on some good "working" music that everyone likes and attack the housework. Set a time limit appropriate to your child's age.

Offering a choice of chores can motivate your child. Would she rather clean the mirrors or dust the furniture? With younger children, you may want to try a positive reinforcement system—stickers for jobs completed, for example. For older children you may want to offer a financial incentive for "extra" jobs that you might otherwise hire someone to do for you. However, don't pay for daily housework that everyone should be responsible for. Your kids need to know that clean dishes are their own reward.

Parents often find that incentives shine brightly for a while and then lose their lustre. Be ready with the next incentive or another creative approach. Often a simple compliment about a job well done will be incentive enough.

Small Steps to Independence

Kids are always eager to take the next step to independence. "When can I go to the store by myself?" soon becomes "When can I go to the mall by myself?" All your parenting skills are directed toward helping children become independent and confident individuals. But starting down that road to independence can be nerve-wracking for parents. How do you decide when your child is ready for the next small step?

"In my day, we were told, 'Here's the neighbourhood. Go forth and enjoy. Just don't leave the neighbourhood.' I don't think things are any more dangerous now. It's just that we're more aware of the danger. I've seen cases where parents go overboard to be protective. Sometimes parents are blind to the fact that their kids are ready for some independence."

GEORGE, FATHER OF TWO

Age is one consideration. A six-year-old isn't ready to spend any time alone, because he's not capable of making complex decisions in the event of an emergency. He also isn't mature enough and still lacks the peripheral vision to cross the street alone safely. Not all older children develop

A new pet can be an important responsibility for a child.

a good sense of responsibility, so ask yourself if your child is ready for the task at hand. If his friends are involved, consider the maturity of the other kids. What will the group dynamics be? Will your child be more responsible or less responsible when he's with his friends?

At the same time, look honestly at your own anxieties. Don't let your dark imaginings of what could go wrong hold your child back from more independent actions. Try to judge the potential risks of a situation objectively. Make your decision based on your child's level of maturity, not your level of anxiety.

Before you let your child go out into the wide world alone, make sure to review the basics of streetproofing. Get him to think about the kinds of real situations he might face. Ask him, for example, what he would do if a stranger offered him a ride or if he ran into someone he didn't like.

SEE PAGE 30

Try a dry run before you let your child go on short outings without you. Suggest she go with a friend to provide support. Let them walk or bike ahead of you while you keep an eye on things from a distance. Watch how she conducts herself and tell her how she did when you both get back home. Here are a few pointers for typical outings that your child may want to try.

Sleeping over

Sleeping overnight at a friend's house is a fun way for kids to build social skills and begin learning about independence. Most kids are ready by about the age of six, or younger if they're staying with a relative they know well. Your child should also be emotionally ready. Ask yourself if he has the self-confidence to last the night away from home. If he usually sleeps with a stuffed toy, you can boost his confidence by letting him know it's OK to take it with him. If your child is still not dry at night, let the other parents know and pack the appropriate supplies. Make sure he knows he can call you if he really needs to come home.

Going to school

Most kids will be ready to go to school without you by about age eight or nine, but consider the distance, the traffic, and the neighbourhood. It should be only a few blocks in a safe neighbourhood without any streets with busy traffic to cross. You might want to work up slowly to letting them go alone. Ensure they travel with a responsible friend or an older sibling.

A trip to the store

Kids enjoy the thrill of spending their own money on the treats and novelties that are an important part of childhood. Make sure they have basic money skills. Do they understand how to make change? Do they know enough to keep their money in their pocket until they need it

A trip to the mall with an older sibling can be a big step to more independence.

and put it back when they're finished? Once they've mastered that, then accompany them part of the way, and wait for them while they go the rest of the way to the store. When you're sure they're fine, then let them go from home to store and back without you. Be sure they know they have to check in with you as soon as they're home.

A trip to the mall

Depending on the size of your community and the size of the mall, it's best to wait until your child is older, perhaps twelve or so, before you let him go to the mall without you. He'll probably want to go with a friend or two. Drop them at the mall entrance, set a firm time limit, perhaps an hour the first time, and agree on a place for you to meet. Make sure they know whom to call if they have a problem.

Going to a movie

For some children, going to a movie without their parents is a sure sign that they're growing up. And letting your child go without you can save you from sitting through the latest clash of the mutant warriors. Many children will be ready for such an outing at around age eleven. Start by taking your child and her friend to the theatre and meeting them when the movie's over. If she's itching to try going to a movie but you don't think she's ready, go along with her and her friends, but agree to sit in a different part of the theatre. Then meet them in the lobby when the lights come up.

Home alone

In many parts of Canada, there's no law setting out a minimum age for a child to be left alone at home without supervision. Most child protection professionals agree that children should not be left on their own for any significant amount of time until they are twelve. But even provinces such as New Brunswick, which sets the minimum age at twelve, recognize that there has to be some flexibility, depending on the circumstances. Here are a few guidelines.

- Ask yourself how mature the child is. Some responsible kids may be ready for brief periods on their own—say, up to an hour or so—at the ages of ten or eleven. Some twelve-year-olds may not be mature enough.

- Ask yourself whether your child is comfortable being by herself. Many kids are happy to stay at home with a sibling or a friend, but not alone.
- Arrange for indirect supervision if you'll be away more than a short time. Have a relative or responsible neighbour look in on the child at a specified time.
- Make sure the child knows what numbers to phone in case of an emergency. If you're not going to be reachable by phone, post the phone numbers of other adults who could help.
- Make sure you can trust your child not to touch or play with the stove or any other potentially dangerous appliances or machinery.
- Drill your child on what to do in case of an emergency.
- Be sure he knows not to answer the phone or door unless it's at the specific times you've arranged for another adult to check on him.

First baby-sitting job

Baby-sitting not only provides kids with an opportunity to earn money, but it also builds self-confidence. Baby-sitting is a major responsibility, and your child must be prepared. Both the Red Cross and the St. John Ambulance offer courses for both boys and girls, in which they teach the basics of looking after children of varying ages and provide guidelines for dealing with emergencies. The Red Cross allows kids to start these courses at age eleven, but parents should check local offices for the recommended age for course participants in their region.

A baby-sitting course gives first-time baby sitters confidence.

Teaching Empathy and Tolerance

You can see it in the school yard, in the way children play and talk to each other. Some children, it's clear, are more concerned for others. They're more sensitive to the feelings of their friends, more concerned about those who are left out, more worried, even, by upsetting news stories they see on TV.

Some children are born more empathetic. They can imagine what others must be feeling in a given situation and respond to them. Children who are empathetic tend to be more cooperative and develop stronger friendships. Research shows that a child who is helpful to others—what social scientists like to call being pro-social—is a child who will not likely display delinquent behaviour as he grows older.

Parents can also help their children develop this important quality, although you can't teach empathy the way you can teach arithmetic. But you can teach it through encouragement and by modelling empathetic behaviour yourself. As often as you can, give your child the message that there's almost always something good about other people. Help her understand how the way she acts and what she says may hurt other people or make them feel better. Look for opportunities to "catch" her being helpful and sympathetic and praise her for it. When you see your daughter spontaneously help her friend with a problem, make a point of telling her how good it must have made her friend feel. But save the mush until after the friend has left to avoid embarrassing your child. Point out how kids in your neighbourhood treat each other to reinforce your message. When another child refuses to share with his friends, talk to your own child about how that kind of behaviour affects others.

Look for opportunities to "catch" your child being helpful and praise her for it.

Even your child's own difficulties with another child can become an opportunity, but one you should treat carefully. When your daughter complains to you about a friend who is being bossy toward her, be sympathetic and offer your support. But when she's feeling better, suggest she think about why the other girl might behave the way she does. Is she having problems at home? Is she trying to make a place for herself in a new school? Is her bossiness a way of hiding her insecurity? Just be careful not to neglect your own child's needs. Make sure you listen and respond to her complaints first before you discuss the other child's possible problems.

Finally, let your children know that they don't have to like everyone. Not everyone can be a friend. But it's not acceptable to be mean to those you don't like, and it's never right to join others who taunt unpopular kids.

Modelling empathy

Talking to your child about empathy is only half the picture; you also need to model empathetic behaviour yourself. The way parents act has a more powerful effect on their children than the things parents say. When your children come to you with their concerns, treat their problems seriously and let them know you care. Treat them the way you want them to treat their friends or their siblings. Let them hear you showing empathy to the other adults in your life. When you're complaining about a boss or criticizing a sister-in-law, they'll be listening for you to say something nice, too. And if you can't, then maybe you shouldn't be saying anything at all.

Dealing with Differences

In most Canadian cities, children will have friends from many ethnic groups and socio-economic backgrounds. The 1996 census showed that 11.2 per cent of Canadians and more than 30 per cent of the population in Toronto and Vancouver, for example, belong to a visible minority. By the time she starts school, your child will have noticed differences in skin colour. She may also have questions about why Mary can't come to play on Sunday morning, or why Prem's mother knows how to make curry but her own mother doesn't. Feed her interest in people from a wide range of backgrounds by reading her stories or watching movies with characters of different races.

Make sure your child's cultural education involves learning about her own ethnic background.

Maybe there is a multicultural festival in your community at which she can taste different foods and see traditional dances from around the world. Take her to a powwow when you're on a camping holiday in Alberta, or to Chinatown for lunch on a visit to Vancouver. Get your takeout from a Greek restaurant, and find opportunities to visit different ethnic specialty shops. Make sure your child's cultural education involves learning about her own ethnic background, even if you don't practise traditional customs or attend religious services. A child who knows about her own culture may embrace other cultures more quickly.

When your child is six and seven, monitor her TV viewing to ensure the programs she watches represent all races fairly; avoid the programs with character stereotypes. As your child becomes a more critical television viewer, around age nine or ten, talk with her about

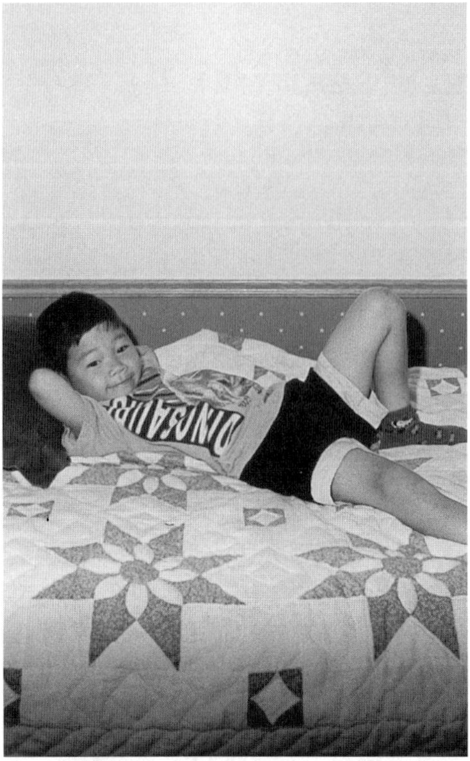

Talk with your child about positive and appropriate images of difference in the media.

the positive and negative ways that the media portray differences, and help her learn about stereotypes and prejudices. She'll soon be able to point out to you the programs in which all the bad guys speak with an accent or all the minority women are domestics. Talk with her about the examples she finds of positive, appropriate media images of difference.

Your own behaviour toward people of other backgrounds, races, and abilities will be the model for your children, so unlearn any bad habits you have. Do you describe the noisy neighbours as "those Italians with the loud radio?" If someone makes a racist joke in your house, do you laugh? Is your dentist or hairdresser or anyone you do business with a person of another race? Try to identify your own prejudices and consciously work against them; your child will learn from you.

All your attempts to prepare your child will not forestall his occasional astonishment at seeing someone or something new in a public place. He may cause you embarrassment by staring at a Muslim woman and asking, "Why is she wearing that thing on her head?" or by pointing to a dwarf and saying, "Look at that man." A quick response from you can stem the tide of questions your child wants to ask and spare the person he's pointing at any further embarrassment: "She wears her head covered as part of her faith. Let's go stand at the back of the bus." Or "Not everyone grows to the same size. You may say good morning to the man, but it's not polite to point at him." Promise to answer further questions when you get home or when you get off the bus. If he doesn't ask, reopen the subject by saying, "I guess you were wondering about why that man in the bank was so small." A simple explanation will satisfy him, but remind him that it can hurt other people's feelings to have their differences pointed out in public. You will have delivered the message that, in your family, respecting others who are different from you is important.

Misbehaviour and Acting Out

Raising kids means dealing with behaviour problems. If a certain amount of misbehaviour is normal, how much should you react to and how much should you let go? Learn to rely on your intuition. Although books and experts can provide guidelines, you know your child and the situation best.

Consider your child's personality. Some children are naturally more compliant and cooperative; others are more determined to test every rule.

Consider the circumstances. Like adults, kids aren't at their best when they're sick, stressed out, or tired. A move to a new house, a new baby brother or sister, or problems at school could each trigger undesirable behaviour.

If misbehaviour is minor, just ignoring it might be the best policy.

If the misbehaviour is minor—your eight-year-old leaves his school bag in the hall again or your ten-year-old "bugs" her older sister—just ignoring it might be the best policy. But when the behaviour is harmful to the child, to the family, or to others, don't overlook it. Parenting experts often suggest two different approaches to dealing with misbehaviour—behaviour modification and variations on Parent Effectiveness Training.

Behaviour modification, as it is now practised, uses discipline and rewards to discourage some behaviours and encourage more desirable ones. Discipline should take the form of withholding a privilege or deducting money from the child's allowance. It should be fair and appropriate for the circumstances. Children have a keen sense of fairness and react very strongly to what they see as an injustice. You can also let your child experience the logical consequences of his behaviour, which shouldn't be thought of as a punishment but as another way to modify behaviour.

Although previous generations of parents may have used spanking as a form of discipline, most experts now agree that physical punishment is not effective because it makes a child fearful and more likely to use physical force himself to get his own way with other children.

Rewards for good behaviour are considered more effective than punishments for misbehaving. These rewards can take many forms. Some parents like to record their children's good behaviour on a chart, perhaps with a point system or gold stars. The accumulation of a certain number of stars or points brings the child a special reward. The system also allows parents to "catch" their children behaving well. When you see your daughter sharing with her little brother or helping him with his homework, encourage her by acknowledging what you've seen: "Joey sure enjoyed it when you spent that time with him." But you don't need to do it every time.

Parent Effectiveness Training, a system developed by American psychologist Thomas Gordon, is widely taught in Canada as well as in the United States. Gordon points out the weaknesses of reward and discipline, saying that both lose their impact over time and, if not accompanied by discussions, don't help the child understand *why* certain behaviours are undesirable.

Gordon recommends that parents use "I messages" to tell their children how they and those around them feel about the children's behaviour, rather than criticizing the children for their behaviour. For example, if your son sneaks off to the corner store without telling you, you might say, "When you went to the store on your own, I got very worried because I didn't know where you were, and you could have been hurt." Such statements avoid making the child defensive, but let him know exactly why his behaviour was not acceptable. Keep it simple and to the point. Explaining feelings can sometimes help your child get out of his own head and into the experience of others. Behaviour modification and Parent Effectiveness Training have their strengths and limitations. Most parenting experts agree that it's best to use a combination of the two.

Behaviour Expectations

Part of handling misbehaviour is making sure your children know what you expect. Don't just tell your kids to stop teasing each other. Tell them you expect them to treat each other kindly. Tell your six-year-old that you expect her to wash her hands before she comes to dinner. Tell your ten-year-old that you expect him to say thank you to the store clerk. Be sure your expectations of your child are reasonable for his age. Here are strategies for dealing with the behaviour problems that try the patience of most parents.

Teasing

It may not be dangerous or especially destructive, but teasing probably drives more parents crazy than any other behaviour. Siblings tease one another because they feel their brother or sister is getting more parental attention. They may tease children outside the family because they have fears and doubts about themselves, and they try to make themselves feel bolder.

If siblings do tease one another, give them a chance to work it out, but they may need your guidance to do so. Intervene if one of them is being hurt by vicious name calling or physical fighting. Separate the children, and give your attention to the victim first. Talk to the teaser later to hear his side of the story. Don't always favour the younger child. Yes, your twelve-year-old should be more mature than your six-year-old, but if you regularly let the younger one tease the older one, you will create resentment that may lead to even more friction between them. Try to deal with the situation in an even-handed manner.

SEE PAGE 156

If your child teases a non-family member, get him to think about how the teasing makes the victim feel. Tell him that it's acceptable not to like someone else, but it's never acceptable to be mean. If the teasing persists or is especially hurtful, find out what the problem is. You might say, "Either you and Bobby play without teasing today or maybe Bobby shouldn't come over at all." If it turns out that your child and Bobby don't really like one another, the problem is solved.

Temper tantrums

Most children outgrow temper tantrums by kindergarten or grade one, but for a few children, tantrums persist well into middle childhood. Some children have shorter fuses than others and take longer to learn to manage their anger. Others are slower to learn to express themselves in words, which means their anger can explode as a tantrum. If your child is acting out in several ways—fighting, bullying, or hitting—you need to consider a different course of action. But if you're just dealing with the occasional temper tantrum, here are some suggestions.

SEE PAGE 125

- If you want your child to do something and he resists to the point that a tantrum is obviously building, state your request firmly once more, then leave the room. This way you avoid a confrontation, and your child may calm down and comply with your request after waiting a few minutes.
- If your child does launch into a tantrum, don't respond with anger. Stay calm and ignore his behaviour. You may want to go to another part of the house, giving yourself a time-out. Or you can remove him from the situation by sending him for a time-out. Make it no more than five minutes. Or you may sit quietly with a child who is very young to calm his frustration. Later, when he's calm, urge him to talk about his feelings of anger and help him to think of ways he could have resolved the situation using words instead of howls of rage.

Aggressive behaviour

By the age of six, most children have learned enough self-control to express their anger in words and to negotiate with other kids for what they want, at least most of the time. But some children occasionally resort to kicking, hitting, yelling, or destroying other children's property.

SEE PAGE 96

When children behave aggressively toward others, they need to experience clear consequences for their actions. If your seven-year-old daughter hits a friend during a visit, you should first attend to the injured party, then end the visit. Tell both children they can play together again, but not today because hitting hurts people, and the rule in your family is "no hurting."

Talk to your child about what happened and help her to put into words what made her lash out. Help her with suggestions: "It really makes you angry when people don't follow the rules of the game, doesn't it?" Then ask her to think of how she might have handled the situation without hitting. Behave calmly yourself. You can't teach a child self-control by losing control yourself.

For some kids, aggressive behaviour has serious underlying causes. Kids may be aggressive because they've seen adults, especially their parents, behave that way. In some cases, the child hasn't learned self-control because his parents haven't set clear limits for him. In other cases, if he has been spanked for misbehaving, he may think that it's OK to hit others. The child may be under stress or lack attention, feeling that he's alone because his parents have little time for him. If the child's aggression is a serious, frequent, or long-term problem, discuss your concerns with your family doctor and consider requesting professional help.

Lying

A six-year-old who says he can run faster than anyone else in his class isn't necessarily lying; he's enjoying a fantasy. However, a six-year-old who says he didn't take the money from the loose-change jar is probably lying.

Children usually lie because they fear their parents' anger if they tell the truth. Sometimes they feel overwhelmed by problems and lie to cover them up. When you catch your child in a lie, immediately point it out to him. Tell him that knowing the truth is very important to you and that the consequences of his actions will always be less severe when he tells the truth than when he tries to cover up with a lie. Tell him how glad you are when he tells you the truth. All kids are going to misbehave at times, but they need to know that when they tell the truth about their behaviour, you will treat them fairly when you let them deal with the consequence of their behaviour. For the six-year-old who helped himself to the loose-change jar, for example, you might require him to pay back what he took, plus a loonie more for lying about it.

Stealing

When a young child steals, it may be a way of showing off, of trying to increase popularity, or it may simply mean she acted on an impulse. Avoid your own impulse to shame and embarrass her. It's much more effective to tell her that taking what belongs to someone else is stealing, and stealing is wrong. It's also important that she make restitution, but in a way that's not humiliating. Have your child return the stolen object or use her own money to pay for it if it can't be returned. Give her support by going with her. Don't make a big scene. Return the object or pay for it, tell her the issue is settled, and don't bring it up again. In most cases, that will be enough of a lesson. But if your child steals repeatedly, ask for professional help.

Siblings

The sibling relationship is often the first real peer relationship a child has, particularly if the age gap is just a year or two. This relationship can offer a safe, predictable environment as each child learns to interact with another child close in age. Siblings deal with all kinds of feelings, ranging from admiration and affection for each other to jealousy and anger. They can learn to share and to see another person's point of view; they can also learn how to stand up for themselves, but also how to compromise in order to resolve conflicts. They may learn how to make a friend or, in some cases, how to deal with a foe.

"What's great about it is that they care about each other and feel for each other. Kathleen will help him if he has a problem. If she's sad, Alex will get me to cheer her up. When one is truly upset, the other doesn't want them to be upset. They want life to be normal. He worships her; she's fond of him. As a sibling, you learn about being part of a group. You learn about your own position and when you need to give in."

MARGARET, MOTHER OF TWO

Conflict between siblings is inevitable, but parents can reduce jealousy and competition between siblings by the way they treat each child and by the way they allow each child to treat the other.

Siblings help each other learn to share and see another person's point of view.

Settling Sibling Disputes

Most squabbles between siblings generally develop and continue by mutual consent. Allow your children to settle such disputes between themselves. But let them know they must observe the family rules of no hurting, and make it clear what types of behaviour are off limits—abusive name calling, physical fights, and damaging the other's personal possessions.

Parents have to make their own judgment calls as to when and how to intervene, and you must be careful about taking sides. If you always defend the younger or weaker one, you disempower that child. It's preferable to teach each sibling to take responsibility for working out conflicts. They need to learn how to hear the other's side of the story and viewpoint about the situation. As children learn how to listen to all sides of a story, they develop the skills needed to solve problems and resolve conflicts. They learn to be assertive, rather than just aggressive or passive, in creatively working out a solution that includes part of what each one wants, but that both can at least live with.

Fair, but Not Equal

Most parents with more than one child would not be surprised to learn that, according to behavioural geneticists, the personalities of siblings are about as varied as the personalities of unrelated children. One child in a family may be cheerful and easygoing, happier as a follower than as a leader. The other child may be an attention-seeking perfectionist who loves to take charge. Or one child may be shy and physically awkward, while the other is boisterous and athletic.

Experts say that it's a mistake to treat each sibling exactly the same way. The key to success is to explain your desire to be fair in responding to each one's needs. This means treating each one as an individual, which might require some disparities, but the treatments balance out in the end. An aggressive child may need more limits placed on his activities and behaviour to contain him, but a timid child may need more encouragement to try new experiences and to take risks.

As you become aware of each child's strengths and weaknesses, you must avoid comparing your children and describing one more favourably than the other. Comparing children is toxic to their relationship both with you and with each other. No matter what words you use, they will probably feel resentful and envious of each other, which might lead to bitter sibling rivalry. Show equal respect for the individual qualities of each child, and let them know you expect them to admire and respect each other.

Sibling rivalry may turn into abuse when, through repeated acts, one child becomes the oppressor and the other the victim. When one child overpowers, punches, kicks, chokes, or actually injures the other, that's physical abuse. A pattern of nasty name calling or ridiculing, of vicious swearing or terrorizing also becomes emotionally abusive.

"It's easier to be Katie than Molly. Katie was a sunny baby, bubbly from the beginning. Molly was intense from the word Go. It's a challenge when one kid is easygoing while the other is difficult and acts out. As parents, you try not to exaggerate the disparity."

HUGH, FATHER OF TWO

As with any adult-child abuse, the abuse of one sibling by another, whether physical, emotional, or sexual, can cause lasting damage and lifelong problems for both the victim and the perpetrator. Parents sometimes fail to recognize the seriousness of physical, emotional, or sexual abuse between siblings because they believe that fighting between siblings is normal. If you're concerned that your children's relationship may be abusive, you must take action. Give each child an opportunity to express his feelings without being interrupted. Establish clear guidelines for their behaviour toward each other and set out the consequences you will impose as discipline. Be sure to follow through. Consider also whether your children should be at home alone together after school, or whether they should be separated until their relationship improves.

It may help if parents spend more one-on-one time with the child who's the aggressor. Often there's something else going on in the child's life or in your relationship with him that causes him to take out his anger and resentment on his sibling. When you help him deal with his problems—whether at school, with friends, or with you, you may find that his relationship with his sibling gradually improves.

Sibling friendship can last a lifetime.

Friendships

Making friends is an important social skill for children in the six- to twelve-year-old age group to develop as they try to fit comfortably into their environment and into the general society. At about six, children begin forming more complex relationships. They've learned to be more cooperative and less aggressive in their play, and they're better able to put their ideas and feelings into words. At the same time, they're ready to start looking for more support and companionship outside of the family.

It's also at the age of six that differences between the sexes become more apparent. Boys want to play mostly with boys, and girls with girls. There's also a difference in the styles of friendship. Girls tend to have closer, longer-lasting relationships with a few other girls. As they grow older, they're more likely to exclude others from their circle of friends. Boys may have intense friendships with one or two other boys but also have a wider circle that changes and shifts rapidly.

How friendships form

Children are drawn to each other for reasons they may be unaware of. A child's friends tend to share characteristics that the child has or admires. They also tend to have similar temperaments and styles of play. Children who prefer active games are more likely to stick together, while common interests such as music or hobbies can lead other children to a close bond. That need for similarity explains why childhood friendships are sometimes intense but short-lived.

> "When Alicia's friends suddenly wanted nothing to do with her, I was upset and desperate to solve the problem. But I figured it might only make the situation worse. It was Alicia and her friends who solved the problem on their own. Alicia invited them to her birthday and that rekindled the friendship. Unless it's really a horrible situation, kids can work things out."
>
> KAREN, MOTHER OF TWO

What kids need or want in friendship is complex, says Linda Rose-Kintner of McMaster University in Hamilton, Ontario, and sometimes opposites attract. As the child grows and his needs and interests change, so may his friendships. Although the children don't realize it, their parents also play a role. Dr. Rose-Kintner's studies show that children tend to hang out with others who share their parents' core values. But what's important is the strength of the relationship their parents form with them, which gives them the ability to form other lasting relationships.

You can help foster friendships by providing a welcoming home for your child's friends. Let your children know it's all right to bring their pals over. Resist the temptation to complain about their music, and don't intrude too much on their games. Have snack food on hand. Welcoming kids to your home has a couple of advantages: It gives you a chance to get to know your children's friends and their parents. That's important to give you early warning of potentially troublesome relationships. If your children feel comfortable bringing their friends home when they're young, the foundation will be laid for the teen years. Although they'll want more independence then, they'll still feel comfortable hanging out at home with their friends.

Best friends

While friendships may change often, it's also common for a child to have a best friend. These two usually share the same interests and the same view of the world, and they rely on each other for approval and companionship. They are truly kindred spirits, as Anne of Green Gables says. Don't worry that by spending time with one best friend your child is missing out on relationships with other kids. Most experts agree that a special close friendship is good for kids, as long as the two have a basically positive influence on each other.

Best friends share the same interests and the same view of the world.

Multi-age friendships

Children tend to hang out with others their own age, but sometimes they can form a close bond with a child who is several years older or younger. The age discrepancy may cause some parents to feel uncomfortable, but it's not necessarily anything to worry about. In today's smaller families, few children get to know children of different ages as they did in the larger families of the past, so the relationship may be beneficial. However, it's important to monitor it to be sure that the older child doesn't take advantage of the younger one. If your child is the older one in the relationship, encourage her to continue her relationship with others closer to her own age, and ensure that she isn't escaping from problems with her peers. If the friendship between children of different ages is a smooth and constructive one, don't worry about it.

Problem friends

Sometimes parents are dismayed to find their child has become friends with a kid who bullies other children, misbehaves at home, or gets into trouble at school. Nobody wants his child to have such a negative relationship, but what's the best way to handle it? First, take a look at your own family situation; children usually look for others who are like them and who share their values, or others whom they admire. Ask yourself if there's anything in your family's situation that might affect your child's choice.

Sometimes kids form a friendship with another who is much younger or older.

Although you want to discourage your child's harmful friendship, don't waste time criticizing the friend or forbidding them to get together. Criticism may make your child feel the need to rise to his defence, or the two may find ways to continue the banned relationship anyway. Concentrate instead on your own child's behaviour when he's with his friend. If you don't see a change, you may not have anything to worry about. In one Swedish study, researchers paired delinquent kids with very positive children and had them spend time together. They found that neither group had much effect on the behaviour of the other. However, if your child's behaviour is changing for the worse, take action. Tell him you're unhappy about it. Remind him of the limits and expectations you have for him in your household. Tell him if you're worried about what might happen to him if he acts like his friend, and make sure he understands where the behaviour could lead. Make it a logical argument, not an emotional one, and avoid attacking the friend. That will forestall your child's impulse to jump to his friend's defence.

At the same time, do whatever you can to encourage more desirable friendships. Help arrange activities with other children, and encourage your child to invite them to your house. The damaging friendship will likely sputter and die on its own.

You are the major influence on the friends your child chooses, and you need to know who she is spending her time with.

You are the major influence on the friends your child chooses, but as she grows older, she is less influenced by her parents' opinions. You still need to be aware of who she's spending time with and what they're doing. Meet the friend's parents if possible. Their values and attitudes could be an early warning of trouble.

When your child doesn't have friends

It's heartbreaking for parents to see their child left out of activities or ignored by others. It's also hard on the child who is left feeling lonely, inadequate, and full of self-doubt. There are many reasons why a child might have no friends.

Create opportunities for your child to make friends, and create a welcoming climate for her friends in your home. Get your child involved in organized activities that both pique her curiosity and provide opportunities to meet others with similar interests. Contact parents of other children in her class or on your street to arrange after-school play or weekend outings.

Find an opportunity to watch your child interact with others. Perhaps you could volunteer to help out on a school trip. If you spot relationship problems that are causing trouble, discuss them at home. Ask your child how he feels about a particular behaviour that you've seen. Get him to think about what he wants from a relationship and how he expects to bring that about. If his behaviour is causing him problems, ask how he might have behaved differently. Also ask your child's teacher how your child interacts with others and where the problems lie, if there are any. Teachers are often the first to spot trouble.

Develop a few simple strategies that your child could use to overcome her problem. Give her suggestions about how to initiate conversations or to deal with her shyness. Help her practise the skills at home first, if she's willing. Young children are still learning about social interaction, and what's obvious to you is quite new to them. Be involved, but don't intrude. It's natural to want to fix the problem yourself, but your child will be resentful and embarrassed if you push too hard or complain about the situation in front of her peers. And if you take care of everything, she won't learn how to deal with social situations herself.

SEE PAGE 135

The Culture of Kids

Your children may live with you, share your values, and have many of the same interests, but children also live in a parallel world of their own that has its own toys, its own games and movies, even its own sense of humour. Kids have always lived in this world separate from adults. What's different for today's kids is that their separate culture has spawned huge entertainment industries with well-oiled marketing machinery. Many parents worry about what effect all this attention is having on their kids.

With the number of movies, music, games, and toys aimed at children, it's hard to remember that children's culture is a relatively new phenomenon. Since the Second World War, children's toys and children's entertainment have exploded into multi-billion-dollar industries. The average child in the six- to twelve-year-old group now watches about 18 hours of television a week. During that time, he may see as much as 5 hours of commercials for products, which creates his appetite for a never-ending stream of new toys. Not only does the advertising accelerate demand, but the programs do, too. Many cartoon shows are created by the toy manufacturers who feature animated versions of their products in the programs.

SEE PAGE 105

When Canadian kids watch TV, they may experience the world largely from an American perspective, since American programming dominates the channels. Some major Canadian toy manufacturers produce American toys under licence, rather than develop toys that reflect the Canadian scene.

"There is simply too much that needs doing at the present time in our house. After school, the kids play, do homework, practise music. I want my children and me to always be able to step outside whatever we're doing, to look at each other, to ask each other questions, to remember this is our time, our rhythm of life. It's difficult to imagine spending these few precious years sitting together in a room, not looking at each other, and losing the freedom to talk or ask questions because of a TV program."

WINSTON, FATHER OF SIX

How does this exposure to television programs and the products advertised affect kids? Stephen Kline, a professor of communications at Simon Fraser University and author of *Out of the Garden: Toys and Children's Culture in the Age of TV Marketing* (Garamond Press, 1993), a critique of modern marketing to children, says children's imaginative play is now largely scripted by advertisers. He feels that while kids once created their own culture through fantasy play and whatever props they could find, they now need a certain toy to play a certain way or to act out the characters that the toys represent.

But in *Kid Culture: Children & Adults & Popular Culture* (Second Story Press, 1994), Toronto-based author Kathleen McDonnell argues that children don't always follow the script laid down by toy makers. Instead they use it as a starting point for their own imaginative games. Even the Barbie doll, often criticized as creating sexual stereotypes, isn't used in the way marketers imagine or parents fear, she says. The doll is instead the centre of an imaginary universe where females rule supreme and do whatever they please.

"It feels kind of funny not watching TV. I sometimes get teased and I'm not up-to-date with shows. If ever I have kids, which isn't likely, I'll let them have one show a day together."

IZAK, AGE 11

McDonnell also pleads for a little less rhetoric about the sometimes antisocial tone of some children's entertainment. Child culture, she points out, has always had a tinge of subversion, be it rude bathroom humour that grownups hate or satirical songs about teachers. And, in spite of much research on violence in television programming, it has not been proved that there is a cause-and-effect relationship between violence on TV and childhood violence, which is another concern that many parents have.

Children live in a parallel world of their own that has its own toys, games, even its own sense of humour.

Fascination with pop heroes is an aspect of children's culture that baffles parents. It's not unusual for children to develop intense crushes on a particular movie star or music performer, especially as they approach the teen years. While seeing your child mooning over a pop idol may irritate you, it's seldom unhealthy. Some experts think it may even be a positive and necessary part of development.

These fascinations are good practice for handling the intense emotions your child will experience in just a few years in real relationships. Since there's little chance she'll ever get to meet or spend time with her idol, it's a practice relationship at a safe distance. Unless your child's other behaviour changes—she stops eating or sleeping—don't worry about her pop star crushes. Whether it hurts their imagination or not, whether it affects their behaviour or not, pop culture has become an integral part of children's play. They relate to each other by discussing the latest episodes of their favourite program, the details about their star of choice, or the capabilities of their newest toy.

So what should a parent do? Probably the best answer is to carefully monitor your child's exposure to manufactured kid culture. Children are resilient and, with direction, can become quite sophisticated in analyzing how marketers attempt to reach them. Help them negotiate the highly commercial world of child culture. Here are a few pointers.

- Take the time to play with your children often. While playing whatever game or activity they involve you in, you pass on your values and attitudes in a subtle and natural way. You also gain insight into your children's world.
- Watch television programs and movies with them, and talk about the incidents you see or the actions and conversations that don't reflect your values or opinions.
- Try to choose toys on the basis that they will have long-lasting value for your child, but don't be too restrictive. If he says he wants a toy that he has seen on television, take him with you to the store to see it before you commit to buying it. He may find the real thing less appealing than the version in the animated commercial. Don't be afraid to let him know what you can afford and what you can't, and which toys, such as a war toy, don't reflect your values.
- Select programs for your child's TV viewing to limit his exposure to commercials and, more importantly, to give him more time for his own imaginative play.

Smoking

All parents realize the health and safety hazards of smoking and want to protect their children from it, even if they themselves smoke. But the attraction of smoking is complex, and there's no simple strategy you can use to prevent your child from starting. Although smoking is often viewed as a teen problem, it actually first becomes an addiction in childhood. A 1994 national study by Statistics Canada showed that 8 per cent of kids between the ages of ten and twelve years were beginning smokers. In that same age range, 3 per cent of children were already regular smokers.

"Everyone at my school tried smoking by the end of grade seven. It's something I would never do. My dad started smoking when he was my age and now he's dead."

MIRIAM, AGE 14

Smoking persists as a problem, despite years of anti-smoking campaigns and the revelations about tobacco manufacturers. The Addiction Research Foundation in Ontario has conducted a comprehensive survey every two years since 1977. It surveys students in grades seven through thirteen and asks whether they've smoked more than one cigarette in the previous twelve months. The numbers hit a peak in 1979 and steadily declined until 1991. But after 1991, the figures shot up again to the point that, by 1997, they were back close to the 1979 high. In 1997, almost 29 per cent of girls and 26 per cent of boys reported smoking.

What factors lead children to smoke? One answer is in their own homes. Canadian studies show that children who have a parent who smokes are more likely to start themselves. Having friends who smoke is another important factor. One study showed that 46 per cent of kids aged ten to fourteen who called themselves casual smokers had five or more friends who smoked. Only 1 per cent of casual smokers had no friends who smoked. But perhaps the biggest factor of all is school. The strongest predictor of how many grade six students at a school will smoke is how many grade eight students at that school light up. Although all schools are officially No Smoking areas, older kids are very precise about standing just over the line between school property and public property, perhaps on

Help Your Child Quit

Ultimately, you can't stop your child from smoking if she's determined to do it. However, you can increase the chances she'll quit. Only about half of the kids who start smoking go on to become regular smokers. You still have a good chance of steering your child away from a harmful lifetime habit. Here are a few tips.

- If you smoke, stop. It's hard for your child to quit if there's smoking in the home.
- If you can't quit, at least don't smoke in the house. Be sure to tell your child how much you want to quit and how you're worried about your own health because of cigarettes.
- Never let anyone else smoke in the house or on the property.
- Limit your child's access to cash. Let her know that you will buy her things that she would normally buy with her allowance, and give her money for specific activities—money to go to a movie, for example. But eliminate the cash in her pocket that allows her to buy cigarettes.
- Talk with your child about the choices. Be sure he knows the damages that smoking causes to his own health and the health of those he spends time with. Also, try to discover what it is that attracts your child to smoking, and what might overcome that attraction.
- You might promise to reward your child with something you know she really wants on the condition that she quit smoking and stay smoke-free until she is twenty-one. Almost everyone who becomes a regular smoker gets hooked before the age of twenty-one.

the sidewalk. Younger kids may just look up to the coolest kids in the school—the grade eights—and want to be like them.

One of the reasons it's so hard to fight smoking is that the habit appears to offer social benefits from the kids' point of view. A groundbreaking 1998 study by a Toronto anthropologist, Grant McCracken, shows that smoking has very clearly defined rituals that make social interactions much easier. The way you light a cigarette, the way you hold it, even the way you throw it away, are all clearly defined skills that kids carefully practise. Mastering the rituals not only smooths over social interactions but helps create a worldly personality for the smoker at a time when most kids don't feel especially confident. In a kid's world, smoking is one of the fastest ways to improve his image. It's also a convenient way to rebel. The more the adult world tells kids not to smoke, the more attractive it becomes.

Try fighting the powerful allure of the smoking ritual using several different strategies. Talk with your child about the smokers and the smoking you see on television or in movies or when you're out together. Show how cigarettes are used to break the ice or to cover up awkward moments. It helps de-glamorize the whole process when you show how strictly the smokers follow conventions. There's nothing worse than finding out how conventional your behaviour really is when you're trying to be a rebel.

If you smoke, give it up, especially if your child is approaching the teen years.

Point out how the advertising by tobacco companies associates their product with glamorous people and exciting events when it's really a product that, when used as directed, kills 50 per cent of its customers. The reality behind the glamour is that smokers smell bad, they cough frequently and develop bronchial problems from ordinary colds, 1 in 6 will get lung cancer, and half of them will die of a smoking-related illness.

Other strategies: If you smoke, give it up, especially if your child is approaching the teen years. If you can't give it up, at least don't smoke in your own home. Ask for a nonsmoking table when you're out with your children. Talk with your children about your own battle with cigarettes. If your child hasn't started smoking, try role-playing games in which you're a friend trying to get him to start. That will give him a chance to rehearse what to say when there's real-life pressure. If your child already smokes, find out who's selling the cigarettes and report the shop owner.

Find out what your child's school is doing about the problem, especially if a lot of the older students smoke. If there isn't an anti-smoking campaign in the school, start one. If possible, encourage nonsmoking teens to talk to younger students about their own decision not to smoke. And get involved in anti-smoking campaigns in your community. It's easier for a child to resist smoking if she lives in a relatively smoke-free environment.

God Questions

Where is God? Does God sneeze? What happens to us when we die? Why did God let my dog die?

All kids ask questions about God. And if you're like many Canadian parents, you find it very difficult to answer them. Your religious information may be thin. You may not have attended a religious service other than a wedding or a funeral since you were a child yourself. Church attendance has steadily declined in Canada since the Second World War. Today, less than a quarter of Canadians attend religious services weekly.

One could assume from our lack of interest in religious services that Canada is essentially a nation of non-believers. Hardly! The 1993 Religion Poll of 4,510 Canadians, conducted by Angus Reid Group and Professor George Rawlyk of Queen's University in Kingston, Ontario, took the most comprehensive look at faith in Canada ever. They discovered that 80 per cent of Canadians believe in God and only 9 per cent define themselves as atheists.

God talk

You know that your child has spiritual questions when he uses the word God. But his spiritual concerns are just as likely to be about the meaning of life, death, and suffering. Why does Grandma have cancer and feel so bad that she has to be in the hospital all the time? His religious questions can also centre on forgiveness and hope. Why should he forgive Daddy for leaving and going to live with another family?

If you're unsure about your own beliefs, you may inadvertently change the subject when your child asks about God or give a dismissive reply that closes the door on discussion. If you don't want God to become a taboo topic in your home, encourage your child's questions by sharing your own feelings and beliefs. Even if you've had little religious training, you still have beliefs.

Try responding to your child's God questions with "I, too, have wondered about that," or "I've come to believe…," or "I'm still working on that question, but I think…." Don't worry that you can't give your child definitive answers. Neither can the wisest priest or minister or rabbi. Spirituality develops through a process of asking questions, discussing the varied answers that all religions provide, and pondering your own beliefs.

For many children and adults, the tough question about God is "Why doesn't God stop bad things from happening?" Your child may envision God as sitting on a cloud watching people suffer. Many Christians believe that when a person suffers, God suffers, too. They turn to God for healing comfort. Your child may want to know how you feel in situations like this.

Other people feel that God works in their lives every day, even on the bad days. This idea may feel right to your child, and he'll be delighted at the opportunity to share all sorts of experiences that he considers miracles. Or your child may find the idea that God is involved in all the activities of her everyday life so unappealing that it sends her into a fit of the giggles.

If you can help your child feel comfortable talking about God, you may open a window onto her spirituality. You also help prepare her to deal with a crisis, should it occur. When there's a severe illness, death, or other tragedy in her life, she may have urgent God questions, and she'll know she can turn to you to talk them through.

Developmental Stages of Faith

Children are realists, but they combine that with elements of fantasy to explain the new and different to themselves. Some kids see God as a man with a long beard who lives on a fluffy white cloud. Other kids hold God closer and imagine him or her skateboarding beside them. By adulthood, you may have incorporated both images and feel God as a presence beyond you, yet close. Often the faith of a child is very pure. Children want to believe that God cares for us and turns our suffering into good.

Early childhood (before age 6)
At this age, children see God as the person who made everything. They may consider prayers as a magical way of getting what they want.

Middle childhood (ages 6 to 10)
At this age, kids unconditionally accept the existence of God, but may find it difficult to imagine God's presence in their own life. Their interest in cause and effect often prompts the question "If God created everything, who created God?"

Late childhood (ages 10 to 13)
As children enter puberty, doubts and confusions about God begin to appear. A child may feel frightened that God doesn't exist and, in the face of injustice and suffering, may point to his apparent absence or disinterest. Older children want reasoning and logic where mystery exists. Their emerging critical thinking abilities may make them either demand proofs or struggle with the concept of accepting on faith alone.

Mom, do you want to say a prayer?

Canadians practise a quiet, very private faith. More Canadians pray regularly than attend religious services. The Religion Poll revealed that on any one day in Canada, almost a third of Canadians pray. Those Canadians who pray the most live in the Atlantic provinces, where 37 per cent pray daily. In British Columbia, only 20 per cent pray daily. An interesting finding of the Religion Poll is that 49 per cent of Canadians "feel that God always answers their prayers."

Almost all the world's religions expect their adherents to communicate with their god or gods through prayer or meditation. If your child wants to share her prayers, encourage her. If she seems reluctant, assure her that no two people pray the same way. Some use memorized prayers to start, then chat to God as casually as they would to their next-door neighbour. Other people's prayers are full of ritual and ancient words. If your child shows an interest in learning new prayers and you don't know any, look for a book of children's prayer in a library or bookstore.

Your child will look to you for spiritual guidance.

If prayer is a part of your life, help your child learn how you pray. Try to put into words for her your own experience of prayer. Do you look in on your sleeping children at night and thank God for them? Do you pray for strength before you walk into a hospital room to visit a dying relative? If you're both comfortable with the idea, try praying out loud. The grace, or prayer of thanks, you offer before a meal can help your child recognize the sacred in everyday life. Difficult times for a family bring family members together, and you may want to pray as a family. When Grandma's sick, pray together to ask God's help in coping with the illness. Let your child know that no problem is too small or too big for prayer. Also ask your child to consider that while it's wonderful to be able to talk to God, it's also important to listen to God. All religions ask us to listen. When you listen, you move from trying to control God to letting God direct you.

Just as you would in any other area of parenting, get professional help if you find it difficult to address your child's spiritual concerns. You don't need to shoulder the theological challenge alone. Phone up a local minister, rabbi, or priest. You don't need to belong to a mosque, synagogue, or church to receive counselling there. If your child is struggling with a spiritual issue specific to suffering or illness, you may want to consult a hospital chaplain. And some police and fire departments have chaplains to offer counselling to people caught up in a crisis.

Religion in a Multicultural World

In Canada, families worship God, Allah, Jehovah, Brahma, Yahweh, to name a few. But the majority of Canadians, 78 per cent, identify themselves as Christian. Another 1 per cent identify themselves as Jewish, and half a per cent claim adherence to each of the Hindu, Muslim, and Buddhist religions.

The chances are that your child has at least one friend who celebrates a faith different from yours. In helping your child understand different religions, you may find the analogy of a diamond useful. Explain that there isn't just one right way to look at a diamond. Every facet has a different sparkle, and every religion sparkles in its own way. Every facet of the diamond is similar, as are many beliefs of the world religions. All religions believe in something greater than the individual, and believe that all life is one. In almost every religion the golden rule—do unto others as you would have them do unto you—pops up. All religions preach that human beings should love one another.

A Child's Point of View: My Heart and Soul

My feelings can be easily hurt as I learn to negotiate new relationships with friends and at school. I'm learning about right and wrong and developing a moral code.

Age Six

- My mother is no longer the centre of my world. I am.
- As I work on building up my independence, my feelings toward my parents go from one extreme to the other. One minute I worship them; the next I'll say I hate them.
- I need to be the centre of attention. I act up when I feel ignored, and I show off in front of company.
- I'm not a good sport. I need so desperately to win every game that I'll cheat or change the rules. I blame others when things go wrong.
- I start many things but I don't have the patience to finish them.
- I can switch from being loving and affectionate to being rebellious and bossy.
- I don't always tell the truth, and I might take something that belongs to somebody else, but I'm not purposely lying or stealing. I'm still trying to figure out these concepts.
- Even if I have friends of the opposite sex on my street, at school I generally play only with friends of the same sex.
- At mealtimes, I often get distracted. At bedtime, I have trouble settling down.
- My feelings are easily hurt. I cry at the slightest thing. I need a lot of reassurance that you still love me.

Age Seven

- I sometimes appear gloomy, as if I'm carrying the weight of the world on my shoulders.
- I need a lot of personal space—my own desk at school and my own place at the dinner table. If I'm sharing a bedroom, I'll want to divide my half from my sibling's.
- Sometimes I withdraw into myself so much that I tune everyone else out.
- I have many fears and worries—that a robber will break in, that a tornado will hit, that my family will run out of money.
- I worship my teacher—I may even develop a crush—but I might complain that my teacher picks on me or doesn't like me.

- I may balk at my parents' displays of affection toward me in public, especially in front of my friends.
- I spend a lot of time watching and listening.
- I'm content to stick around home doing things by myself, like bouncing a ball, skipping, or playing a computer game.
- I'm able to take on more responsibility for household chores.
- Despite my melancholic moods, there are times when I still like to clown and act silly.

Age Eight

- I'm busy, active, and outgoing once again.
- I'm no longer happy playing by myself. I want your undivided attention. Sometimes it seems that I can't get enough of you, and I follow you from room to room.
- I'd rather have negative attention, even when you're annoyed with me, than no attention at all.
- I brag, exaggerate, and make up stories.
- I can be belligerent and aggressive. I sometimes act as if I have a chip on my shoulder. I'm especially quarrelsome with my parents and my siblings.
- I'm ready for new adventures. I don't shrink from a challenge.
- When I make a mistake, I'm very hard on myself.
- My room often gets messy. I don't have the patience to put away my clothes, so I'll just leave them where they drop.
- I'm starting to become conscious of the way I look to other people.
- I'm very sensitive to criticism. I take the smallest admonishment as a personal slight. I need a lot of praise.
- I'm learning about right and wrong, not just good and bad.

Age Nine

- I'm moody, anxious and sensitive.
- It's a struggle for me to pull away from my dependence on my parents. Sometimes I'll be rebellious, other times withdrawn.
- I worry a lot. I'm particularly afraid of not doing well in school.
- I'll sometimes appear lost in my own little world.
- My outside interests continue to develop. There isn't enough time in the day for me to do all the activities I want to do.

- I spend more time with my friends, although my relationships are complex and shift often. Today's best friend may not be speaking to me tomorrow.
- My friends and I spend a lot of time teasing and insulting one another. Some take it very personally.
- I'm more self-conscious about how I look. I may want to change my appearance—grow out my bangs or switch from track pants to jeans.
- I'm less interested than ever in the opposite sex.
- I'm as demanding of myself as I am of others. Sometimes I get so frustrated with my limitations that I burst into tears.
- My emotions become deeper and stronger.

Age Ten

- I'm comfortable with myself most of the time. Life is good.
- I have few worries or fears, and I don't cry much.
- My parents are once again the centre of my world. I confide in my mother and I idolize my father.
- I'm attracted to almost any group activity. My friends and I love to form clubs, although after the initial, thrilling business of thinking up a name and making rules, we'll probably forget to hold meetings.
- My emotions are on a pretty even keel, but I can explode in anger, stamping my feet, shouting, and even swearing under my breath. My rage blows over quickly.
- I take a new interest in pets. I might say that when I grow up I want to be a veterinarian.
- I want to try everything. Even when I know that my schedule is too full, I'm reluctant to give up any activity.
- I have a strict moral code. If admission to an event is cheaper for kids under ten, I'd rather have you pay full price for me than lie about my age.
- My sense of empathy for people in difficult situations is growing. I'm starting to see that other people have problems.

Age Eleven

- Even if I show no outward signs of puberty, the changes are going on inside. My emotions are all over the place. I can become instantly enraged, then laugh hilariously, then withdraw. I'm often unaware of the turmoil my outbursts cause.
- The flip side to my roller-coasting emotions is that I'm spontaneous and have bursts of energy that can be put to good use. I participate enthusiastically in charity events like walkathons.

- When I feel bugged by a younger sibling, I can be cruel and even violent.
- I might cry more than I have in years.
- Fears that I thought I'd conquered may return. I might need a night-light, although I'd die of embarrassment if my friends found out. I might suddenly feel insecure or even homesick at a sleepover.
- I argue with my parents over just about anything. I can be a harsh, relentless critic. But my family is still very important to me.
- I test limits. I might try cheating on a test or stealing from a store, just to see if I can get away with it.
- I don't take kindly to being baby-sat.
- When I'm away from home, at my grandparents' or at a summer camp where I feel secure, I can behave just fine. My rebelliousness just falls away.

Age Twelve

12

- I'm feeling more secure now, more in control of myself.
- I'm becoming interested in forming friendships with members of the opposite sex, but I'm clumsy in going about it. I might try teasing them, grabbing things from them at school, or phoning them (with my friends there for moral support) and saying goofy things.
- I spend more time just hanging out with friends, walking with them, or standing around and talking.
- My sense of identity and individuality may seem to be growing stronger at home, but when I'm with my friends it gets lost in the group.
- I'm content to go to family gatherings as long as I can bring a friend.
- I'm very susceptible to fads in clothes, hairstyles, and music. I'm also vulnerable to the lure of drugs. I almost certainly know someone my age who smokes, drinks, or uses illegal drugs.
- I go to school dances at which most people don't dance, at least not with a member of the opposite sex.
- When I've done something wrong, I'm usually willing to take the blame.
- I can handle more responsibility now. I might be ready to take on baby-sitting jobs.

Parenting through Family Highs and Lows

4

The one constant about family life is change. Our kids change every day and so do the circumstances of our lives together. Most families must deal with crises—unemployment, illness, substance abuse, separation and divorce. You can't protect your children from every crisis, but you can help them deal with problems appropriately. And through it all, mothers and fathers can learn to parent together as a team—even parents who are no longer a marriage team.

Teamwork—every expert agrees it's vital to good parenting. The majority of Canadian kids do have the benefit of at least two adults to look after their needs. Approximately 80 per cent of kids between birth and the age of eleven live with the two adults who are their biological parents, and both kids and parents live together in one usually happy family. The remaining 20 per cent of children in this age group live in families in which they are the responsibility of one or more adults who either live separate lives or who have come together to form a new family.

There may be a team of two or more adults to raise the children, but there are many different configurations that make up a family. Some of the advice that follows applies to two parents, but lots of it applies to any family configuration. One of the most important features of good parenting is open communication.

Can We Talk?

Experts agree that in order to parent effectively together, the adults have to communicate with one another. The lone parent may prefer to think these topics through on her own or to discuss issues with a sibling or friend. What does "communicate" entail?

- *Think about and talk to one another about how you were parented.* As your child reaches different milestones or behaves in certain ways, you may find your first reactions spring from memories of your own parents' behaviour. Some reactions may still be appropriate, but some won't. Talk about how your parents treated you; be open to each other's views of what methods worked for particular situations in the past and what didn't; and discuss whether the methods and reasoning would work for you and your children in current situations.
- *Work from shared information.* To parent children well, you each need to understand how children develop physically, intellectually, and emotionally, and what you might expect at each stage. Tell each other about the changes you've noticed in your child—both the new levels of maturity and the kind of behaviours that make you uncomfortable. Select the kind of parenting resources that

you both respond to, whatever the medium: books, videos, TV programs, discussion groups or formal associations, newsletters, or other media or human resources.

- *Discuss together how you'll handle the key decisions about your children's growth and development.* If, for example, your child has learning difficulties, discuss how you might find the best educational setting for him and how you'll organize family time to support remedial efforts.
- *Share your expectations for your family life.* One of the pleasures of parenting is the creation of family-time rituals that become special to your family. Describe in words what each of you wants for your family life together and for your children's future.
- *Share your expectations of each other.* Parenting is full-time work for many years, and requires much thought and effort. For survival as both the parents and the homemakers, partners have to pull their weight on the team.
- *Share your expectations of and for your children.* You may have different expectations for each of your children, as you recognize the characteristics and talents that make each of them unique human beings.

Which Kind of Family?

Experts have identified three different types of family structures, but many parents blend different approaches to different aspects of family life into their particular parenting style.

The authoritarian family Mom and Dad make the decisions and teach their kids to comply with their rules. This type of family can function reasonably well when the children are very young, but the parents may not be aware that they aren't helping their children learn to make decisions of their own. These families may run into conflicts as the kids enter puberty. Unless the parents adopt a more democratic parenting style, considerable friction may occur.

The permissive family One or both adults allow the children to do whatever they want and to decide about such things as their own mealtimes, bedtime, and TV programs. In these families, conflicts often arise between the parents, or alliances form between the more permissive parent and one or more of the children. The children do not develop the sense of security usually fostered by regular routines and a structured family life.

The authoritative family This is the healthiest parenting style. In this family, the adults agree between themselves on basic ground rules for raising the children, but then negotiate with kids over the smaller issues. The family is working toward a fuller democracy, with the idea that kids need to continually stretch their boundaries.

In Our Family

In healthy families, parents communicate their values to their children, not just by what they say but by what they do. But what are your values and how do you make them clear? When you explain to your kids why certain behaviours are right and others are wrong, try using an "In our family,…" statement to articulate your own values. Here are some examples.

"In our family, …

- no one hurts another person."
- we don't have to like everybody, but we can't be mean to anybody."
- we like a sense of humour."
- kids can ask their parents anything."

What do parents do when they can't agree

You don't have to agree about everything to do with your kids. Even an eight-year-old can deal with a difference of opinion about whether or not he needs a treat while the family is out for a walk. But the more important the guideline or the behaviour, the more essential it is for parents to agree. Your eleven-year-old should know that both parents want him to call them to explain and ask permission before he goes from Tom's house to a movie on a Friday night. If he doesn't let you know where he is at all times, he will face the same consequence from either of you.

Even when you can't agree on some aspect of parenting, agree to let the parent who feels most strongly about the topic have a chance to try his or her way first. If the parenting strategy isn't successful, you can usually still try the other parent's way. Because kids get anxious if they think they're the cause of discord between their parents, have your discussions in private. Then let your child know that although you have different points of view, you've agreed on one solution.

Family Meetings

The family meeting—to some it sounds awkward or bureaucratic, but many families find it works. The family meeting offers a chance to air complaints, to work out schedules, to assign family chores, to deal with problems, and to plan vacations. As families cope with increasingly busy lives and complex schedules, family meetings provide one calm moment when everyone can touch base and deal with issues that might otherwise simmer for weeks.

Some families prefer to hold their meetings on a regular basis. Others hold them occasionally as the need or the opportunity arises. But experts agree it's a mistake to have family meetings only when there's a crisis, because when emotions are high, it's difficult to deal effectively with an issue. Periodic family meetings can defuse crises before they develop.

Plan your meeting for a time and place when everyone is likely to be relaxed—after dinner is often good. Make it a fun occasion by having a special treat. Draw up an agenda ahead of time, and encourage the children to include their items so that they know they're part of the process. If your meetings are going to be successful, you must establish a few rules from the start.

- Everyone gets a chance to bring up issues.
- When someone is having his say, no one else can interrupt, no matter how they feel. You don't want the meeting to deteriorate into a noisy shouting match.
- The family meeting is not a time to belittle or embarrass anyone.
- Keep the meeting short, perhaps no more than half an hour.

Although parents might run the family meetings at first, they should eventually let a child chair a meeting he or she has requested. Don't set yourselves up as judges. The idea of family meetings is to work out solutions to problems, not to assign blame or decide punishments. Encourage everyone to contribute to the solution. If one problem is that the dog always tracks mud onto the carpet, don't just blame the one who let him play in the mud. Look for a solution: Restricting the dog to the back porch until he's been washed down? Then try it out and discuss how it's working at the next family meeting.

> **Family meetings get kids involved in planning and organizing, which encourages their development of self-discipline.**

Family meetings are also a great opportunity to plan together, whether you're figuring out who needs a ride where in the next week, or working out the details of a summer vacation. Such meetings get kids involved in planning and organizing instead of leaving it all up to Mom and Dad, which encourages their development of self-discipline. Discussing household chores at a family meeting also gives the kids more of a say in what needs to be done, when, and how often, and increases the chances that they'll do their share without grumbling.

What if your too-sophisticated twelve-year-old turns up her nose at attending anything so un-cool as a family meeting? Explain that she doesn't have to attend, but make it clear that she'll lose the chance to have her say. Whatever the rest of the family decides, she'll just have to live with: If you do try holding family meetings, keep these principles in mind.

- Don't raise sensitive or private issues that don't concern the family as a whole. Such issues are best dealt with only between the parents and the child involved.
- Be careful not to just cut off the youngest family members who might add what others think are impractical suggestions to the discussion. Help them think through their ideas and possibly turn them into something a little more realistic.

Parents Together

A strong relationship with your spouse is the bedrock of your child's family life and influences how your child will eventually relate to his own partner. But the rush of daily life, especially during the busy years of Brownie packs, soccer teams, and dance lessons, may push the adult relationship into second place. But it's important for a couple to love and support one another, so let your Saturday night date be as important as any of your children's events if it keeps your relationship strong.

In a recent national survey, parents reported that their Number One stress is finding enough time to spend with their kids. One way to increase the time you spend with your children is to involve them in the daily activities of running the home—preparing meals, tidying up, looking after the pets, and doing the laundry. This way, the whole family becomes a team in maintaining the home front as a refuge from the rest of the hectic world.

In building a family team, it's important that the adults be co-captains. Kids between the ages of six and twelve need to know their parents are in charge. Gradually give your child more and more independence and opportunities to make her own decisions. Although your role is to eventually do yourself out of a job, make it a slow and steady process.

Parenting is best handled as a team effort, not just because it helps to share this major responsibility, but because men and women bring different influences to the family and affect their children's development in different ways. Children tend to do better when they're exposed to both parenting styles, as the research reveals.

The Special Role of Fathers

Evidence is mounting that the involvement of a father has a greater influence on his children than previously acknowledged. It appears that a father's interest increases a child's social development, his sense of self-worth, and his chances of academic success. The reason seems to be that his involvement in child-rearing is different from a woman's. Fathers influence their children's social confidence because they are the first "stranger" in their child's life, unlike mothers whom infants appear to regard as an extension of themselves. A good relationship with this first "other," the father, sets the groundwork for dealing with strangers later. As a dad, you play a significant role in your children's emotional health and the development of their sense of self-worth. As the children grow older, fathers tend to push them to take chances in situations in which mothers tend to urge more caution. Both approaches are important to the children's development.

Dads, of course, provide boys with something that women can't—a model of what it's like to be a man. Children learn more from what you do than from what you say, although both actions and communication are important. Show them how a man conducts himself with dignity, integrity, and respect for others.

Girls also seem to rely on their fathers in developing a sense of their own femininity. A girl's relationship with the opposite sex seems to be based on how well she gets along with the first male in her life—her dad. A daughter learns from her father that she is worth being loved by a male. If you have a loving relationship with your daughter, she'll have a better chance of creating a good relationship with a male partner in later life.

> "Being at home with the kids has been a terrific experience. They add a richness and texture to your life, and when you're with them, it's like a privilege."
>
> RUSS, A FATHER OF TWO WHO WORKS AT HOME

Some studies suggest that the average father spends only 15 to 20 minutes a week in one-on-one discussions with his kids. One of the most effective ways of becoming an involved father is to spend more one-on-one time with your children in real two-way conversations. When you're a father who's genuinely engaged in raising his children, you're doing something good for your children as well as for yourself. Kids are sponges who soak up love, and when they get enough of it, they aren't shy about giving it back to you.

How to Be a Better Dad

Dr. Neil Campbell, who founded Dads Can, has 10 + 1 Tips for being an involved father.

1. Support and respect the mother of your children.
2. Work together as a team, sharing equally in all child-rearing tasks.
3. Spend time with your children.
4. Show love and affection toward your children.
5. Protect your family.
6. Spend time together as a family.
7. Tell your story.
8. Promote and encourage your place of work to be father-friendly.
9. Be an example.
10. Being an involved father is for life.
11. Dads can do it! Believe in yourself and your potential to be an active, caring father. Every child deserves a loving, involved father.

Everyone in the family needs to share chores, like walking the dog.

You can also share the workload around the house. Statistics Canada studies continue to show that, on average, women do more housework and spend more time with the children, even when both parents are working. That's a recipe for fatigue, and it's bad for the mother, the children, and the whole family relationship. The time you spend with spouse and children in meal preparation or cleanup, in walking the dog, in keeping house and home in good shape is also good talking time.

The Special Role of Mothers

Researchers have made some important observations about maternal influence. It appears that mothers have a stronger role than fathers in teaching children the skills of social interaction. Women tend to put more emphasis on building and maintaining relationships, both inside and outside the family. They also tend to have a more flexible style of discipline than fathers and are more open to negotiation as a means of reconciling conflicts. Children learn from them how to handle the give-and-take that's part of any strong relationship. As a mom, you also tend to have an important influence on the academic performance of your children because you likely spend more time with them, even if you have a job outside the home. Moms also more often take on the role of guardian of the family's health.

A mother plays a major role in her daughter's developing self-esteem. Girls look for role models as they try to figure out how they fit into society, especially how they relate to men. When you provide a strong model of confidence and equality with the men in your life, your daughter is likely to adopt the same attitudes.

Your daughter relies on her mother to be a model of how to be a mother.

Your daughter relies on her mother to be a model of how to be a mother herself. She learns to maintain strong family relationships, to care for other family members, and to continue family traditions, whether it's a family picnic on Canada Day or hosting a gathering of the extended family during the summer holidays. Take care lest you inadvertently teach your daughter that a mother's role is to sacrifice for the family. That's the message she might get if her mother automatically calls on her first for help around the house or when she sees that her mother takes on most of the responsibilities for the family's everyday care. Be sure that both partners are involved in running the household and that both sons and daughters share household responsibilities.

Mothers can provide a healthy model for girls who worry about their body image. Girls are more likely to become preoccupied about their size and weight if their mother has the same obsession. Talk to your daughter about the images on TV and in magazines and reassure her that there is no one "acceptable" body type. Encourage your daughter to care about her grooming, but don't be judgmental about what you see as her physical shortcomings.

Throughout his childhood, your son probably was happy to spend time with his mother, chattering all the while. As he gets older and begins to focus more on friends, he still wants and needs lots of your attention. But by the time he's about nine or ten, your boy may pretend that he doesn't need you—partly because of society's messages about how boys should behave and partly to avoid teasing. He may squirm and fuss if you continue to kiss him goodbye as he leaves for school. But at the same time, he'd be disappointed if you didn't. Just don't do it in front of his friends!

Mothers model many skills for their daughters, including good fishing techniques!

Many mothers play a major role in demonstrating important qualities—sensitivity, compassion, caring—that help their sons develop as complete human beings. Boys also learn from their mothers about the nature of relationships with the opposite sex. If a boy has a bad relationship with his mother, the first woman in his life, it may lead to troubled relationships with women later on. Boys who grow up without their own mothers or with mothers who aren't emotionally available to them tend to be less secure and more emotionally fragile. But boys rely on maternal sensitivity to recognize and respond to them as they develop. Teaching your son how to relate to the world emotionally will also prepare him to be a better, more involved father one day.

When There Is a Crisis

When there's a crisis in the family, children know it, whether you tell them or not. If Mom and Dad are talking in their room with the door shut, if family routines are disrupted, if a parent seems upset or withdrawn, children will notice. Don't let them jump to conclusions. More than one family has been confronted with a child asking, "Are you and Daddy getting a divorce?" when the real problem has been less traumatic—for example, Dad has lost his job, and Mom and Dad have been talking in private about money. Whatever the crisis, find a good time to tell your children what's going on in a way appropriate to their age.

When your family faces the long illness or death of a family member, or one parent's loss of a job, or divorce and remarriage, it can mean a big adjustment for everyone. Families who have established good patterns of communication seem to handle crises better than others. If children know they can talk to their parents about their emotions—including anger, fear, and grief—and be greeted with understanding rather than disapproval, they will have a first outlet for their distress.

One of the most important parenting skills is that of responsive listener—a parent who listens to the anxiety behind the children's questions and comments. A parent who listens closely to what his child shows as well as what he says can help the child explore his emotions by asking gentle questions. An open-ended question like "How do you feel about Daddy leaving?" is too difficult for a troubled child to answer. But if you say, "Were you sad or angry when you woke up this morning and thought about Daddy?" he is more likely to name his emotions. In difficult situations it can also be helpful to ask, "What was the worst thing about today?" or "What was the best thing?" Even the child who doesn't like to answer these questions can benefit from being asked, if you respect his wish not to be pushed.

Don't let your child be forgotten as you become engrossed in the details of a separation or coping with bereavement. Your detachment may pose a risk, especially for the child who reacts by withdrawing and appears not to be troubled because he's quiet. If you don't feel equipped to handle your child's trauma alone, ask someone else who cares for your child—a spouse, relation, or friend—to step in for you. Let the house go, and accept offers of casseroles and other support from the neighbours so that you can free your time to spend with your children.

How Stress May Appear

SEE PAGE 128

All crises are different, and the reactions of individual children vary with their age, their temperament, and their life experiences. Many of the ways children express stress are different from adult reactions. Your children may exhibit either physical symptoms or behavioural changes, although both may occur, and the problems are not age-specific. Here are examples of physical symptoms.

- gastric upsets such as tummy ache or loss of appetite
- sleep problems such as nightmares and insomnia
- overactivity and inability to concentrate
- bedwetting and bowel accidents
- headaches

Other symptoms of stress are behavioural. Signs of depression such as withdrawal or loss of energy can be seen in children as young as three. But sadness and anger can come out in other forms, such as disruptive behaviour and overactivity. Some children regress to an earlier stage of development, and they need a great deal of reassurance and physical contact, although they might have become quite independent. If a child is worried about the situation at home, she may be afraid to go to school, although she had earlier been a happy student. She is expressing her fear that something dire may happen at home if she's not there to stop it. Other behavioural problems may be caused by stress:

- tantrums
- defiance and negativity
- antisocial behaviour such as destroying things or hurting others
- dependent and clinging behaviour
- ritualized attachment to routine, such as needing the same foods or actions every day
- difficulty separating from parents or caregivers
- being fearful at night
- inability to accept discipline
- being accident-prone

Signs of depression such as withdrawal or loss of energy can be seen in children as young as three.

These patterns of behaviour come and go in well-adjusted children and are a problem only if they persist. In eight- to ten-year-olds, for example, behavioural problems may increase the child's stress. If negativity and aggressive behaviour persist in this age group, it may affect the child's ability to make or keep friends, an important skill for this stage of development. A child who is unsuccessful at making friends will become isolated and may become more troubled as a result.

A child's inability to concentrate may also mushroom into full-fledged academic problems. At age eleven or twelve, children begin to realize that others may not put the same value on school as their parents do. A child who's unable to concentrate because of a family crisis may become lost in the more complex subjects and be unable to keep up with the progress of her class. She may be more inclined to share her problems with a close friend than with you, and you might encourage her to do so.

As peer relationships become more important, she may stake out a new identity for herself as the class clown. Another child might become a risk taker, not just trying new stunts on his skateboard but taking chances that could end his life. Some children become depressed and withdrawn, even suicidal. It can be difficult to distinguish the child who is seriously depressed from the moody preteen, but any abrupt changes in your child's choice of friends, her academic achievement, or her interests in life should set off alarm bells.

Some children express grief and loss in the same way that adults might. They have a brief troubled period, then begin to deal with their problems more effectively, and eventually get on with life. Other children are unlikely to concentrate on their grief or anger as adults do. They may run off and play and seem to forget the crisis for a time. Children who have experienced more than one shock within a short period of time are at greater risk. So if parents have divorced and the child has had to move, then Grandma dies, you are more likely to see extreme distress.

In a time of crisis, respond to your child's unique way of expressing stress.

Generally, if the child's behaviour is disruptive to the family or if he seems troubled for a long time, you may want to seek professional help. Many school boards have child psychologists on staff or on call, or you might ask for a referral through your family doctor or your religious leader. Publicly funded mental health centres in all provinces offer both family therapy and psychotherapy for children. If there's a waiting list, there are many family therapists and psychologists in private practice. Check your health plan to see if it covers part of the treatment for your child or family.

SEE PAGE 220

Bibliotherapy sometimes offers a successful alternative to professional treatment. Joseph Gold, in his book *Read for Your Life: Literature as a Life Support System* (Fitzhenry & Whiteside, 1990), says that "Language is the human link between thought and feeling; story is the most memorable organization of language." Reading children's books whose stories focus on fictional children struggling with problems provides opportunities for you to talk together about their feelings and yours. But be sensitive to the situation and to your child's feelings; it would be too difficult for you both to read a story about death in the midst of your own grief. Many other resources in print and media highlight strategies for easing your family through particular crises.

When Parents Separate and Divorce

Short of the death of a parent, there is no shock greater for most children than the separation or divorce of their parents. Even if there had been obvious discord, the news can be a blow to the children. Parents should expect grief, anger, and anxiety, tears or blank withdrawal, or any other physical or behavioural symptoms of stress. There will be a difficult period for their children, which might occur right after the separation or several months later as the implications of what has taken place slowly dawn on the children. Although you, as individuals, will be experiencing a stressful time, be sure to listen and respond to your children.

How to Tell the Children

No matter how acrimonious your separation and possibly your subsequent divorce, it's important that you and your spouse tell the children together. In private, discuss what and how you will tell them. If practical, choose a morning on the weekend when both of you will be around for the rest of the day to answer questions and deal with strong emotions. Sit down together, turn off the TV, and ignore the phone. Agree that the two of you won't argue during the discussion with your children. It's important that both of you speak to them, or they'll get the impression that one parent initiated the divorce and the other one opposes it. They need to know:

- That you have reached the decision together that you will separate, if this is your initial talk. Include the information that you may decide to divorce, if necessary.
- That you made an effort to resolve your differences, if you tried mediation or counselling.
- That you are separating from each other, not from the children. You are both still their parents and will remain in their lives; reassure them that you both still love them.
- That this is an issue for the adults, and it's not the children's responsibility. Nothing they could have done would have stopped this.
- That it's OK to cry or to feel mad.
- When the separation will take place.
- What changes the children will face in their day-to-day lives.
- Where each parent will live.
- When and where the children will see the parent who moves out.

About 10 per cent of Canada's adult population is separated or divorced, and 1 in 5 of all children lives with a lone parent. Canada's rate of divorce has led to the establishment within some schools of counselling groups for the children of divorcing and divorced parents. Your child is likely to know several other children whose parents have split up, and it can help him to spend time with these children.

Children need both their parents. It's best for the children to see both Mom and Dad regularly—unless a parent is abusive or abandons the family. Although you no longer share a marriage, you still share children and should make major decisions together regarding their welfare. The separations that create the least stress for children are those in which the parents work out an amicable custody arrangement and continue communicating with one another after the split. The most hurtful are those in which parents continue their conflict after the divorce, using their children as pawns in a power game.

School-age children benefit from knowing exactly what arrangements will be made for them to visit a noncustodial parent. Don't use the children as messengers. Communicate by phone to make arrangements, or, if you cannot talk civilly, exchange information about the children's schooling, clothes, and friends by sending notes back and forth. Your child should not feel she has to choose sides, so don't criticize your ex in your child's hearing, and avoid blaming the divorce on the other parent. Help keep the children's extended family relationships alive. Create opportunities for them to see both sets of grandparents and cousins.

SEE PAGE 228

Families in Transition and other family service associations across the country can direct you to support groups and counselling in your community. There is ample literature available about handling separation and divorce within the family; there are also excellent books for children on these topics.

Remarriage and Stepparenting

When parents begin to date again after a divorce, they should be cautious about how they introduce the individuals to their children. Only romantic partners you believe may take a significant role in your life should be brought into your child's life. If he becomes attached to another adult, it may be harder for him to let go than for you, if you decide to end the relationship. If you've been alone with your child for a long time after your divorce, he may also be extremely jealous of your new partner. He may wonder, "Where do I belong in this new relationship?" or worry about losing your love to another.

Most children harbour a fervent wish that their parents will be reunited, even years after a divorce. Your child probably won't treat the news that you plan to remarry with the joy you would like. Even if she likes your new fiancé, she may be troubled over how your remarriage will affect her relationship with Daddy. Be quick to reassure her that she has only one Daddy and that your new husband doesn't expect to take his place. Don't be surprised if she compares your new loved one with Daddy.

School-age children like to have concrete information about how changes will affect them. Outline any new living arrangements well in advance, especially where you will live and how often she will see her father. Then give your child a role in the wedding ceremony. Many children enjoy the festivities and begin to welcome the prospect of again being in a family with two parents.

"I was happy when I thought that the boys liked me, and I liked to please them, but I also experienced strong desires for them to go away—to disappear. The most difficult aspect of all was the realization that Dan was a father."

LORRAINE, STEPMOTHER OF TWO BOYS

Blended families, even those in which two sets of children have to live together, often enjoy a brief honeymoon when everyone gets along, but conflicts may emerge as everyone gets to know one another. Stepparents have the doubly difficult job of learning to live with both a new partner and his or her children. Becoming a stepparent is new territory, which most adults enter without any guide map. You have an idea about being a parent from your own childhood, but few people have models for being a stepmom or stepdad. Talk things over carefully with your new partner before the marriage. Couples who address potential issues beforehand prove more successful in getting the children to accept a new parental figure in their lives.

Because 84 per cent of all stepchildren in Canada live in a family that is formed by a mother forging a relationship with a new man, it becomes his responsibility to make the most adult adjustment. His first challenge is to understand how being a stepdad differs from being a dad. Stepfathers often enter new families believing they know how dads should act, but few stepfathers can immediately assume the role of an authority figure for their stepchildren.

SEE PAGE 177

One of the most effective parenting styles is called "adjunctive parenting." In this style, the stepparent supports the parenting initiatives already established and does not create new rules. For example, if a twelve-year-old tells her stepfather that she'll be home at a certain time, the stepfather would reply, "How late does your mother let you stay out?" and then insist that the same rule still applies. This style of parenting allows you and your partner to develop skills in consistent parenting without the children becoming resentful because someone who is "not really Dad" is setting out new rules.

You and your partner should establish some problem-solving strategies, such as the family meeting during which you ask the children how you all can solve the problem of homework or chores not being done. As stepparent, listen to and support your wife or husband in the decisions reached as a family. Your own strong feelings about how children should behave may have to wait.

Younger children are likely to adapt to a remarriage more quickly than the older ones. If you are the biological parent, be alert for signs that your children feel neglected. Be sure to spend time alone with them so that they know they don't have to compete with the new spouse for your attention. Many blended couples underestimate how long the process takes—on average, it takes two to four years for children to accept a stepparent as a decision maker in their lives.

Building history together is important. Encourage children to continue "traditions" and rituals from their former family life, but also establish your own as a blended family. If your Victoria Day custom was to have a fireworks display in the back yard with all the neighbours there, involve the children in preparing for this new and exciting ritual. In two years they'll be asking for the big day. At the same time, you may have to be ready to melt into the background or even make other plans during the birthday celebration at which the children want both their biological parents present.

Building history together means building family traditions.

When a Parent Loses a Job

When Mom or Dad loses a job, it can throw off the whole balance of the family. It's not just the effect of having a parent home all day, but the uncertainty over money, awareness that the family might have to move, and the need for everyone in the family to accommodate a new job search. Many parents greet the loss of a job by vowing it will not affect the children. But school-age children know their parents' jobs support them and your family life together. They'll worry about the future even as you reassure them that nothing will change.

People who counsel families during job loss recommend that you and your partner talk privately first about how to tell the children and what reason to give for the loss of a job. In today's climate of downsizings and mass layoffs, you may not even know why you were fired. But the children will ask, so give them an explanation appropriate to their age and one that you're prepared to have them broadcast around the neighbourhood and the school yard. Your children shouldn't be asked to keep it quiet. Losing a job no longer has the stigma it once had. Nor is it a bad thing for everyone around you to know you're looking for new work—the public knowledge just means that you have more eyes and ears looking for job leads. Notify the children's teachers that one parent is unemployed, not just because of any change in child-care arrangements but because the stress the family undergoes may show up in the children's school work.

You may be surprised at the strength of your children's reaction to a job loss. Some will be compassionate, as was the seven-year-old who asked her mother, "Are you sad you're not going to work today, Mommy?" Some will be angry at the company who dared to fire the person they admire most in life. Others may direct their anger at the jobless parent: "You mean you missed my concert, and you came home late all last summer because of that job, and you still got fired?" Still others will just put forward their own concerns: "Does this mean I'll have to give up camp this year?"

"Now that you're going to be home more, Mommy, could you bake homemade bread like we had in P.E.I.?"

JENNY, AGE 11, TO HER CAREER-CONSCIOUS MOTHER

Children may seem to absorb the information, then forget about it. You and your partner must take the time to deal with your own emotions, but don't become so preoccupied that you cannot see your children's reactions. Be alert for signs that they are worrying about the effects of unemployment on your family. If your son spends a lot more time

How Kids Can Help

1. Help with chores around the house.
2. Stay quiet when a parent is on the phone.
3. Never play silly games when answering the phone.
4. Always write down phone messages carefully.
5. Read the classified ads to help with a job search.
6. Do research on the Internet on companies where your parent has an interview.
7. Understand that there may be changes.
8. Understand your unemployed parent may have bad days. Ask him how he's doing.
9. Be respectful of spending restraints.
10. Talk it over with friends whose parents have also lost a job.

alone or appears to avoid coming home, he may be upset by the level of tension in the home.

During a long period of unemployment, money will become a major concern. You and your partner should discuss your financial situation privately, then inform the children of any aspects that may affect them. Warn them, for example, if you have to restrict your spending on birthday or holiday presents. Children are usually willing to accommodate this kind of change when you explain why it's necessary. However, if every dinner table conversation revolves around money at this time, it can be stressful for children. Try to make a budget and live within it.

When unemployment drags on to the point at which you have to sell property or possessions for money to live on, try to prepare the children for the changes to come. Promise them that they will know if a big change is to come. That way, they can put aside their worries until there is something important enough to worry about. Let them know as soon as you know if you have to move to another city to take a new job. Smooth the move by showing them pictures of their prospective new hometown and allowing an advance visit, if practical.

If the stress becomes too much for your family, seek help. An excellent resource is the book *Surviving Your Partner's Job Loss* by Jill Jukes and Ruthan Rosenberg, published in 1993 by the outplacement firm Murray Axmith & Associates (available through the firm in Toronto). Some outplacement firms also offer family counselling. If you've not received outplacement help, perhaps a religious or youth group leader, or a teacher or counsellor at your children's school might help your children deal with their stress.

When a Parent Is an Alcoholic

The conspiracy of silence surrounding alcohol or drug addiction within the family can do as much damage to a child as the substance addiction itself. Often the partner of an alcoholic puts all his efforts into fighting or covering the addiction, and the children may become lost in the family struggle. Alcoholism is *often* associated with abuse, whether physical, sexual, or emotional, and with subsequent family breakdown. It is *always* associated with the neglect of children by the addicted parent. As a result of the parent's broken promises, harsh words, and the threat of abuse, the children learn not to trust, not to feel, and not to talk about their problems.

"What happens is that you think, 'If only I was better in school, my mother wouldn't drink. If only I didn't annoy her, she might be better.' I would get so angry at her yet, at the same time, I thought I was to blame."

LUCILLE, ADULT CHILD OF AN ALCOHOLIC

Children's reactions to the stress of alcoholism vary with the age and sex of the child and their temperament. One child may become withdrawn, another aggressive, still another may become depressed and unable to concentrate in school. The responsible eldest child may take on the role of superachiever, excelling in school, taking care of younger children, and otherwise filling in for an absent parent. As she covers for the family, doing her utmost to make everything appear normal, she neglects her own hurt and need. Another child might become withdrawn and unable to communicate with anyone, because her trust has been destroyed by the unacknowledged turmoil in her family. Some children become scapegoats and act out aggressively both at home and in school. Or one may become the class clown whose jokes and hijinks call attention to himself and away from the problems at home. It takes a long time for these children to relearn appropriate patterns of behaviour.

Children need one very resilient parent to help them overcome the effects of a partner's alcoholism. One important step is to acknowledge the problem in an age-appropriate way. School-age children can see the difference between what happens in their family life with an alcoholic parent and what happens in that of a nonalcoholic parent. Telling them what's going on can help re-establish healthy patterns of communication.

There's no agreement among addiction counsellors about the best way to describe alcoholism to children. Some adopt the Alcoholics Anonymous method of describing it as a disease: "Daddy behaves that way because he's sick. He cannot control himself when he's drinking." Although your children may wonder why Daddy can't just get a pill from the doctor, describing alcoholism as a disease helps the child feel less responsible for the drinking parent. You might tell a younger child that Daddy is "stuck on drinking like a magnet on a piece of steel. He can't let go." The message you give your child should be geared to his level of understanding. Your child needs to have an explanation for the alcoholic partner's denial of his condition, and to know that the parent's condition is not the child's fault. "We can't make Daddy well. He has to get help for himself."

Covering constantly for an alcoholic partner is a mistake and one your children will see through. If your wife has a problem with drugs or alcohol, urge her to seek counselling. If she's reluctant, point out the effect that she's having on the children, something most alcoholics deny. If she does take treatment, participate in all the family counselling available, whether you believe that you'll stay together as a family or not. Through the provincial health-care system, some provinces fund residential treatment programs that include family counselling. In Ontario, Renascent Centres offer a 21-day, live-in program at no charge for men SEE PAGE 222 and women willing to take treatment. The Alberta Alcohol and Drug Abuse Commission, which is publicly funded, will initiate family counselling while encouraging the addicted parent to get involved in treatment. Alcoholics Anonymous and its family support groups like Al-Anon/Alateen offer effective follow-up in most communities. You can seek help through a family doctor or a mental health centre if you're unsure where to go.

Children of alcoholics grow up fast. They feel responsible for their parent's drinking and for the future of their family, but they also feel SEE PAGE 177 powerless. Authoritative parenting by the nonalcoholic parent might help alleviate some of the child's burden. An authoritative parent makes it clear that she's the adult, the person with authority, but she's willing

What Kids Need to Know about Alcoholism

1. It's not your fault. Your parent doesn't drink because of something you do or don't do. No matter how perfect you are, you can't change it.
2. You can't fix it. Forget about watering down the booze or talking your parent into seeking treatment. That's not your responsibility.
3. You can learn to deal with it. Find a friend, relative, or teacher you can talk to. At home, find a safe place for yourself.

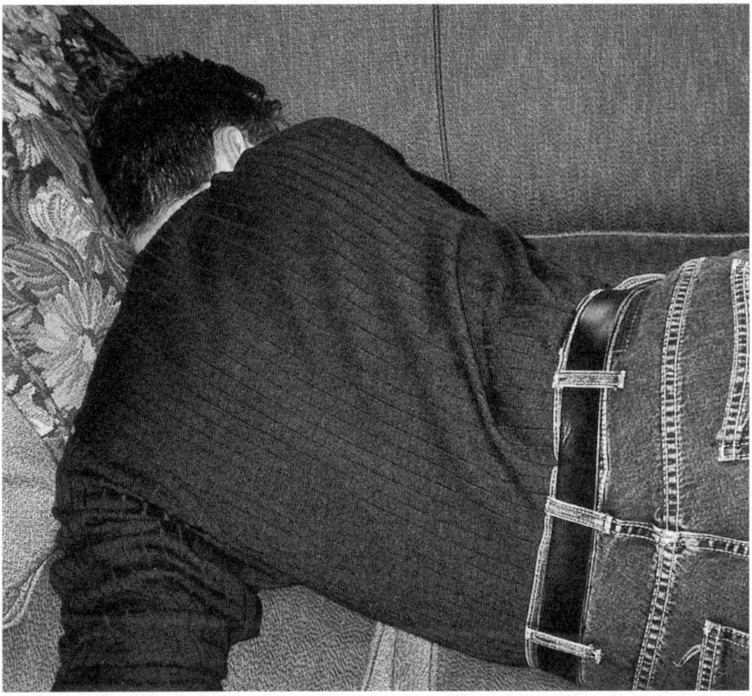

Alcoholism is always associated with the neglect of children by the addicted parent.

to negotiate with the child on the rules and the consequences of breaking them. This parenting style can help children to maintain consistency in day-to-day routines and family rituals.

Children of alcoholics should be helped to develop coping strategies for the kind of situations they face.

- If Dad starts drinking when you're out together, call home and I'll come and get you both.
- If Mom passes out at home, call Grandma to get help until I get home.
- Speak to a favourite aunt or uncle for advice and comfort.

Children of alcoholics, if given permission to express their doubts and fears, can learn and become stronger through their experiences. If you think that you're not equal to the role of helping your child, look around your community for others who can help—perhaps a coach, a teacher, or a leader in your religious group. Your children need as many models as possible of how to be healthy adults.

When a Family Member Is Ill or Dying

When a family member has a long or serious illness, it may disrupt family life. Perhaps Mom goes out every evening to visit her sister in hospital, ending the familiar bedtime routine. Or a sibling with a serious illness consumes more of the parents' time and attention. Or if Dad is troubled about sickness in his family overseas, children notice that he's not as ready to play as usual.

"I figured out it was cancer. I had read a book about a girl with cancer. Now I was hearing words like chemotherapy and radiation. But my parents didn't say what Dad had. I was wondering if maybe the grownups didn't know what was going on."

MIRIAM, AGE 14

Children should be told about illness in a way that they will understand: "Aunt Emma has cancer. That's a disease that makes her very sick and weak." This may be enough for your six-year-old, but an eight-year-old will want to know about how cancer acts on the body, and a twelve-year-old may be interested in the details of chemotherapy. Let them know how it might affect their lives: "I'll go to see her every night to cheer her up, so Daddy will put you to bed." Often a family illness will bring out the child's fears about disease. Reassure him that he cannot "catch" cancer and that he won't have to go to the hospital just because he's ill with a cold. When a family member has a terminal illness, a child might interpret every upset tummy as a sign that he, too, might be ill.

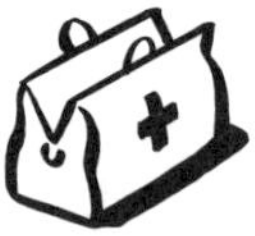

If the family member faces the probability of death within a short period of time, prepare your children for that probability. Otherwise, when the death occurs, they may feel betrayed, as if everyone but them knew what was going to happen. Don't take away their hope that the loved one will recover, but introduce the idea that death might be the end result: "Grandma is in the hospital. She's had a stroke, and we're worried that she might die. The doctors are doing everything they can."

When you're caring at home for someone who's ill for a long time, seek out all the help you can to keep family life stable for your children. Enlist school friends and neighbours to take them to school or to their swimming lessons. If you can afford it, hire someone to manage the household so that you can concentrate on the family and your sick spouse or child. The children will feel less lost if they can help in some way. Suggest your six-year-old draw a picture for the sick family member. An older child might help by taking water to Daddy in bed or by reading him part of the paper. Your eleven-year-old may be able to help more around the house or walk to the corner store for supplies. If someone in your family is dying, nothing you can do will ease the pain of a terminal illness in a parent or sibling, and you may want to get counselling for your children or yourself.

When a Loved One Dies

Until recently, it was common to hear that children did not grieve, even over the death of a close family member. Although children may react to a death differently from an adult, they do grieve deeply. What adults may feel as a hollow in the heart may feel like a tummy ache to a grieving child. They may lose appetite, have trouble sleeping, be unable to concentrate in school or revert to earlier behaviours like bedwetting or tantrums. Children cannot concentrate on their grief as adults do. They may seem to bounce back, laughing and wanting to play with friends or return to school right after a death. But they will return to do the work of grieving later—in some cases years later.

Your most immediate question may be whether to take the children to the funeral home with you or whether they should just attend the service. Your answer will emerge out of your culture and family traditions, but don't exclude your children because you fear that they won't understand or that they will be too upset.

How to Tell Them

People who work with bereaved children recommend you use the words *death* and *died*, rather than euphemisms such as *passed on* or *gone to heaven* that might be confusing to children. Try to tailor your message to your child's level of understanding. Sit close beside him and touch him as you speak.

First, give a little warning of what you are about to say: "I have some bad news to tell you." Then, say what has happened: "Grandpa died suddenly last night." Third, give a cause of death: "He had a heart attack. That's when the heart stops beating." This will be enough information for most children, as they try to absorb the news. But leave the door open to all the questions that will arise later in your child's mind. "Do you have any questions about Grandpa?" If you feel you cannot handle these questions, direct your child to someone accessible who can: "I am feeling sad today. You can ask Aunt Bea."

Experts are divided over whether children aged six to twelve should see a dead body. Some say viewing a body is traumatic for a child, others that children will not find it frightening with the right preparation. If you have an open casket and set visiting hours, give your child a choice. Many funeral homes have playrooms where children can stay. You should also ask your child whether she wants to attend the funeral service. Describe for her what will happen and what will be expected of her.

"Usually, before I go to bed I look at a photo of me and my dad together. I tell him what's going on and what's going to happen tomorrow. I say, 'Guess what? I'm doing so well on such and such a thing.' Like about a year after he died, I won this big spelling bee in front of the whole school. I was disappointed he didn't get to see that."

JASON, AGE 11, WHO LOST HIS DAD AT AGE 6

Psychologists who work with bereaved families encourage them to include their children in the activities surrounding visits to the funeral home and in the funeral service so that they will witness how adults grieve for and honour the dead. Before she makes a choice, let your daughter know what car she will ride in, how the service will be conducted, and who she will sit with. Explain that people cry or react in different, very personal ways, and it's OK either to cry or not.

Take care of your own emotions by accepting some of the many offers of help from your family and friends at this time. Honour your child's wishes to go back to his normal routine if that's reassuring for him. If you're not ready to resume the daily rounds, you might enlist a neighbour to walk him to school.

Families with open patterns of communication seem to deal better with grief. Don't be afraid to let your child see you cry sometimes. Talk about Grandma and your good memories of her. Keep a picture of her in the living room. Don't be surprised if your child asks when Grandma will visit again. He may have absorbed the information that Grandma is dead, but he may not be mature enough to understand that this means the end of his relationship with her.

A child of six may not see death as final and may imagine the dead person living somewhere else. Children aged seven to ten may realize that the dead person no longer exists in the familiar body, but may continue to converse with the person as if their relationship could continue. They may see the death as final, but may not think it was inevitable; they're more likely to press for reasons why medicine couldn't save the loved one.

At this age, children may worry about their own death and may need reassurance that Uncle Harry's leukemia cannot spread to them. They may also ask gruesome questions about what happens to the body—which is normal, so don't interpret the questions as an unhealthy preoccupation with death. The mature eleven- or twelve-year-old may have an understanding of death and is more likely than a younger child to think deeply about the afterlife.

Children who have experienced the death of someone very close, such as a sibling or parent, may continue to speak to that person in fantasy games, carrying on the relationship years after the death. They continue the work of grieving well into adulthood, with fresh bouts of sorrow as they reach each new stage of maturity.

Unfortunately, parents who have lost a child or a partner may be "absent" emotionally to the rest of their family because of their own grief. If one parent has died, it's difficult to re-establish familiar routines. The family may have to move and accept a reduced lifestyle with less money. Such children may need extra support. Grief counselling may be available through the school, a hospice, your religious organization, and through all mental health facilities. Groups such as Bereaved Families of Ontario also offer bereavement therapy for children.

SEE PAGE 223

Families who talk openly about their grief make it easier for kids to deal with it.

When a Child Faces Discrimination

Whether short or plump, dark-skinned or light-skinned, born with tight, curly, black hair or straight, red hair, a wearer of glasses or of leg braces, your child may be teased about some aspect of his physical appearance at school. How well he deals with it will depend on his own personality, his level of self-esteem, and how you prepare him for the occasional roughness of the world.

Every child should be grounded in his own family history and culture. Festivals, celebrations, and family events are an excellent time for him to discover what makes your family so special. Encourage your children to talk to their grandparents and other family members about the old ways. Such conversations help them accept and love your family's differences when the dominant culture may seem to ignore them or to devalue them.

If you are a visible minority, you might have to work extra hard to help your children counteract the negative attitudes that some people show toward those who look or worship the way you do. Recount stories about

Help your child understand that racism springs from ignorance.

public figures, media stars, or people in the history of your culture or your home country who could be role models for your child. When you watch TV with your child or see discriminatory stereotypes in other media, point out the inaccuracies. Talk with your child about discrimination in an age-appropriate way. She should understand that racism springs from ignorance, and that she has the right not to be ridiculed for her appearance and culture. But you don't want your six-year-old to be frightened of the world; save the most horrific details of the Holocaust and "ethnic cleansing" for when she is older.

"When someone speaks a language other than their mother tongue, she usually speaks the second language with an accent. One day, my daughter came home from school and told me, 'Mommy, you talk funny.' I pointed out that people who speak with an accent are very smart because that means they speak more than one language. So the next time she was teased, she knew what to say: 'Yes, my mother speaks with an accent. She comes from another country and speaks four languages. Does your mother speak four languages?' "

RIVA, MOTHER OF TWO

Canadian ministries of education have developed policies and procedures to deal with discrimination. How well these policies and procedures are carried out depends to some extent on your board and your individual school's administration. Most school boards have offered professional development training to educators to learn how to prevent and cope with discrimination. School staff are obliged to stop racial teasing when they encounter it.

Unfortunately, most discriminatory incidents occur out of sight of a supervising teacher. If your child comes home with a story about such an incident, always treat her story seriously. Curb your anger, take a deep breath and calm down—an extreme reaction may discourage her from telling you the next time. Sit down and patiently listen to your child's story without interrogating her. Tell her that the words she heard are hurtful and unacceptable, but reassure her that she has the right not to be bullied. Then ask her what she thinks you should do, or what she wants to do. The "correct" response will depend on your child's age and temperament.

When your child is between the ages of six and eight, consider speaking in the classroom about the festivals and events and perhaps the beliefs that are special to your family. At a later age, your child may be embarrassed to have you visit his classroom, but continue to monitor what he learns by talking with him about his schoolwork, or by participating in a parent group, or by conferring with principals and teachers at his school.

The educators who develop provincial or board curriculums and the related learning and instructional materials work hard to achieve the clearest representation possible of peoples of diverse backgrounds and abilities. If you're concerned, you might check for yourself to see how well the books and materials in your child's classroom and the school's library and resource centre reflect the variety of cultures in Canada.

Make sure your six- to eight-year-old knows where to seek help from an adult. Young children often have to learn school yard skills such as staying with a group for safety in numbers, avoiding troublesome kids, and learning not to cry or react strongly—a strong reaction only encourages a racial bully. You may want to talk to the teacher or principal, even if your child is against it. When your child is in the early grades, it's a good strategy to learn how your school deals with racial incidents.

Check for yourself how well the materials in your child's classroom reflect the variety of cultures in Canada.

An older child is more likely to want to deal with the problem himself. Help him by putting appropriate words in his mouth. "Yes, I have one leg shorter than the other; what's that to you?" You can work together to devise a retort for verbal teasing, without encouraging your child to indulge in name calling: "Curly black hair is beautiful. It's calling other people names that's ugly." Role-playing can help a sensitive child learn ways to stand up for himself and stop being a victim.

If your child is physically hurt or if racial teasing seems to be a pattern in your community, you may be forced to intervene more strongly. Inform the school first; most staff are grateful to know if there's a problem they haven't noticed. Make every effort to work cooperatively with them to solve the situation. Don't be easily put off by administrators who believe there's no problem. You know best what's happening to your child. If necessary, involve the board's consultant on racial issues.

If you don't feel confident approaching these people because English or French is your second language, then take along a friend who can act as an advocate. Sometimes the parents of minority students must group together to make a complaint or to get enough attention from administrators to solve the problems and to help create an atmosphere that is accepting and supportive of their children.

It's a good experience for your children to witness community activism, especially when you're involved. A nine- or ten-year-old may like to hear about people in the news or in your community who are working to end discrimination. Your eleven- or twelve-year-old may be able to express movingly the hurt that results from racial discrimination. It is wonderful to grow up with the idea that many others are working toward a world where we all accept each other.

Family Resources

5

Finding the right information at the right moment is essential to good parenting. Here are national and specialized resources to help you parent well.

Medical Notebook

Allergies

Description and cause

It may take more than one exposure for a person to build up an allergic reaction to a particular substance, or allergen. Examples are allergens in the environment (inhalants like dust and pollen), some foods (like nuts, eggs, or fish), stinging insect venom (like wasps), and medications (like penicillin).

How common are allergies?

Allergies are common and frequently inherited. Two out of ten children have some form of allergy.

Signs and symptoms

Allergies produce many different reactions. Common symptoms are sneezing, itchy eyes and nose, coughing, shortness of breath, and swelling of the skin. Many parents may have observed a connection between a child's reactions and a substance in their environment.

Diagnosis and treatment

The most straightforward treatment is to avoid exposure to whatever substance triggers your child's allergy or allergies. But your child's doctor will be able to determine the best treatment. She may refer you to a specialist to do the skin tests for common allergens. Some doctors may prescribe regular allergy injections to desensitize your child to the triggering substances, but most allergies can be controlled by other treatments, including oral long-acting antihistamines, eye drops, nasal sprays, or inhalers that prevent the allergic reaction.

Anaphylactic shock

Anaphylactic shock (or anaphylaxis) describes a person's extreme physical reaction to a particular allergen. This rare but severe reaction produces one or more of the following symptoms: swelling of the eyes and face, hives all over the body, difficulty breathing, vomiting, diarrhea, and a loss of consciousness. These symptoms may occur at the same time, often developing in less than ten minutes. Death will result if the person is not given adrenaline (epinephrine) and taken to the hospital immediately.

Do children with allergies need special care?

Caring for children with allergies requires an understanding of prevention, management, nutrition, and medication. Ensure that your child avoids the particular substances that trigger her allergies, that all her caregivers are aware of the kind of reaction she experiences when exposed to the substance, and that she wears a MedicAlert bracelet.

If one or more foods trigger your child's allergic reactions, teach her to refuse them, to read carefully the ingredients on food packages, and to watch for her particular allergenic foods when eating at restaurants and at special events such as field trips. Inform your child's school and caregivers or baby sitters of your child's allergies. Always carry an EpiPen yourself, and ensure that one is available to your child whenever she is away from you.

Anemia

Description and cause

Anemia is a preventable condition in which a person's blood has a low number of red blood cells. It's the red blood cells in the bloodstream that have the hemoglobin that carries oxygen to body organs and tissues. The most common cause of anemia in childhood is a diet low in iron. But in some children, anemia develops when blood leaks from the intestines into the stools. Abnormal blood cells, such as in sickle cell anemia and thalassemia, also cause anemia.

Signs and symptoms

The signs that may indicate anemia are a pale colour (lips, palms, skin), fatigue, poor tolerance of exercise, a rapid heart rate, and breathlessness. Children with anemia are usually more susceptible to infections than other children and may exhibit irritability and apathy, a loss of interest in everyday activities.

Medical treatment

Your doctor will determine treatment based on the cause. For example, children with iron-deficiency anemia may need to increase their intake of iron-rich foods (cereals, green vegetables, meats, fish) and take an iron supplement. Anemia is preventable if your child's diet is well-balanced.

Should children with anemia be restricted from participating in regular activities?

No, but they will not have as much energy and they will get tired faster.

Antibiotics

What are germs and what illnesses can they cause?

Germs exist in the air and on everything you touch. The two most common types of germs are bacteria and viruses. Strep throat and skin infections are examples of illnesses caused by bacteria, germs that are living organisms. Colds and flu are examples of illnesses caused by viruses, germs that are not living organisms.

What are antibiotics and how effective are they?

Antibiotics are the drugs or medicines that doctors prescribe to kill bacteria, but antibiotics are ineffective against viruses. In recent years, the bacteria that cause infections in children have become resistant to traditional antibiotics, which has become a major problem. Consequently, newer and more costly drugs must be developed for use against common infections.

Why have bacteria gained a resistance to antibiotics?

The most common reason for bacteria developing resistance to an antibiotic is inappropriate usage. When an antibiotic is prescribed for the wrong reason or for the wrong length of time, it may produce bacteria that are resistant to that antibiotic. For example, if your child is infected with a cold virus and your child's doctor prescribes an antibiotic, even though antibiotics do not cure viruses, the use of the antibiotic can actually encourage resistance to the antibiotic by the bacteria that normally inhabit the child's intestinal tract. If your child subsequently develops a bacterial infection that could have been treated by the antibiotic, you may find that it's ineffective because the normal bacteria have become resistant to the antibiotic that was incorrectly used to treat the cold.

How can I avoid development of antibiotic resistance?

Try to ensure that your child receives appropriate treatment with antibiotics. Don't request a prescription for an antibiotic for a child who has a cold or flu symptoms. When an antibiotic is prescribed appropriately for a bacterial infection, be sure to administer it properly at the prescribed dose for the prescribed duration. Never give your child antibiotics that are prescribed for someone else or left over from an unfinished prescription.

What about secondary infections?

Your child may contract a viral infection like a cold, then on the fifth day develop an earache. The earache represents a secondary bacterial infection, and your child will need an antibiotic, but it will only clear up the secondary bacterial ear infection, not the cold.

Asthma

Description and cause

Asthma is a chronic breathing disorder. The severity of the condition varies from child to child. In most cases, a child's asthma attack is triggered by a common cold virus. Other triggers are allergies to animals, dust, pollen, mould, and wool. Weather conditions (cold air, weather changes), certain odours, smoke and smoking, perfumes, and strenuous exercise can also cause an asthma attack.

Signs and symptoms

Regardless of the cause, symptoms of an asthma attack are the same: coughing and difficulty breathing, accompanied by a wheezing or whistling sound. These symptoms are caused by a spasm of the air passages (bronchi) to the lungs, and are usually followed by swelling, inflammation, and a thickening of lung secretions (mucus). This narrowing of air passages by muscle spasm, mucus, and swelling makes it difficult for the child to breathe out. They must work harder to move air into and out of their lungs. Symptoms may come on fast, immediately after exposure to an allergen, or slowly over days, as with a cold. In both cases, the attacks can be very serious.

How common is asthma?

Asthma is very common, affecting 1 in 10 children. Attacks may be few and far between, or more frequent and severe. Some severely affected children require constant medication, but most children with asthma can lead a normal life with the usual level of exercise and activity.

Medical treatment

You can start treatment for your child by efforts to control environmental factors such as dust and cigarette smoke that act as triggers. Your child's doctor may prescribe medications to relax the child's airways and to prevent inflammation. Common forms of medication include liquids, pills, inhalation puffer (an inhaler with a spacing device), powders, or a compressor (which turns medicine into a vapour). One or more of these medications may be prescribed for use during asthma attacks or every day to reduce the likelihood of an asthma attack.

What special care should I provide for my asthmatic child and how can I prevent attacks?

Parents can do a lot to lower the occurrence of asthma attacks. Keep your home's humidity low (35–40%) to prevent the growth of moulds. Ensure that your child avoids allergic agents such as smoke, dogs, cats, feather pillows and duvets that can cause asthma attacks. Vacuum daily and dust regularly. Children who are allergic to dust mites will benefit from having vinyl or hardwood floor coverings instead of carpets in the home. Enroll your child in swimming classes designed especially for asthmatic children, and encourage them to participate in all physical activities respecting their capacities. Join your local chapter of the Canadian Lung Association or the Asthma Society of Canada.

Bedwetting (Enuresis)

Usually, children have stopped bedwetting by the age of five or six. Enuresis (or bedwetting) is a condition in which a child of this age or older involuntarily urinates while sleeping.

Are the causes emotional?

No, if the child has always wet the bed and has never gone more than six months with dry sleep, the cause is most likely related to deep sleep. Other reasons may be a small bladder or increased production of urine during the night.

Does bedwetting run in the family?

Yes. Scientists have discovered a gene for enuresis. If one parent wet the bed, the chances are 25 per cent that the child will, too. If both parents wet the bed, the chances are 65 per cent.

Treatment

Bedwetting does not always have to be treated, unless it is annoying or disturbing to the child.

Will my child outgrow it?

Yes. By the age of five, 15 per cent of all children wet the bed. Even without intervention, the number declines to 2 per cent by age fifteen.

Colds in Children

Description and symptoms

A child with a cold will appear sick, have a loss of appetite and energy, and may have a fever. The most common and less severe symptoms are coughing, sneezing, and a runny nose. Most children have several colds a year. The terms "bad cold, chest cold, or flu" are often used to describe more troublesome respiratory illnesses with fever, cough, tiredness, and body aches. Other symptoms include sore throat or eyes, hoarseness, or swollen glands in the neck. Vomiting or diarrhea also commonly occur in children with flu-like illnesses.

Can colds be treated with antibiotics?

No. Colds are caused by viruses and so cannot be treated with antibiotics.

How are colds transmitted?

Colds are spread from person to person in the following ways:

- Through the air whenever someone infected with a cold coughs or sneezes.
- Through direct contact whenever someone infected with a cold touches her saliva or runny nose and then touches someone else.
- Through indirect contact whenever someone infected with a cold touches an object and then another person touches it, because cold germs live for hours.

What can parents do?

Offer your child plenty of fluids and encourage rest, at least in the early stages. Note that warm chicken broth is as effective as any over-the-counter medicines. Always wash your own and your child's hands after blowing his nose and before you eat or prepare food.

For relief of aches, pain, and fever greater than 38.5°C (101.3°F), give your child acetaminophen (Tylenol, Tempra, Panadol). Aspirin (acetylsalicylic acid) and other cold medications that contain ASA should never be given for a cold or flu because ASA can lead to brain and liver damage (Reye's Syndrome). Acetaminophen, decongestants, and antihistamines have no effect on coughing.

Recognizing complications

Common colds usually get better after five to seven days, but bad colds may take a few days longer. A cough, usually the last symptom to clear up, gets better one to two weeks after other symptoms go away. Chest colds can be complicated by earache, pneumonia, and asthma. Children should be checked by a doctor if they have any of the following complications: trouble breathing, blue-tinged lips, noisy breathing, coughing up a lot of yellow phlegm, a fever greater than 38.5°C (101.3°F), severe coughing that causes vomiting or very flushed face, skin rash, excessive crankiness or fussiness.

Colds and middle ear infections

Colds can lead to infection of the middle ear, signs of which include fever, earache, crankiness, or vomiting. Pus draining from the ear is a sure sign of infection.

Colds and eye infections

Eye infections frequently accompany colds and ear infections. They may be caused either by viruses or by bacteria. A bacterial eye infection is usually indicated when one or both eyes are stuck shut with dried yellow matter.

Colds and impetigo

This infection may develop from the bacteria normally found on the skin and in nasal secretions. It's indicated by yellow pustules or wide, honey-coloured scabs around the nostrils that spread rapidly to other areas of the face.

Constipation

Description and causes

Causes of constipation include drinking too much milk, eating too many milk products, and not eating enough solid or high-fibre foods. Delaying regular bowel movements for whatever reason, including pain from a crack or tear around the anus, may also cause constipation.

Symptoms

A child who was rushed through the stages of learning to use the toilet can worry and hold back bowel movements. The less frequent a child's bowel movements, the harder and drier the stools and the more difficult or painful they are to pass.

Treatment

Offer your child plenty of fluids, especially water. Don't give them more milk or milk products than is appropriate for their age. Also, ensure your child's diet contains plenty of high-fibre foods—favour fruits over fruit juices, for example. Try to get your child used to a daily toilet routine and provide her with firm foot support at the toilet while she is trying to have a bowel movement. If her constipation persists or is painful, consult your child's doctor.

Dehydration and Diarrhea

Signs and symptoms of dehydration

Dehydration results from the loss of body fluids, which are made up of water and salts. When a sick child vomits and has diarrhea, his body can lose large amounts of body fluids and he can become dehydrated very quickly. A healthy child may vomit or have an occasional loose stool without being in danger of dehydrating. Dehydration can be dangerous, even fatal, if the child is not treated. Symptoms include decreased urination, no tears, dry skin, dry mouth and tongue, sunken eyes, greyish skin.

Signs and symptoms of diarrhea

Although diarrhea is a common occurrence in childhood, it's sometimes difficult to tell the difference between diarrhea and a loose bowel movement, because every child has an individual pattern of bowel movements. If your child has more bowel movements than usual or if her stools are less formed or more watery than usual, consider that she has diarrhea. She may also have a fever, loss of appetite, nausea, stomach cramps, and blood or mucus in the bowel movement.

How is diarrhea transmitted?

Diarrhea germs are spread by person to person, especially from child to child. The spread of the infection can be reduced if children and the adults who care for them practise good hand-washing habits.

What causes diarrhea?

Many different germs cause diarrhea. Usually, it's caused by a virus and so cannot be treated with antibiotics. Occasionally, diarrhea is caused by bacteria such as Campylobacter, salmonella, shigella, and Escherichia coli (E. coli) and can be cured by antibiotics.

What can happen if diarrhea is not treated properly?

Diarrhea drains water and salts from your child's body, and if these are not quickly replaced, your child can become dehydrated and may need to be hospitalized. It's important that a child with diarrhea continue to drink appropriate amounts of fluids to avoid dehydration.

Medication guide

At the start of vomiting or diarrhea (the first 6 hours)

Give your child 15 mL (1 tbsp.) of an oral rehydration solution (ORS) every 10 to 15 minutes until he stops vomiting, and then give the regular amount. If vomiting or diarrhea does not stop after 4 to 6 hours, consult your doctor or take your child to the hospital.

The recovery stage (from 6 to 24 hours)

Keep giving the oral rehydration solution until the vomiting or diarrhea occurs less frequently. After 24 to 48 hours, most children can resume their normal diet. It's important to have your child eat in small, frequent feedings. Don't give her fruit juice or sweetened desserts until the diarrhea has ended. It may take from 7 to 10 days for your child's stools to become fully formed again, which is part of healing the bowel.

What are oral rehydration solutions (ORS)?

Oral rehydration solutions have the right balance of water, salts, and sugar. They are available in drugstores in ready-to-serve preparations, pops, and powders.

What should I avoid giving a child with diarrhea?

Don't give your child Kool-Aid, fruit juice, pop, Jell-O, broth, rice water, or sweetened tea—these will make your child's diarrhea worse. Also don't use over-the-counter medications to stop diarrhea because these prevent your child's body from getting rid of the infection.

At what point should I take my child to the doctor?

Take your child to the doctor when his stools are bloody or black; when your child continues to vomit after four to six hours; when your child has a fever with a temperature greater than 38.5°C (101.3°F); your child has signs of dehydration.

Ear Infections (Otitis Media)

Description and causes

Ear infections are very common in almost all children before the age of three. Ear infections, which often accompany colds, are caused by bacteria travelling from the back of the nose through the eustachian tube to the middle ear, and affected children may complain of an earache. Ear infections are usually not serious, but complications may occur, and the child might become very ill with a high fever, lack of energy, and a loss of appetite.

Diagnosis and treatment

Your child's doctor can diagnose an ear infection after examining her ears; she will probably prescribe an antibiotic to prevent serious complications such as mastoiditis or meningitis. Effective treatment with an antibiotic will mean your child feels better and her fever will be gone within two or three days after starting the treatment.

Some children have frequent ear infections, which may cause hearing loss or a delay in learning to speak clearly. These children may have to have an antibiotic daily for several months. Eliminating exposure to passive smoke will lower the frequency of ear infections.

Some children may need an operation to insert a plastic tube through the eardrum to drain the fluid from behind the eardrum. Once the fluid is drained and the middle ear is aerated, the child's hearing improves.

What complications should I be aware of?

If your child shows any of the following signs, contact your doctor:

- A fever over 39°C (102.2°F) in spite of treatment or a fever that lasts more than three days.
- An earache that gets worse in spite of treatment.
- Excessive sleepiness.
- Excessive crankiness or fussiness.
- A skin rash.
- Rapid or difficult breathing.
- Hearing loss.

Fever in Children

Description and causes

Fever is a sign that your child is fighting an infection or some other illness. Call your doctor if the fever is quite high (39.5°C or 103.1°F or higher) or if the fever persists. Check for fever by taking your child's temperature with a thermometer for rectal, oral, or axillary (armpit) temperature-taking. Digital thermometers can be used for all three. Take care when using a glass thermometer not to let it break in your child's mouth or rectum.

Signs and symptoms

Fever as a symptom of infection indicates your body's attempt to defend itself against infection by inhibiting the production of the infecting germs.

Treatment

The majority of children with a fever have an upper respiratory infection that is non-bacterial (or viral), so an antibiotic is inappropriate. Lowering your child's temperature will make him feel better and less irritable. You can do this by giving your child plenty of fluids, dressing him lightly, and encouraging him to rest. You may also administer acetaminophen. Physical methods such as sponging with tepid water, fanning, or baths in cold water increase a child's discomfort and lead to shivering with the resulting "goose pimples" increasing body temperature. Never use sponging with alcohol.

Acetaminophen (Tylenol, Tempra)

Acetaminophen is available in several forms—chewable tablets, syrup, and drops. If the child is vomiting, acetaminophen can be given by a rectal suppository. Give 10 to 15 mg for every kilogram the child weighs (1 kg = 2.2 lb.). This dose may be repeated every 4 to 6 hours. Do not give it more than 5 times in 24 hours. Since the amount of medicine in a tablet or a teaspoon may vary from product to product, check the amount on the label. Give acetaminophen only if your child's temperature is over 38.5°C (101.3°F). Complications or deaths can occur from acetaminophen overdose or prolonged inappropriate use.

Contact your doctor if your child's temperature is over 39.5°C (103.1°F) and she does not respond to the above methods, or if her fever is accompanied by one or more of the following symptoms: excessive sleepiness, crankiness or fussiness; a skin rash; rapid or difficult breathing.

Do not use Aspirin (acetylsalicylic acid) unless your doctor prescribes it, because ASA can lead to Reye's Syndrome. Avoid it particularly if your child has chickenpox or the flu.

Food Intolerance

Description

If some common foods appear to disagree with your child, she may have an intolerance or an allergy. The two reactions to foods differ. A food intolerance is not an immune system reaction, but the exact cause and mechanism of the reaction is unknown.

Signs and symptoms

After eating a particular food, your child may experience gas, bloating, loose stools, or other symptoms of one of the bodily systems. In the case of reactions to milk, your child may lack the enzyme lactase, which is normally present in the bowel wall. This may be a temporary result from a bout of diarrhea. But during this temporary absence of the enzyme, the child may have a reaction after ingesting a lactose-containing food.

Treatment

To reduce the severity of the reaction, limit his intake of milk or use lactose-free milk, as recommended by your child's doctor. For other foods that your child cannot appear to tolerate easily, eliminate them or decrease their use in his diet. Be sure to assess the overall nutrition provided by the foods he can eat without discomfort.

Food Allergies

A food allergy triggers an immune system reaction when a person eats a specific food or food additive. The reaction may start very suddenly after your child ingests only a small amount of the food—which signals a very serious, life-threatening food allergy. This severe reaction is called anaphylactic shock or anaphylaxis. (See page 204.)

Usually a child has to eat a particular food and have a reaction more than once before parents and doctor can determine if the child is allergic to the substance. For example, the first time your child eats nuts, there may be no reaction. But if there is a reaction to a subsequent exposure, it may well be that the child is allergic to nuts, or a particular nut. Many children outgrow some food allergies, but sensitivities to nuts or to fish are unlikely to disappear.

Symptoms and treatment

Wheezing, hives, vomiting, or diarrhea are all symptoms of food allergies, but such symptoms should send you to consult with your child's doctor. For treatment, see page 204.

What foods frequently trigger allergic reactions?

Wheat, cow's milk, eggs, nuts (particularly peanuts), and fish or shellfish are the most common foods associated with allergies.

Head Lice

Description and causes

Head lice are tiny insects that live on the scalp. They lay nits (eggs), which stick to the hair shaft very near the scalp. Head lice do not spread disease and are not caused by a lack of cleanliness. They are a common condition in children and don't necessitate a visit to the doctor.

How does my child get head lice?

Head lice are spread from person to person by direct physical contact or through lending such items as hats, combs, or hairbrushes or headphones. Head lice cannot jump or fly as do fleas on pets.

Signs and symptoms

Many children with head lice have no symptoms, although some children may complain of an itchy scalp. To find head lice, check your child's hair and scalp.

How do I check my child for head lice?

In a well-lit area, spend a few minutes every week checking your child's head. Look for nits by parting small sections of the hair from one side of the head to the other. The nits appear as whitish-grey or tan specks, about the size of a grain of sand. They are firmly attached to the hair shaft very close to the scalp. It's easy to distinguish lice nits from other whitish specks like dandruff in the hair. Nits are so firmly attached to the strands of hair that they cannot be easily removed, while dandruff can be easily combed or brushed out.

Treatment

There are many effective treatments for head lice. Special shampoos and cream rinses such as NIX contain an insecticide that kills lice. Make sure you follow the product directions and consult your doctor if live lice or new nits are found again seven days after treatment. Don't treat your child if the signs aren't visible, but if one person is infected, treat all household members.

Strep Throat

Description and causes

Strep throat is an infection caused by the Streptococcus pyogenes (strep) Group A bacteria. These infections are more common in children than in adults. The strep bacteria are found in an infected person's saliva and are spread by the droplets made when the person sneezes, coughs, or talks.

Signs and symptoms

Children with strep throat infections often also have a fever. They may complain of a sore throat, a headache, and a stomachache. They may also have swollen, tender glands in the neck and sores around the nose.

Diagnosis and treatment

A doctor usually takes a swab of the throat to diagnose strep throat. It is usually treated with an antibiotic, usually penicillin. The two major complications from strep infections are acute rheumatic fever (a disease of the heart and joints) and acute glomerulonephritis (a kidney disease).

How can I lessen the chances of my child getting strep throat?

If a child with whom your child spends time has strep throat, be watchful for symptoms in your own child. Use appropriate precautions for preventing the spread of infection from coughing and sneezing during colds and flu by good handwashing habits; good dental hygiene may also reduce the opportunities for strep throat.

Sun Safety

What are the dangers?

The hot summer sun can be very dangerous for children, who are more likely than adults to lose body fluid and become dehydrated. Your child's skin can be burned by sunlight or by touching hot surfaces like pavement, metal slides, and cars that have been sitting in the sun. Bad sunburns from spending too much time in the sun, especially without skin protection, have been linked with a higher risk of developing skin cancer later in life.

What should I do to protect my child from the sun?

As much as possible, keep your child indoors or in the shade during the hottest time of the day (10:00 a.m. to 2:00 p.m.). Avoid long exposures to the sun at the start of the spring and summer seasons. Get children used to being in the sun by gradually increasing the amount of time that they spend outdoors over a period of several days. Ensure your child's outdoor play area has a shaded area. Lastly, encourage your child to drink plenty of fluids to replace body fluids lost because of the heat.

Sunburn prevention

Dress your child with sun hats or visors and loose cotton T-shirts to protect her skin from being burned by the sun. Apply a sun block cream with at least SPF 30 (sun protection factor) on all areas of your child's skin that will be exposed to the sun. Keep in mind that sunscreen must be reapplied after your child has played in the water.

Recommended Immunization Schedule for Infants and Children

NATIONAL ADVISORY COMMITTEE ON IMMUNIZATION (NACI), HEALTH PROTECTION BRANCH, HEALTH CANADA

Routine Immunization Schedule for Infants and Children

Age at vaccination	DTaP[1]	Inactivated polio vaccine	Hib[2]	MMR	Td[3]	Hep B[4] (3 doses)
Birth						
2 months	x	x	x			
4 months	x	x	x			
6 months	x	(x)[5]	x			Infancy
12 months				x		or
18 months	x	x	x	(x)[6] or		preadolescence
4–6 years	x	x		(x)[6]		(9–13 years)
14–16 years					x	

DTaP Diphtheria, tetanus, pertussis (acellular) vaccine
Hib *Haemophilus influenzae* type b conjugate vaccine
MMR Measles, mumps and rubella vaccine
Td Tetanus and diphtheria toxoid, "adult type"
Hep B Hepatitis B vaccine

Routine Immunization Schedule for Children under 7 Years of Age Not Immunized in Early Infancy

Timing	DTaP[1]	Inactivated polio vaccine	Hib	MMR	Td[3]	Hep B[4] (3 doses)
First visit	x	x	x	x[7]		
2 months later	x	x	(x)[8]	(x)[6]		
2 months later	x	(x)[5]				
6–12 months later	x	x	(x)[8]			Preadolescence
4–6 years[9]	x	x				(9–13 years)
14–16 years					x	

Routine Immunization Schedule for Children 7 Years of Age or Older Not Immunized in Early Infancy

Timing	Td[3]	Inactivated polio vaccine	MMR	Hep B[4] (3 doses)
First visit	x	x	x	
2 months later	x	x	(x)[6]	
6–12 months later	x	x		Preadolescence
10 years later	x			(9–13 years)

DTaP Diphtheria, tetanus, pertussis (acellular) vaccine
Hib *Haemophilus influenzae* type b conjugate vaccine
MMR Measles, mumps and rubella vaccine
Td Tetanus and diphtheria toxoid, "adult type"
Hep B Hepatitis B vaccine

NOTES:

1. DTaP (diphtheria, tetanus, acellular or component pertussis) vaccine is the preferred vaccine for all doses in the vaccination series, including completion of the series in children who have received one or more doses of DPT (whole cell) vaccine.
2. Hib schedule shown is for PRP-T or HbOC vaccine. If PRP-OMP, give at two, four and twelve months of age.
3. Td (tetanus and diphtheria toxoid), a combined adsorbed "adult type" preparation for use in persons seven years of age or older, contains less diphtheria toxoid than preparations given to younger children and is less likely to cause reactions in older persons.
4. Hepatitis B vaccine can be routinely given to infants or preadolescents, depending on the provincial/territorial policy; three doses at zero, one and six month intervals are preferred. The second dose should be administered at least one month after the first dose, and the third dose should be administered at least four months after the first dose, and at least two months after the second dose.
5. This dose is not needed routinely, but can be included for convenience.
6. A second dose of MMR is recommended, at least one month after the first dose given. For convenience, options include giving it with the next scheduled vaccination at eighteen months of age or with school entry (4–6 years) vaccinations (depending on the provincial/territorial policy), or at any intervening age that is practicable.
7. Delay until subsequent visit if child is under twelve months of age.
8. Recommended schedule and number of doses depend on the product used and the age of the child when vaccination is begun. Not required past age five.
9. Omit these doses if the previous doses of DTaP and polio were given after the fourth birthday.

Selected Canadian Children's Books

Selected and annotated by Janet Abernethy from the recommendations of the librarians of Toronto Public Library, West Region, Spring 1998. The books are listed with title first, but are alphabetized by author, the way readers would find them in a bookstore or library.

Ages Seven and Under

Bonnie McSmithers, You're Driving Me Dithers, Sueann Alderson. Illus. by Fiona Garrick. 1991. Annick Press, Toronto.
A rollicking, repetitive, rhythmic reprimand.

The Very Last First Time, Jan Andrews. Illus. by Ian Wallace. 1985. Groundwood Books, Toronto.
An Inuit girl musters her courage to go below the ice to gather mussels, all by herself.

Franklin in the Dark, Paulette Bourgeois. Illus. by Brenda Clark. 1980. Kids Can Press, Toronto.
The first in the popular series about everyone's favourite turtle.

One Grey Mouse, Kathleen Burton. Illus. by Kim Fernandes. 1995. Kids Can Press, Toronto.
Engaging Fimo art and clever rhyme make this concept book a standout.

Waters, Edith Chase. Illus. by Ron Broda. 1993. Scholastic, Toronto.
Follow a melting droplet of snow on its journey to the sea.

The Rooster's Gift, Pam Conrad. Illus. by Eric Beddows. 1996. Groundwood Books, Toronto.
What a humbling shock when the sun comes up without him! Gentle humour, impressive art.

Out on the Ice in the Middle of the Bay, Peter Cumming. Illus. by Alice Priestly. 1993. Annick Press, Toronto.
A toddler meets a polar bear cub. Unforgettable.

Sody Salleratus, Aubrey Davis. 1996. Kids Can Press, Toronto.
An exuberant Appalachian classic tale retold by a master storyteller.

Simply Ridiculous, Virginia Davis. 1995. Kids Can Press, Toronto.
Ludicrous illogic in a panic to name the baby in this absurdly funny folktale, originally from Africa.

Rumpelstiltskin, Marie-Louise Gay. 1997. Groundwood Books, Toronto.
The classic tale, illustrated with whimsy and verve.

The Fabulous Song, Don Gillmor. Illus. by Marie-Louise Gay. 1996. Stoddart, Toronto.
Frederick doesn't live up to his parents' musical expectations, until he begins to conduct.

The Balloon Tree, Phoebe Gilman. 1989. Scholastic, Richmond Hill, Ont.
A heroic princess saves the realm from her evil uncle. A perennial favourite.

Jillian Jiggs, Phoebe Gilman. 1985. Scholastic, Richmond Hill, Ont.
"Jillian, Jillian, Jillian Jiggs, it looks like your room has been lived in by pigs!" The book that begins the series.
The Wonderful Pigs of Jillian Jiggs. 1988.
Jillian Jiggs to the Rescue. 1994.

Something From Nothing: Adapted from a Jewish Folktale, written and illus. by Phoebe Gilman. 1992. Scholastic, Richmond Hill, Ont.
A worn-out baby blanket is lovingly transformed into progressively smaller items.

Muddle Cuddle, Laurel Dee Gugler. 1997. Annick Press, Toronto.
Daddy's lap can't hold the huge pile of toys, pets, and siblings in this exuberant rhyme.

Cameron and Me, Dorothy Joan Harris. Illus. by Marilyn Mets. 1997. Stoddart, Toronto.
First one, then another new baby! Honest and insightful.

The Charlotte Stories, Teddy Jam. 1994. Groundwood Books, Toronto.
Three cozy stories about Charlotte, a determined little girl who insists on making up her own mind.

Jeremiah and Mrs. Ming, Sharon Jennings. Illus. by Mireille Levert. 1990. Annick Press, Toronto.
Jeremiah's imagination is keeping him awake, and Mrs. Ming's is helping him get to sleep.
Sleep Tight, Mrs. Ming. 1993.

I Want a Dog, Dayal Kaur Khalsa. 1987. Tundra Books, Toronto.
When she can't have a real dog, a small girl creates an imaginary one.

Brenda and Edward, Maryann Kovalski. 1993. Kids Can Press, Toronto.
Two devoted stray dogs live happily in an alley, until Brenda gets lost, then adopted.

Frank and Zelda, Maryann Kovalski. 1990. Kids Can Press, Toronto.
Business at their pizza parlour booms too much when their wishes start to come true.

Kate's Castle, Julie Lawson. Illus. by Frances Tyrrell. 1993. Stoddart, Toronto.
To Kate, her sand castle on the beach is, Oh, so much more than that!

Whatever You Do, Don't Go Near That Canoe, Julie Lawson. Illus. by Werner Zimmerman. 1996. Scholastic, Richmond Hill, Ont.
The story of a magic canoe, fearsome pirates, and candy, told with the rhythm of lapping waves.

Lizzie's Lion, Dennis Lee. 1989. Stoddart, Toronto.
Lizzy's pet lion makes short work of a robber in this delightfully gruesome rhyme.

Gruntle Piggle Takes Off, Jean Little. 1997. Illus. by Johnny Wales. Penguin Books, Toronto.
Fun with word play as a gutsy, young city pig sets out to explore her roots.

The Name of the Tree, Celia Barker Lottridge. Illus. by Ian Wallace. 1989. Groundwood Books, Toronto.
The slow and careful tortoise is the hero of this read-aloud favourite folktale from Africa.

Ten Small Tales, Celia Barker Lottridge. 1993. Groundwood Books, Toronto.
Beautifully told folktales from around the world. A gem.

Brewster Rooster, Berny Lucas. Illus. by Russ Willms. 1993. Kids Can Press, Toronto.
A young rooster practises crowing nonstop, until the farmer threatens to put him in the soup!

Amos's Sweater, Janet Lunn. Illus. by Kim LaFave. 1988. Groundwood Books, Toronto.
An old sheep rebels at being shorn, yet again.

Duck Cakes for Sale, Janet Lunn. Illus. by Kim LaFave. 1989. Groundwood Books, Toronto.
A little old lady takes two yellow ducklings to pretty up her stream, and in no time it's overrun with ducks and eggs. What to do?

Waiting for the Whales, Sheryl McFarlane. Illus. by Ron Lightburn. 1993. Orca Book Publishers, Victoria.
A grandfather and granddaughter lovingly share the wonders of nature over many years.

Sadie and the Snowman, Allen Morgan. 1995. Kids Can Press, Toronto.
How a clever girl manages to make her snowman last, and last, and last.

David's Father, Robert Munsch. Illus. by Michael Martchenko. 1988. Annick Press, Toronto.
Julie is surprised to find her friend's father is a giant.

The Paper Bag Princess, Robert Munsch. Illus. by Michael Martchenko. 1980. Annick Press, Toronto.
The princess rescues the priggish prince, then dumps him. Munsch's best.

Thomas' Snowsuit, Robert Munsch. Illus. by Michael Martchenko. 1985. Annick Press, Toronto.
Thomas absolutely refuses to be stuffed into his snowsuit. Hilarious.

Have You Seen Josephine? Stéphane Poulin. 1986. Tundra Books, Toronto.
A little boy explores old Montréal in his search for his cat, Josephine.

The Party, written and illus. by Barbara Reid. 1997. Scholastic, Richmond Hill, Ont.
Winsome Plasticine illustrations and fun-filled rhyme capture cousins at play at a family reunion.

Two by Two, written and illus. by Barbara Reid. 1992. Scholastic, Richmond Hill, Ont.
Masterful Plasticine art tells the story of Noah's ark.

Farmer Joe's Hot Day, Nancy Wilcox Richards. Illus. by Werner Timmerman. 1987. Scholastic, Richmond Hill, Ont.
Farmer Joe complains about the heat until his wife comes up with a clever plan.
Farmer Joe Goes to the City, 1990.
Farmer Joe Baby-Sits. 1997.

The Rats Came Back, Ross Seidel. 1995. Annick Press, Toronto.
A clever turnabout in which Granny rewards the helpful rats.

Red Is Best, Kathy Stinson. Illus. by Robin Baird Lewis. 1992. Annick Press, Toronto.
A much-loved classic in which a small girl knows the value of the colour red.

Wild in the City, Jan Thornhill. 1995. Owl Books, Toronto.
A gentle picture puzzle of city animals.

The Wildlife ABC: A Nature Alphabet, Jan Thornhill. 1988. Owl Books, Toronto.

Woodland Christmas, Frances Tyrell. 1995. Scholastic, Richmond Hill, Ont.
Elegant and vivacious illustrations of "The Twelve Days of Christmas" with a cast of Canadian animals.

Thor, W.D. Valgardson. Illus. by Ange Zhang. 1994. Groundwood Books, Toronto.
Thor has never been ice-fishing and has no interest in it. But when his grandfather needs his help, Thor surprises everyone, and returns home a hero.

Chin Chiang and the Dragon's Dance, written and illus. by Ian Wallace. 1992. Groundwood Books, Toronto.
A small boy longs to dance the celebrated dragon's dance with his grandfather, but when the New Year comes, he's afraid.

The Lighthouse Dog, Betty Waterton. Illus. by Dean Griffiths. 1997. Orca Book Publishers, Vancouver, B.C.
That Newfoundland pup is one huge disaster—and a lifesaver.

Zoom at Sea, Tim Wynne-Jones. Illus. by Ken Nutt. 1983. Groundwood Books, Toronto.
Zoom is a cat who loves the sea and magically finds an ocean in his house.
Zoom Upstream. 1992.
Zoom Away. 1993.

Ages Eight to Twelve

The Auction, Jan Andrews. Illus. by Karen Reczuch. 1992. Groundwood Books, Toronto.
A poignant picture story in which a boy and his grandfather pay tribute to happier times while packing up the farm.

How Come the Best Clues Are Always in the Garbage? Linda Bailey. 1992. Kids Can Press, Toronto.
The first in the lighthearted mystery series about the intrepid young sleuth Stevie Diamond, a girl.

'Til All the Stars Have Fallen: Canadian Poems for Children, ed. by David Booth. Illus. by Kady MacDonald Denton. 1989. Kids Can Press, Toronto.
Touching, funny, thoughtful, wise, happy, and warm. An exceptionally fine poetry collection—a must for every family.

The Great Race, David Bouchard. Paintings by Zhong-Yang Huang. 1997. Raincoast Books, Vancouver, B.C.
A richly illustrated and highly satisfying version of the fable of the Chinese Zodiac.

The Incredible Journey, Sheila Burnford. 1961. McClelland & Stewart, Toronto.
The heartwarming classic of the courage and loyalty of two dogs and a cat who trek across the wilds of Ontario to return home.

The Runaways, Kristin Butcher. 1997. Kids Can Press, Toronto.
The homeless vagabond camped out in the deserted mansion is hiding a secret.

The Hockey Sweater, Roch Carrier. 1984. Tundra Books, Toronto.
A mix-up results in the ultimate embarrassment—having to wear a Leafs sweater in small-town Quebec. Nostalgic.

Maple Moon, Connie Crook. Illus. by Scott Cameron. 1997. Stoddart, Toronto.
A small boy discovers maple syrup and saves his tribe from hunger.

How Smudge Came, Nan Gregory. 1995. Red Deer College Press, Red Deer, Alta.
A tender picture book in which a young woman with Down syndrome longs to keep a stray puppy.

Tikta'Liktak, James A. Houston. 1965; reissued 1990. Harcourt Brace, Toronto.
Stranded on a desolate island, a young Inuit hunter fights for survival.

Space Trap, Monica Hughes. 1994. Groundwood Books, Toronto.
Valerie has been caught and caged to be sold as animal contraband by outlaw aliens. How can she get home?

That Scatterbrain Booky, Bernice Thurman Hunter. 1981. Scholastic, Richmond Hill, Ont.
The Great Depression was hard on the whole family, but nothing could keep the irrepressible Booky down for long. The first of a popular trilogy.

False Face, Welwyn Wilton Katz. 1987. Groundwood Books, Toronto.
Two teens unearth a magic Iroquois mask and struggle against its power.

Tales of a Gambling Grandma, Dayal Kaur Khalsa. 1986. Tundra Books, Toronto.
A grandmother remembers coming over from Russia, marrying, gambling for extra money, and loving her granddaughter.

No Coins, Please, Gordon Korman. 1984. Scholastic, Richmond Hill, Ont.
Artie turns the Juniortours trip across the country into one great money-making scheme after another, much to the chagrin of the counsellors—and the FBI.

The Twinkie Squad, Gordon Korman. 1994. Scholastic, Richmond Hill, Ont.
The misfits become the "in" clique in this fast-paced school farce.

The Zucchini Warriors, Gordon Korman. 1990. Scholastic, Richmond Hill, Ont.
Bruno and Boots try to lead the Macdonald Hall football team to victory. Part of Korman's hilarious Macdonald Hall saga.

A Thief among Statues, Donn Kushner. Illus. by Nancy Jackson. 1993. Annick Press, Toronto.
Brian is shocked when a statue in the church not only speaks to him but also assigns him a most important and difficult task.

The Olden Days Coat, Margaret Laurence. Illus. by Muriel Wood. 1979. McClelland & Stewart, Toronto.
An old coat in an attic trunk takes a young girl back in time.

Bats about Baseball, Jean Little and Claire McKay. Illus. by Kim LaFave. 1995. Penguin Books, Toronto.
A picture book of clever word play with baseball lingo to delight fans young and old.

The Belonging Place, Jean Little. 1997. Penguin Books, Toronto.
A young Scottish orphan feels insecure in her adopted family until they emigrate to Canada.

Charlotte, Janet Lunn. 1998. Tundra Books, Toronto.
When her Loyalist cousins are exiled from New York, Charlotte defies her rebel father to bid them farewell, and her life is changed forever.

Mama's Going to Buy You a Mocking Bird, Jean Little. 1984. Penguin Books, Toronto.
Jeremy's world comes crashing down when his father is diagnosed with terminal cancer. One of Jean Little's best-loved, heartwarming novels.

Ticket to Curlew, Celia Barker Lottridge. Illus. by Wendy Wolsak. 1992. Groundwood Books, Toronto.
A gentle story of friendship and the struggle to settle on the Prairies.
Wings To Fly. 1997. The sequel to *Ticket to Curlew.*

Double Spell, Janet Lunn. 1986. Penguin Books, Toronto.
Eerie, inexplicable things begin to happen after the twins buy an antique doll.

The Root Cellar, Janet Lunn. 1981 and 1996. Penguin Books, Toronto.
For orphan Rose, the farmhouse cellar is a door to the past, where she finds the friendship she needs.

The House of Wooden Santas, Kevin Major. Wood carvings by Imelda George and photography by Ned Pratt. 1997. Red Deer College Press, Red Deer, Alta.
Jesse's mother has moved them to the country to begin her new life as a wood carver. Jesse broods until the Santas work their magic.

The City Underground, Suzanne Martel. 1994. Groundwood Books, Toronto.
Almost one thousand years ago, humankind retreated beneath Earth's surface to survive nuclear destruction. Luke breaks the law, sneaks outside, and totally changes his world.

Canadian Fairy Tales, Eva Martin. Illus. by Laszlo Gal. 1984. Groundwood Books, Toronto.
Twelve traditional tales from the British, Irish, and French peoples who settled in Canada. Each tale is transformed by life in the new land.

Josepha: A Prairie Boy's Story, Jim McGugan. Illus. by Murray Kimber. 1994. Red Deer College Press, Red Deer, Alta.
An immigrant boy, unable to speak English, leaves school to work on the farm. Poignant.

The Orphan Boy, Tollolwa Mollel. Illus. by Paul Morin. 1995. Stoddart, Toronto.
The Maasai legend about the planet Venus. A tale of love, curiosity, and the importance of keeping your word.

Anne of Green Gables, 1908, and **Anne of Avonlea**, 1909, by Lucy Maud Montgomery. Reissued in 1992. Nimbus Publishing, Halifax.
The spunky, articulate, red-headed orphan continues to inspire girls around the world in Canada's most famous classics.

Owls in the Family, Farley Mowat. 1961; reissued 1989. McClelland & Stewart, Toronto.
This laugh-out-loud favourite first novel will touch your heart.

Biscuits in the Cupboard, Barbara Nichol. Illus. by Philippe Béha. 1997. Stoddart, Toronto.
Clever, lighthearted rhymes, all written by dogs. Guaranteed to bring smiles.

Dippers, Barbara Nichol. Illus. by Barry Moser. 1997. Tundra Books, Toronto.
The summer of 1912 was already an unusual one for Margaret, and then along came those furry creatures with wings!

The Secret Wish of Nannerl Mozart, Barbara Nichol. 1996. Second Story Press, Toronto.
Amadeus's sister was every bit as talented as her famous brother.

The Always Prayer Shawl, Sheldon Oberman. 1994. Boyds Mills Press, Honesdale, PA.
Memory, tradition, and love across the generations.

The White Stone in the Castle Wall, Sheldon Oberman. Illus. by Les Trait. 1994. Tundra Press, Toronto.
There is one white stone in the grey wall around Casa Loma. This is the story of how it got there.

Silverwing, Kenneth Oppel. 1997. HarperCollins Publishers, Toronto.
Shade, a young bat, defies tradition, battles foes, and makes strange friends on his perilous journey to rejoin his colony. An amazing animal fantasy with a sequel on the way.

Awake and Dreaming, Kit Pearson. 1996. Penguin Books, Toronto.
Helped by the ghost of an author, a mistreated, bookish child finds herself living with the family of her dreams.

A Handful of Time, Kit Pearson. 1988. Penguin Books, Toronto.
An old pocket watch takes Patricia back in time to the summer when her mother was twelve.

Jacob Two-Two Meets the Hooded Fang, Mordecai Richler. Illus. by Fritz Wegner. 1975; reissued 1997. Tundra Books, Toronto.
A fun-filled satirical poke at adult pomposity, set mostly in the children's prison.
Jacob Two-Two's First Spy Case. 1995.
Mystery and intrigue as Jacob, with the help of the spy next door, foils the villains in another satirical spoof.

The Hiccup Champion of the World, Ken Roberts. 1995. Groundwood Books, Toronto.
Maynard was a normal boy until he got the hiccups.

Days of Terror, Barbara Smucker. 1979. Penguin Books, Toronto.
A Mennonite family's traumatic journey from the horrors of the Russian revolution to their new life in Canada.

Incredible Jumbo, Barbara Smucker. 1990. Penguin Books, Toronto.
When Jumbo, the African elephant at the London Zoo, is sent to America to be part of the circus, young Todd follows.

Selina and the Bear Paw Quilt, Barbara Smucker. Illus. by Janet Wilson. 1995. Stoddart, Toronto.
Each piece of the quilt her grandmother made holds a precious family memory. The quilt consoles Selina when she moves to Canada.

Underground to Canada, Barbara Smucker. 1977. Penguin Books, Toronto.
The exciting and compassionate story of the hazardous journey faced by two girls as they flee from slavery in Mississippi to the safety of Canada.

The Mare's Egg: A New World Folk Tale, Carole Spray. Illus. by Kim LaFave. 1981. Camden Press, Camden, Ont.
A gullible settler is fooled into trying to hatch a horse from a pumpkin.

The Doll, Cora Taylor. 1992. Douglas & McIntyre, Vancouver, B.C.
Meg welcomes the magic of the doll that takes her back in time to the security of a loving pioneer family.

Julie, Cora Taylor. 1992. Scholastic, Richmond Hill, Ont.
Julie struggles to understand the psychic gift that brings such joy and such loneliness.

Summer of the Mad Monk, Cora Taylor. 1994. Douglas & McIntyre, Vancouver, B.C.
Might the local blacksmith be the notorious Rasputin?

Before and After: A Book of Nature Timescapes, Jan Thornhill. 1997. Owl Books, Toronto.
A spot-the-difference look at seven different biomes and how they have changed after varying passages of time.

Morning on the Lake, Jan Waboose. Illus. by Karen Rezueh. 1997. Kids Can Press, Toronto.
A picture book in which a boy and his grandfather share precious moments with nature.

The Sandwich, Ian Wallace, Angela Wood. 1985. Kids Can Press, Toronto.
Vincenzo loves his mortadella and provolone sandwiches, but the other kids laugh. What's a guy to do?

Ghostwise: A Book of Midnight Stories, Dan Yashinsky. 1997. Ragweed Press, Charlottetown.
Canada's master storyteller has collected memorable and haunting tales from across the country.

Ghost Train, Paul Yee. Illus. by Harvey Chan. 1996. Groundwood Books, Toronto.
A sombre fantasy about the Chinese men who died building the railroad through the Rocky Mountains.

Roses Sing on New Snow: A Delicious Tale, Paul Yee. Illus. by Harvey Chan. 1991. Groundwood Books, Toronto.
A mere girl surprises everyone when she not only wins the contest for the best dish in Chinatown but also teaches the governor a lesson.

Tales from Gold Mountain: Stories of the Chinese in the New World, Paul Yee. Illus. by Simon Ng. 1989. Groundwood Books, Toronto.
Original tales of the brave and sometimes tragic role the Chinese played in the making of Canada. Haunting.

Books about Books and Reading

Parents will find within many of the following books bibliographies that offer brief descriptions of dozens of children's books, Canadian, American, and international.

Creating a love of reading, J.D. O'Leary. 1991. National Literacy Secretariat, Ottawa.
A 24-page booklet for parents.

Everybody's favourites: Canadians talk about books that changed their lives, Arlene Perly Rae. 1997. Penguin Books, Toronto.

Great books for boys: More than 600 books for boys 2 to 14. 1998.
Great books for girls: More than 600 books to inspire today's girls and tomorrow's women. 1997.
Both by Kathleen Odean. Ballantine Books, New York

The New republic of childhood: A critical guide to Canadian children's literature in English, 3rd ed., Sheila Egoff and Judith Saltman. 1990. Oxford University Press Canada, Toronto.
Historical bibliography to 1990 on pages 315–348.

Only connect: Readings on children's literature, 3rd ed., Sheila Egoff, Gordon Stubbs, Ralph Ashley, and Wendy Sutton. 1995. Oxford University Press Canada, Toronto.

The Read-aloud handbook, 4th ed., Jim Trelease. 1995. Penguin Books, Toronto.
The ultimate "how-to" book for raising readers and bringing families closer together. Includes a giant treasury of the best books for read-aloud.

Specialized Sources and Web Sites

Canadian Children's Book Centre CCBC
35 Spadina Road
Toronto, ON M5R 2S9
(416) 975-0010
Fax: (416) 975-1839
E-mail: ccbc@sympatico.ca
<http://www3.sympatico.ca/ccbc/>
A national nonprofit organization founded in 1976; promotes and encourages the reading, writing, and illustrating of Canadian children's books; offers the services of a comprehensive reference library of contemporary Canadian children's books as well as background on authors, illustrators, book production and publishing—by phone, fax, or mail.

CCBC offers a touring program, a school readings program, author and illustrator visits. Individuals, schools, and interested organizations can support the CCBC by becoming members. Members receive a comprehensive list of book awards, a regular newsletter, Children's Book News, *announcing annual activities like Children's Book Festival, Freedom to Read Week, and Book Day. Check out the Web site.*

Canadian Children's Literature CCL
University of Guelph
Guelph, ON N1G 2W1
(519) 824-4120 x3189
Fax: (519) 837-1315
E-mail:ccl@uoguelph.ca
<http://www.uoguelph.ca/englit/ccl/index.html>
Founded in 1975, CCL is a bilingual journal of criticism and review covering Canadian books and other media for children and young adults. Provides essential information not only for librarians and educators but also for everyone who cares about children's reading.

Canadian Children's Literature Service
National Library of Canada
395 Wellington Street
Ottawa, ON K1A 0N4
(613) 996-2300 or 996-7774
Fax: (613) 995-1969
E-mail: clsslj@nlc-bnc.ca
<http://www.nlc-bnc.ca/>
Set up in 1975, the service maintains a collection of books (in English and French and other languages published in Canada) for children and young people aged sixteen and under. Services are offered to the general public as well as to students and those with a professional interest. The service promotes its book collections with exhibits and publications like "Read Up On It: Books to Share."

CANSCAIP
Canadian Society of Children's Authors, Illustrators and Performers
35 Spadina Road
Toronto, ON M5R 2S9
(416) 515-1559
Fax: (416) 515-7022
<http://www.interlog.com/~canscaip/>
The largest organization in Canada supporting creative work for children and young adults; works with the CCBC on a variety of activities, exhibits, and workshops; offers a newsletter and annual meetings.

The Children's Book Store CBS
2532 Yonge Street
Toronto, ON M4P 2H7
(416) 480-0233
Fax: (416) 480-9345
Toll-free fax: 1-888-480-9345
E-mail: cbs@inforamp.net
<http://www.toronto.com/cbs>
Established in 1974 by former librarian Judy Sarick, CBS was the first bookstore in Canada devoted exclusively to children's books. Known throughout North America, CBS offers many services beyond selling books and media.

Children's Literature Web Guide
David K. Brown
Doucette Library of Teaching Resources
University of Calgary
Calgary, AB T2N 1N4
(403) 220-6295
<http://www.acs.ucalgary.ca/~dkbrown/>

The 1999 Canadian Encyclopedia, Student Edition. Young Learner's CD-ROM. McClelland & Stewart, Toronto.

Kidsworld Magazine
Editorial Office
108-93 Lombard Avenue
Winnipeg, MA R3B 3B1
(204) 942-2214
Fax: (204) 943-8991
E-mail: kidsworld@kidsworld-online.com
<http://www.kidsworld-online.com>

National Library of Canada
Forthcoming Books
<http://www.nlc-bnc.ca/forthbks/efbintro.htm>

OWL Books/Greey de Pencier Books
179 John Street, Suite 500
Toronto, ON M5T 3G5
(416) 340-2700
Fax: (416) 340-9769
E-mail: owlbooks@owl.on.ca
<http://www.owl.on.ca/>
OWL magazine (Ages 8 and up; since 1976)
Chickadee magazine (Ages 6–9; since 1979)
OWL/TV (since 1985)
FAMILY (For parents; since 1991)
OWLKids Online (since 1996)
Chirp magazine (Ages 2–6; since 1997)
CyberSurfer: The OWL Internet Guide for Kids

@Sympatico NetLife
Canada's Home Internet Magazine
Links Editor: Adrienne Webb
E-mail: a_webb@bc.sympatico.ca
Six issues a year; a good source of interesting Web sites for children. Magazine comes with a subscription to the Internet service Sympatico.

Selected Canadian Associations and Organizations

Many of these resources offer information, fact sheets, and publications.

Ability OnLine Support Network
<http://www.ablelink.org/public/default.htm>
Provides links to other disability/health-care Web sites.

AboutFace
123 Edward St., Suite 1003
Toronto, ON M5G 1E2
1-800-665-3223
E-mail: abtface@interlog.com
<http://www.interlog.com/~abtface>
Provides support for individuals and families who are affected by facial differences.

Adult Children of Alcoholics
20 Bloor St. E., Box 75061
Toronto, ON M4W 3T3
(416) 593-5147
E-mail: ccrumb@passport.ca
<http://www.adultchildren.org>

Al-Anon/Alateen
Al-Anon World Service
Virginia Beach, VA.
1-800-443-4525
<http://www.al-anon.org>
Provides a calendar for all local groups worldwide.

Al-Anon Information Services
1771 Avenue Rd., Box 54533
North York, ON M5M 4N5
(416) 410-3809
1-800-443-4525
<http://web.idirect.com/~alanon>

Alberta Alcohol and Drug Abuse Commission
10909 Jasper Ave., 2nd Floor
Edmonton, AB T5J 3M9
1-800-280-9616
Youth Services: (403) 422-7383

Alcoholics Anonymous AA
234 Eglinton Ave. E., Suite 202
Toronto, ON M4P 1K5
(416) 487-5591
Fax: (416) 487-5855
<http://www.alcoholics-anonymous.org>
Check for local groups in the Business Section of your telephone book.

Allergy/Asthma Information Association AAIA
30 Eglinton Ave. W., Suite 750
Mississauga, ON L5R 3E7
(905) 712-2242
1-800-611-7011
Fax: (905) 712-2245

The Alliance for Children and Television ACT
60 St. Clair Ave. E., Suite 1002
Toronto, ON M4T 1N5
(416) 515-0466
Fax: (416) 515-0467
E-mail: acttv@interlog.com
<http://www.act-canada.com>

Association for Bright Children ABC
Ontario ABC
2 Bloor St. W., Suite 100-156
Toronto, ON M4W 2G7
(416) 925-6136
E-mail: abc_ontario@on.aibn.ca
<http://www.kanservu.ca/~abc>

Association of Canadian Publishers
110 Eglinton Ave. W., Suite 401
Toronto, ON M4R 1A3
(416) 487-6116
Fax: (416) 487-8815
E-mail: info@canbook.org
<http://www2.publishers.ca/acp/default.html>
Provides contact info on member publishers and their catalogues of books and learning materials.

Asthma Society of Canada
130 Bridgeland Ave., Suite 425
Toronto, ON M6A 1Z4
(416) 787-4050
1-800-787-3880
E-mail: asthma@myna.com
<http://www.asthmasociety.com>

Attention Deficit Disorder Ontario Foundation
<http://www.addofoundation.org/>
Attention Deficit Hyperactivity Disorder
<http://www.mhnet.org/guide/adhd.htm>

Autism Society Canada
2281 Yonge St., Suite 206
Toronto, ON M4P 2C7
(416) 483-3566
Fax: (416) 922-1032

Bereaved Families of Ontario
562 Eglinton Ave. E., Suite 401
Toronto, ON M4P 1P1
(416) 440-0290
Fax: (416) 440-0304
E-mail: BFO@InfoRamp.net
<http://www.InfoRamp.Net/~bfo/>

Big Brothers & Sisters of Canada
3228 South Service Rd., Suite 113E
Burlington, ON L7N 3H8
(905) 639-0461
1-800-263-9133
E-mail: bbsc@bbsc.ca
<http://www.bbsc.ca/>
For children 6 to 16 years of age.

Boys and Girls Clubs of Canada
7100 Woodbine Avenue, Suite 405
Markham, ON L3R 5J2
(905) 477-7272
Fax: (905) 477-2056
<http://www.bgccan.com/>

British Columbia Confederation of Parent Advisory Councils
1185 West Georgia St., Suite 1540
Vancouver, BC V6E 4E6
(604) 687-4433
Fax: (604) 687-4488
E-mail: bccpac@direct.ca
<http://www.bccpac.bc.ca>

Cable in the Classroom Association
350 Sparks St., Suite 909
Ottawa, ON K1R 7S8
(613) 233-3033
Fax: (613) 233-7650
E-mail: information@cableducation.ca/
<http://www.cableducation.ca/>

Call Mom
1-800-993-9984
E-mail: callmom@mts.net
<http://www.mts.net/callmom>
National help line on parenting dilemmas and household conundrums.

Canada Safety Council
1020 Thomas Spratt Place
Ottawa, ON K1G 5L5
(613) 739-1535
E-mail: csc@safety-council.org
<http://www.safety-council.org>
Check Traffic Safety Section.

Canada's SchoolNet
<http://www.schoolnet.ca>
SchoolNet's mandate is to facilitate the connection to the Internet of all 16,500 schools and 3,400 libraries in Canada by 1999.

Canadian AIDS Society CAS
130 Albert St., Suite 900
Ottawa, ON K1P 5G4
(613) 230-3580
Fax: (613) 563-4998
E-mail: casinfo@web.net
<http://www.cdnaids.ca>

The Canadian Association of the Deaf
251 Bank St., Suite 203
Ottawa, ON K2P 1X3
Voice/TTY: (613) 565-2882
Fax: (613) 565-1207
<http://www.cad.ca>

Canadian Association of Family Resource Programs
30 Rosemount Ave., Suite 101
Ottawa, ON K1Y 1P4
(613) 728-3307
Fax: (613) 729-5421
E-mail: info@frp.ca
<http://www.cfc-efc.ca>
A national association of resource centres that offer parenting courses, peer support, and other programs.

Canadian Association for Health, Physical Education, Recreation, and Dance CAHPERD
1600 James Naismith Dr.
Gloucester, ON K1B 5N4
(613) 748-5622
Fax: (613) 748-5737
E-mail: cahperd@itm.activeliving.ca
<http://www.activeliving.ca/cahperd>

Canadian Association of Speech Language Pathologists and Audiologists CASLPA
130 Albert St., Suite 2006
Ottawa, ON K1P 5G4
(613) 567-9968
1-800-259-8519
Fax: (613) 567-2859
E-mail: caslpa@caslpa.ca
<http://www.caslpa.ca>

Canadian Automobile Association CAA
Check for local groups in the Business Section of your telephone book.
1-800-268-3750
Traffic Safety: Child Safety
School Safety Patrol Program.
<http://www.caa.ca>

Canadian Cancer Society
10 Alcorn Ave., Suite 200
Toronto, ON M4V 3B1
(416) 961-7223
Fax: (416) 961-4189
also **National Cancer Institute of Canada**
Cancer Information Service: 1-888-939-3333
<http://www.cancer.ca/>

Canadian Child Care Federation CCCF
30 Rosemount Ave., Suite 100
Ottawa, ON K1Y 1P4
(613) 729-5289
1-800-858-1412
Fax: (613) 729-3159
E-mail: cccf@sympatico.ca
<http://www.cfc-efc.ca/cccf>

Canadian Cystic Fibrosis Foundation CCFF
2221 Yonge St., Suite 601
Toronto, ON M4S 2B4
National Office: (416) 485-9149/1-800-378-2233
E-mail: infor@ccff.ca
<http://www.ccff.ca/~cfwww/index.html>

Canadian Dental Association CDA
1815 Alta Vista Dr.
Ottawa, ON K1G 3Y6
(613) 523-1770
Fax: (613) 523-7736
E-mail: reception@cda-adc.ca
<http://www.cda-adc.ca>

The Canadian Dermatology Association CDA
774 Echo Dr., Suite 521
Ottawa, ON K1S 5N8
(613) 730-6262
1-800-267-3376
Fax: (613) 730-1116
E-mail: cda.albagli@rspsc.edu
<http://www.derm.ubc.ca/jcms/CDA-ACD.html#Top>

Canadian Diabetes Association CDA
15 Toronto St., Suite 800
Toronto, ON M5C 2E3
(416) 363-3373
National Toll-Free: 1-800-BANTING
(ON) 1-800-361-1306
Fax: (416) 214-1899
E-mail: info@cda-nat.org
<http://www.diabetes.ca>

Canadian Down Syndrome Society
811-14th St. N.W.
Calgary, AB T2N 2A4
(403) 270-8500
E-mail: cdss@ican.net
<http://home.ican.net/~cdss/index.html>
Down Syndrome Association of Metro Toronto
<http://www.dsamt.toronto.on.ca>

Canadian Education Association
252 Bloor St. W., Suite 8-200
Toronto, ON M5S 1V5
(416) 924-7721
Fax: (416) 924-3188
E-mail: cea-ace@acea.ca
<http://www.acea.ca>
The CEA produces an annual handbook with names and addresses of all education entities across Canada.

Canadian Education on the Web
<http://www.oise.utoronto.ca/~mpress/eduweb.html>

Canadian Fitness and Lifestyle Research Institute CFLRI
185 Somerset St. W., Suite 201
Ottawa, ON K2P 0J2
(613) 233-5528
Fax: (613) 233-5536
E-mail: info@cflri.ca
<http://activeliving.ca/cflri/cflri.html>

Canadian Home and School Federation
(incl. Parent-Teacher Association)
858 Bank St., Suite 104
Ottawa, ON K1S 3W3
(613) 234-7292
Fax: (613) 234-3913
E-mail: chsptf@cyberus.ca
<http://cnet.unb.ca/cap/partners/chsptf/>

Canadian Institute of Child Health CICH
885 Meadowlands Dr. E., Suite 512
Ottawa, ON K2C 3N2
(613) 224-4144
Fax: (613) 224-4145
E-mail: cich@igs.net
<http://www.cich.ca>

Canadian Liver Foundation CLF
National Office
#200, 365 Bloor St. E.
Toronto, ON M4W 3L4
(416) 964-1953
1-800-563-5483
Fax: (416) 964-0024
E-mail: clf@liver.ca
<http://www.liver.ca>

Canadian Living: Your Family Magazine
25 Sheppard Ave. W., Suite 100
Toronto ON M2N 6S7
(416) 733-7600
1-800-265-5371
Fax: (416) 733-3398
E-mail: letters@canadianliving.com
<http://www.canadianliving.com>
Christine Langlois is Canadian Living*'s Health and Family editor and moderator of its Health and Family forum online.*

Canadian Living Foundation CLF
Breakfast for Learning
25 Sheppard Ave. W., Suite 100
Toronto ON M2N 6S7
(416) 733-7600
1-800-627-7922
Fax: (416) 218-3631
E-mail: clf@sympatico.ca
<http://www.canadianliving.com/bfl>
Founded in 1992, CLF is the only national organization promoting and helping to fund school nutrition programs.

Canadian Lung Association
#508, 1900 City Park Dr.
Gloucester, ON K1J 1A3
(613) 747-6776
Fax: (613) 747-7430
E-mail: info@lung.ca
<http://www.lung.ca>

Canadian MedicAlert Foundation
#301, 250 Ferrand Dr.
Toronto, ON M3C 3G8
(416) 696-0267 or (416) 696-0142
National English: 1-800-668-1507
Toll-free Fax: 1-800-392-8422
E-mail: medinfo@medicalert.ca
<http://www.medicalert.ca>

Canadian Mental Health Association CMHA
2160 Yonge St., 3rd Floor
Toronto, ON M4S 2Z3
(416) 484-7750
Fax: (416) 484-4617
E-mail: cmhanet@interlog.com
<http://www.icomm.ca/cmhacan>

Canadian National Institute for the Blind CNIB
1929 Bayview Ave.
North York, ON M4G 3E8
(416) 486-2500
E-mail: irc@lib.cnib.ca
<http://www.cnib.ca>

Canadian Naturopathic Association
4174 Dundas St. W., Suite 303
Toronto, ON M8X 1X3
(416) 233-1043
Fax: (416) 233-2924
E-mail: cdnnds@interlog.com

Canadian Network for New Media Learning
Suite 1002, 10611–98 Avenue
Edmonton, AB T5K 2P7
(403) 424-4433
Fax: (403) 424-4888
E-mail: clc@mrg.ab.ca
<http://www.mrg.ab.ca/clc/>
Offers services and courses for distance education learners.

Canadian Paediatric Society CPS
2204 Walkley Rd., Suite 100
Ottawa, ON K1G 4G8
(613) 526-9397
Fax: (613) 526-3332
E-mail: info@cps.ca
<http://www.cps.ca>

Canadian Parents Online
<http://www.canadianparents.com>
Offers chat forums, product information, and Canadian experts to answer questions.

Canadian Parks and Recreation Association CP/RA
1600 James Naismith Dr., Suite 306
Gloucester, ON K1B 5N4
(613) 748-5651
Fax: (613) 748-5854
E-mail: cpra@activeliving.ca
<http://activeliving.ca/activeliving/cpra.html>

Canadian Publishers' Council
250 Merton St., Suite 203
Toronto, ON M4S 1B1
(416) 322-7011
Fax: (416) 322-6999
<http://www.pubcouncil.ca/>
Provides contact info on member publishers and their catalogues of books and learning materials.

Canadian Red Cross
National Office
1800 Alta Vista Dr.
Ottawa, ON K1G 4J5
Western Zone: (403) 541-4400
Ontario: (905) 890-1000
Quebec: (514) 362-2929
Atlantic: (506) 648-5000
<http://www.redcross.ca>

Canadian Resource Centre on Children and Youth CRCCY
180 Argyle Ave., Suite 316
Ottawa, ON K2P 1B7
(613) 788-5102
Fax: (613) 788-5075
E-mail: crccy@newforce.ca
<http://www.magi.com/~crccy/>
The CRCCY amalgamates the resource collections of the former Canadian Council on Children and Youth and the former Canadian Child Welfare Association.

Canadian Sleep Society CSS
380 Yonge St., Suite 5055
Toronto, ON M3N 3N1
(416) 483-6260
<http://bisleep.medsch.ucla.edu/WFSRS/CSS/css.html>
A professional association of clinicians, scientists, and technologists.

Canadian Teachers' Federation CTF
110 Argyle Ave.
Ottawa, ON K2P 1B4
(613) 232-1505
Fax: (613) 232-1886
E-mail: info@ctf-fce.ca
<http://ctf-fce.ca>

Canadian Toy Testing Council
22 Hamilton Ave. N.
Ottawa, ON K1Y 1B6
(613) 729-7101
Fax: (613) 729-7185
<http://www.toy-testing.org>
The 1998 Toy Report lists 1,700 toys, including educational software.

CanConnect
<http://canconnect.globalx.net/>
Part of Industry Canada's SchoolNet, CanConnect offers such programs as Computers for Schools and the SchoolNet Youth Employment Strategy.

Centre for Addiction and Mental Health
In 1998 incorporated the
Addiction Research Foundation ARF
33 Russell St.
Toronto, ON M5S 2S1
INFO-ARF: (416) 595-6111
Ontario only: 1-800-463-6273
<http://www.arf.org/>
One of North America's pre-eminent facilities for research into addiction. Offers an Information Package on Youth and Alcohol.

Centre for Health Promotion
University of Toronto
The Banting Institute
100 College St., Rm. 207
Toronto, ON M5G 1L5
(416) 978-1809
Fax: (416) 971-1365
E-mail: centre.healthpromotion@utoronto.ca
<http://www.utoronto.ca/chp/>

Child Care Advocacy Association of Canada CCAAC
323 Chapel St., Third Floor
Ottawa, ON K1N 7Z2
(613) 594-3196
Fax: (613) 594-9375
E-mail: ccaac@iSTAR.ca
<http://home.iSTAR.ca/~ccaac>

Child & Family Canada CFC
<http://www.cfc-efc.ca>
An umbrella organization with links to 41 non-profit organizations committed to the well-being of Canada's children and their families.

Child Find Canada
PO Box 6611, RR4
Cornwall, PE C0A 1H0
(902) 626-3152
In Canada and U.S.: 1-800-387-7962
Fax: (902) 626-3153
E-mail: childcan@aol.com
<http://www.childfind.ca>

Childhood Cancer Foundation Candlelighters Canada
55 Eglinton Ave. E., Suite 401
Toronto, ON M4P 1G8
(416) 489-6440
1-800-363-1062
E-mail: staff@candlelighters.ca
<http://www.candlelighters.ca>

Child Welfare League of Canada CWLC
180 Argyle Ave., Suite 312
Ottawa, ON K2P 1B7
(613) 235-4412
Fax: (613) 788-5075
E-mail: cwlc@newforce.ca
<http://www.cwlc.ca>
The CWLC's 71 member agencies offer services and programs on issues relating to the well-being of children and youth.

The Children's Wish Foundation of Canada
95 Bayly St. W., Suite 404
Ajax, ON L1S 7K8
(905) 426-5656
1-800-267-WISH
Fax: (905) 426-4111
E-mail: wishes.national@sympatico.ca
<http://www.childrenswish.ca>
Dedicated to fulfilling a favourite wish for children ages 3 to 17 afflicted with a high-risk, life-threatening illness.

The Clarke Institute of Psychiatry
250 College St.
Toronto, ON M5T 1R8
(416) 979-2221
E-mail: webmaster@cs.clarke-inst.on.ca
<http://www.clarke-inst.on.ca/>
A division of the Centre for Addiction and Mental Health affiliated with the University of Toronto.
Child and Family Studies Centre
(416) 979-2221 x2255
One of Canada's largest child centres for research, education and treatment of attention deficit disorder, the epidemiology of language disorders, learning disabilities and anxiety,

gender identity disturbance, oppositional defiant disorders, and children at risk for mood disorders.

SHIFT School and Home Interventions bringing Families Together
(416) 979-4747 x 2255
One of the Clarke's programs for children aged 6 to 11 with serious behaviour problems, and their families.

The College of Family Physicians of Canada CFPC
2630 Skymark Ave.
Mississauga, ON L4W 5A4
(905) 629-0900
Fax: (905) 629-0893
E-mail: info@cfpc.ca
<http://www.cfpc.ca>

Concerns Canada
Alcohol and Drug Concerns, Inc.
4500 Sheppard Ave. E., Suite 112
Toronto, ON M1S 3R6
(416) 293-3400
Fax: (416) 293-1142
E-mail: concerns@sympatico.ca
Offers services, publications, and educational programs for drug education in grades 4–6 and 7–8.

The Council for Exceptional Children CEC
Canadian Office
1010 Polytek Ct., Unit 36
Gloucester, ON K1J 9J2
(613) 747-9226
Fax: (709) 745-9282
<http://www.cec.sped.org/>

Council of Ministers of Education, Canada
252 Bloor St. W., Suite 5-200
Toronto, ON M5S 1V5
(416) 964-2551
Fax: (416) 964-2296
E-mail: cmec@cmec.ca
<http://www.cmec.ca>
Provides links to provincial ministries and departments of education.

Crohn's and Colitis Foundation of Canada
#301, 21 St. Clair Ave. E.
Toronto, ON M4T 1L9
(416) 920-5035
1-800-387-1479
E-mail: ccfc@netcom.ca
<http://www.ccfc.ca>

Dads Can
St. Mary's Annex, Room 411
35 Grosvenor St.
London, ON N6A 1Y6
(519) 646-6095
1-888-DADS CAN
E-mail: ncampbell@julian.uwo.ca
<http://www.dadscan.org>
Promotes responsible and involved fathering.

Dietitians of Canada
480 University Ave., Suite 604
Toronto, ON M5G 1V2
(416) 596-0857
Fax: (416) 596-0603
E-mail: centralinfo@dietitians.ca
<http://www.dietitians.ca/>

Easter Seals Society Canada
511-90 Eglinton Ave. E.
Toronto, ON M4P 2Y3
(416) 544-1715
Fax: (416) 932-9844
E-mail: national.council@esmodnc.org

Educational Computing Organization of Ontario ECOO
<http://www.oise.on.ca/ecoo>

Epilepsy Canada
#745, 1470 rue Peel
Montréal, QC H3A 1T1
(514) 845-7855/1-800-860-5499
Fax: (514) 845-7866
E-mail: epilepsy@epilepsy.ca
<http://www.epilepsy.ca>

Families in Transition
2 Carlton St., Suite 917
Toronto, ON M5B 1J3
(416) 585-9151
E-mail: fit@idirect.com
For families going through divorce.

Family Service Canada
383 Parkdale Ave., Suite 404
Ottawa, ON K1Y 4R4
(613) 722-9006/1-800-668-7808
Fax: (613) 722-8610
E-mail: fsc@igs.net
<http://www.cfc-efc.ca/fsc/>
A network of over 100 family-serving member agencies in communities across Canada.

Hamilton Health Sciences Corporation
Family Resource Centre
Children's Hospital at Chedoke/McMaster
Box 2000, Hamilton, ON L8N 3Z5
(905) 521-2632
<http://www.cmh.on.ca/~frc/frc.htm>
Offers services and publications for parents.

The Hanen Centre
252 Bloor St. W., Suite 3-390
Toronto, ON M5S 1V5
(416) 921-1073
Outside GTA: 1-800-380-3355
Fax: (416) 921-1225
E-mail: info@hanen.org
<http://www.hanen.org>
Offers program materials, workshops and presentations, and training for speech language pathologists, parents, and teachers of children with developmental delays and language impairment.

Health Canada
<http://www.hc-sc.gc.ca>
Health Protection Branch HPB
Product Safety Directorate
Vancouver (604) 666-5003
Toronto (416) 973-4705
Montreal (514) 646-1353
Health Promotion & Programs Branch HPPB
<http://www.hc-sc.gc.ca/hppb/>
Canadian Hospital Injury Reporting and Prevention Program CHIRPP
National Clearinghouse on Family Violence
1-800-267-1291
Not a crisis line; offers referrals and information on family violence.
Publications Branch
Health Canada, Ottawa, ON K1A 0K9
(613) 954-5995
Also check the Blue Pages for regional offices of Health Canada.

Heart and Stroke Foundation
National Office
222 Queen St., Suite 1402
Ottawa, ON K1P 5V9
(613) 569-4361
<http://www.hsf.ca>
HeartSmart Kids
<http://www.hsf.ca/funpack/index.html>
Check the 1998 Heart and Stroke Report Card on the Health of Canada's Kids.

The C.M. Hincks Treatment Centre for Children's Mental Health
440 Jarvis St.
Toronto, ON M4Y 2H4
(416) 924-1164
Fax: (416) 924-8208
E-mail: centre.hincks@utoronto.ca
<http://www.interlog.com/~hincks/homex.htm>

The Hospital for Sick Children
555 University Ave.
Toronto, ON M5G 1X8
(416) 813-1500
<http://www.sickkids.on.ca/>
Centre for Health Information & Promotion
(416) 813-5819
Poison Information Centre
1-800-268-9017

The Kidney Foundation of Canada
5165 Sherbrooke St. W., Suite 300
Montreal, QC H4A 1T6
(514) 369-4806/1-800-361-7494
Fax: (514) 369-2472
E-mail: comm-mktg@kidney.ca
<http://www.kidney.ca>

Kids Help Foundation
439 University Ave., Suite 300
Toronto, ON M5G 1Y8
How to help, to volunteer, to contribute:
(416) 586-5437
Fax: (416) 586-0651
E-mail: info@kidshelp.sympatico.ca
<http://kidshelp.sympatico.ca>
Kids Help Phone/Jeunesse J'écoute
1-800-668-6868
A national Toronto-based, bilingual telephone service available 24 hours a day free of charge to any child or teenager in distress.

Learning Disabilities Association of Canada LDAC
323 Chapel St., Suite 200
Ottawa, ON K1N 7Z2
(613) 238-5721
Fax: (613) 235-5391
E-mail: ldactaac@fox.nstn.ca
<http://educ.queensu.ca/~lda>
LDAC publishes helpful materials for parents.

Media Awareness Network
1500 Merivale Rd., 3rd Floor
Nepean, ON K2E 6Z5
(613) 224-7721/1-800-896-3342
Fax: (613) 224-1958
E-mail: info@media.awareness.ca
<http://www.media-awareness.ca>
A Canadian nonprofit organization offering on its Web site resources to help teachers, students, parents, and others better understand media information, electronic entertainment, and the new technologies.

Multiple Sclerosis Society of Canada
#1000, 250 Bloor St. E.
Toronto, ON M4W 3P9
(416) 922-6065/1-800-268-7582
E-mail: info@mssoc.ca
<http://www.mssoc.ca>

Muscular Dystrophy Association of Canada
#900, 2345 Yonge St.
Toronto, ON M4P 2E5
(416) 488-0030/1-800-567-CURE
Fax: (416) 488-7523
<http://www.mdac.ca>
Offers information on neuro-muscular disorders and on regional offices and chapters.

Music for Young Children
(613) 592-1144/1-800-561-1MYC
E-mail: myc@myc.com
<http://www.myc.com/>

National Eating Disorder Information Centre
200 Elizabeth St., College Wing 1-211
Toronto, ON M5G 2C4
(416) 340-4156
Fax: (416) 340-4736
<http://www.infonautica.com/nedic>

National Institute of Nutrition NIN
#302, 265 Carling Ave.
Ottawa, ON K1S 2E1
(613) 235-3355
Fax: (613) 235-7032
E-mail: nin@nin.ca
<http://www.nin.ca>
Offers a wide range of information on food and nutrition to Canadian consumers.

The Neurological Centre
2805 Kingsway
Vancouver, BC V5R 5H9
(604) 451-5511
E-mail: tnc@iSTAR.ca
<http://home.iSTAR.ca/~tnc>
Looks after children with physical challenges or developmental delays.

New Directions
542 Mount Pleasant Rd., Suite 203
Toronto, ON M4S 2M7
(416) 487-5317
Fax: (416) 487-5170
An organization focused on divorce and remarriage.

One Parent Families Association of Canada
National Office
6979 Yonge St., Suite 203
Willowdale, ON M2M 3X9
(416) 226-0062
E-mail: oneparent@titan.tcn.net
<http://www.tcn.net/~oneparent>

Ontario Coalition for Better Child Care
500A Bloor St. W., 2nd Floor
Toronto, ON M5S 1Y8
(416) 538-0628
Fax: (416) 538-6737
E-mail: ocbcc@web.net

Osteoporosis Society of Canada
33 Laird Dr.
Toronto, ON M4G 3S9
(416) 696-2663/1-800-463-6842

Parentbooks
201 Harbord St.
Toronto, ON M5S 1H6
(416) 537-8334/1-800-209-9182
Fax: (416) 537-9499

Parenting Today
2762 Wall St.
Vancouver, BC V5K 1A9
(604) 258-9074
Fax: (604) 258-9075
E-mail: k_lynn@home.com
<http://members.home.net/kathylynn>
Offers parent education services.

Parents of Multiple Births Association POMBA
240 Graff Ave.
Stratford, ON N5A 7V6
(519) 272-2203
E-mail: office@pomba.org
<http://www.pomba.org>

Parents without Partners
Check for local groups in the Business Section of your telephone book.

The Renascent Centres
1240 Bay St., Suite 404
Toronto, ON M5R 2A7
(416) 964-1207
<http://www.cleanandsober.com>
An Ontario resource that offers counselling and a 21-day live-in program at no charge for alcohol and addiction treatment for men and women.

Ronald McDonald Children's Charities of Canada
McDonald's Place
Toronto, ON M3C 3L4
(416) 443-1000
1-800-387-8808
Fax: (416) 446-3650
Provides information on R.M. Houses across Canada.

Royal Canadian Mounted Police RCMP
Missing Children's Registry
Box 8885
Ottawa, ON K1G 3M8
(613) 993-1525
Fax: (613) 993-5430
E-mail: mcr.nps@sympatico.ca
Child CyberSEARCH™ Canada
1-888-326-5352
<http://www.childcybersearch.org/>

St. John Ambulance Canada SJA
National Headquarters
312 Laurier Ave. E.
Ottawa, ON K1N 6P6
(613) 236-7461
Fax: (613) 236-2425
E-mail: nhq@nhq.sja.ca
<http://www.sja.ca>
Check for local branches in the Business Section of your telephone book. SJA offers First Aid products, training, and services.

The Sex Information and Education Council of Canada SIECCAN
850 Coxwell Ave.
Toronto, ON M4C 5R1
(416) 466-5304
Fax: (416) 978-8532
E-mail: sieccan@web.net
A publicly funded council of sexuality researchers and counsellors.

Sleep/Wake Disorders Canada SWDC
National Office
3080 Yonge St., Suite 5055
Toronto, ON M4N 3N1
(416) 483-9654
1-800-387-9253
Fax: (416) 483-7081
E-mail: swdc@globalserve.net
<http://www.geocities.com/~sleepwake/>
A national charitable organization providing information, encouraging research, and establishing self-help groups.

SmartRisk Foundation
658 Danforth Ave., Suite 301
Toronto, ON M4J 5B9
(416) 463-9878/1-888-537-7777
E-mail: choose@smartrisk.ca
<http://www.smartrisk.ca>
A national nonprofit injury-prevention organization based in Toronto.

Sport Medicine and Science Council of Canada
1600 James Naismith Dr., Suite 314
Gloucester, ON K1B 5N4
(613) 748-5671
Fax: (613) 748-5729
E-mail: smscc@smscc.ca
<http://www.smscc.ca>

Stay Alert ... Stay Safe SASS
2180 Yonge St., 17th Floor
Toronto ON M4P 2V8
(416) 480-8225
Fax: (416) 480-8556
<http://www.sass.ca>
Founded in 1987, one of five national programs funded by the Canadian Tire Child Protection Foundation, SASS offers a streetproofing program for children aged 7 to 11 years.

Transport Canada
<http://www.tc.gc.ca>
Canadian Motor Vehicle Safety Standards
<http://www.tc.gc.ca/actsregs/mvsa/tocmvs.htm>
Keep Them Safe
<http://www.engr.usask.ca/tc/tcanada/crs/keep.html>
Road Safety Information Centre
<http://www.engr.usask.ca/tc/tcanada/rsic.html>
Road Safety Directorate
330 Sparks St., Tower C
Ottawa, ON K1A 0N5
(613) 998-1978/1-800-333-0371
E-mail: RoadSafetyWebMail@tc.gc.ca
<http://www.engr.usask.ca/tc/tcanada/rsd.html>

The Vanier Institute of the Family
94 Centrepointe Dr.
Nepean, ON K2G 6B1
(613) 228-8500
Fax: (613) 228-8007
E-mail: vif@compuserve.com
<http://www.cfc-efc.ca/vif>

World Health Organization
<http://www.who.ch/>

World of Dreams Foundation Canada
999 De Maisonneuve W., Suite 675
Montréal, QC H3A 3L4
(514) 985-3003
1-800-567-7254
Fulfills dreams for critically and chronically ill children across Canada.

YM/YWCA
Check for local branches in the Business Section of your telephone book.

Selected Canadian Resources for Parents

alphabetized by title

Active children, healthy children: An active living guide for parents. (Booklet) Health Canada.

The Affective curriculum: Teaching the anti-bias approach to young children, Nadia Saderman Hall and Valerie Rhomberg. 1995. ITP Nelson, Toronto.
Pages 171–192 list Canadian, American, and international resources.

All shapes and sizes: Promoting fitness and self-esteem in your overweight child, Teresa Pitman and Miriam Kaufman, MD. 1994. HarperCollins Canada, Toronto.

Anaphylaxis: A handbook for school boards. (Booklet). Canadian School Boards Association, Ottawa. (613) 235-3724.

Anne Lindsay's new light cooking, Anne Lindsay in cooperation with Denise Beatty, RD, and the Canadian Medical Association. 1998. Ballantine Books, Toronto.

Battling the schoolyard bully: How to raise an assertive child in an aggresive world, Kim Zarzour. 1994. HarperCollins Canada, Toronto.

Becoming vegetarian: The complete guide to adopting a healthy vegetarian diet, Vesanto Melina, RD, Brenda Davis, RD, and Victoria Harrison, RD. 1994. Macmillan Canada, Toronto.

The Body image trap: Understanding and rejecting body image myths, Marion Crook. 1991. Self-Counsel Press, North Vancouver, BC.

Bone vivant! Jan Main with the Osteoporosis Society of Canada. 1997. Macmillan Canada, Toronto.

- **Canada's food guide to healthy eating.** 1992.
- **Focus on children six to twelve years: Background for educators and communicators.** 1997.
- **Using the food guide.** 1992.
- **Using food labels to choose foods for healthy eating.**
- **Food guide facts: Background for educators and communicators.**
- **Vitalité: Healthy eating and self-esteem: The body-image connection**

Publications, Health Canada
Ottawa, ON K1A 0K9
(613) 954-5995

The Canadian allergy and asthma handbook, rev. and updated by Canadian allergists Dr. Barry Zimmerman, Dr. Milton Gold, Dr. Sasson Lavi, Dr. Stephen Feanny, with Eleanor Brownridge, RD, FCDA. 1996. Random House Canada, Toronto.

The Canadian babysitter's handbook: The essential guide for everyone entrusted with the care of babies & young children, Caroline Greene, St. John Ambulance. 1995. Random House Canada, Toronto.

Canadian child welfare law: Children, families, and the state, ed. Nicholas Bala, Joseph P. Hornick, and Robin Vogl. 1991. Thompson Educational Publishing, Toronto.

Canadian Living's Best: Kids in the kitchen, 30 Minutes and Light, and **Vegetarian Dishes** (and others in the series), Elizabeth Baird and the food writers and test kitchen of *Canadian Living* magazine. 1998. Ballantine Books, Toronto.

Career intelligence: Mastering the new work and personal realities, Barbara Moses. 1997. Stoddart, Toronto.

Chalk around the block, Sharon E. McKay and David MacLeod. 1993. (Kit) Somerville House Books Limited, Toronto.

Changes in you and me: A book about puberty, mostly for boys. 1997.
Changes in you and me: A book about puberty, mostly for girls. 1997. Both books by Paulette Bourgeois and Martin Wolfish, MD. Sexual health consultant: Kim Martyn. Illus. by Louise Philips and Kam Yu. A Somerville House Book, Andrews and McMeel, A Universal Press Syndicate Company, Kansas City, KA.

Child care: A practical guide, 3rd ed. 1991. St. John Ambulance.

Child care CD, a resource guide for child care centre directors. 1996. Canadian Paediatric Society, Ottawa. (Professional)

Childhood asthma: A handbook for parents, 4th ed., Gerard J. Canny and Henry Levison. 1993. Centre for Health Information and Promotion, The Hospital for Sick Children, Toronto.

Children as peacemakers, Esther Sokolov Fine (York University), Ann Lacey, Joan Baer. 1995. Teacher to Teacher Series, Heinemann, Portsmouth, NH.

Children with school problems: A physician's manual, ed. A. Mervyn Fox, MD, BS, FRCPC, MRCPCH, DCH, and William J. Mahoney, MD, FRCPC. 1998. Canadian Paediatric Society, Ottawa. (Professional)

A Child's grief, videocassette, 54 min., English or French. 1994. Bereaved Families of Ontario. Magic Lantern Communications Ltd., Oakville, ON. 1-800-263-1818.

Child well being: A guide for parents and children. An animated interactive CD-ROM. 1996. Canadian Paediatric Society, Ottawa.

Cinderella revisited: How to survive your stepfamily without a fairy godmother, Dr. Peter Graham Marshall. 1993. Whitecap Books Ltd., North Vancouver, BC.

Clueless in the kitchen: A cookbook for teens, Evelyn Raab. 1998. Key Porter Books, Toronto.

The Complete Canadian health guide, June Engel and The University of Toronto Faculty of Medicine. 1993. Key Porter Books, Toronto. (Reference)

Cooking vegetarian, Vesanto Melina, RD, and Joseph Forest. 1996. Macmillan Canada, Toronto.

Could do better: Why children underachieve and what to do about it, Harvey Mandel. 1995. HarperCollins, Toronto.

Crohn's disease & ulcerative colitis, Fred Saibil, MD. 1996. Key Porter Books, Toronto.

Cybersense and nonsense. 1998. A computer animated game to develop children's critical capacities; downloadable from Media Awareness Network <http:www.media-awareness.ca>

Dads Can Video Series:
Now I'm a Dad (Feelings about being a father). 24 min. 1997.
The Masculine Mystique (Images of men in society). 24 min. 1997.
Magic Lantern Communications Ltd., Oakville, ON. 1-800-263-1818

Eating for performance, videocassette, 24 min. Sport Nutrition Advisory Committee, Sport Medicine Council of Canada, Ottawa.

Food to grow on: Give your kids a healthy start in life, 1st ed., Susan Mendelson and Rena Mendelson. 1994. HarperCollins Canada, Toronto.

Ghosts from the nursery: Tracing the roots of violence, Robin Karr-Morse and Meredith Wiley. 1998. Publisher's Group West Inc., Toronto.

God in the classroom: The controversial issue of religion in Canada's schools, Lois Sweet. 1997. McClelland & Stewart, Toronto.

Growing up in Canada: National longitudinal survey of children and youth, D. Ross, K. Scott, M. Kelly. 1996. Human Resources Development Canada and Statistics Canada, Ottawa.

Harassment: Take positive action, Scarborough Board of Education brochure. Student and Community Services, (416) 396-7516, Toronto.

The HeartSmart shopper: Nutrition on the run, Ramona Josephson. 1997. Douglas & McIntyre, Vancouver, BC.

HIV/AIDS and child care: Fact book and facilitator's guide, A project of the Canadian Child Care Federation; funded by Health Canada through the National AIDS strategy. 1995. (Professional)

How to break bad news: A guide for health care professionals, Robert Buckman, MD, and Yvonne Kason. 1992. Johns Hopkins University Press, (University of Toronto Press, Toronto).

Human growth and development: The childhood years, John J. Mitchell (University of Alberta). 1990. Detselig Enterprises Limited, Calgary, AB.

I can't stop crying: It's so hard when someone you love dies, Rev. John D. Martin and Frank D. Ferris, MD. 1992. Foreword by Robert Buckman, MD, PhD. Key Porter Books, Toronto.

I don't know what to say: How to help and support someone who is dying, Dr. Robert Buckman. 1988; 16th printing, 1998. Key Porter Books, Toronto.

I don't want to go to school today: A guide for parents, Greg Anderson. 1993. Trilobyte Press, Oakville, ON.

I'll be the parent. You be the kid, Paul Kropp. 1998. Random House of Canada, Toronto.

An Introduction to food and weight problems, National Eating Disorder Information Centre.

It takes two to talk: A parent's guide to helping children communicate, 3rd ed. rev., Ayala Manolson. 1992. A Hanen Centre Publication, Toronto.

Keep your child safe, Canadian Paediatric Society. 1990. Ross Laboratories Ltd., Montreal, QC.

Keys to parenting your anxious child, Katharina Manassis, MD, FRCP, The Hospital for Sick Children. 1996. Barron's Educational Series, Inc., Hauppage, NY.

Kid culture: Children & adults & popular culture, Kathleen McDonnell. 1994. Second Story Press, Toronto.

The Lactose-free family cookbook, Jan Main. 1996. Macmillan Canada, Toronto.

Learning Disabilities Association publications
A guide to understanding learning and behavior problems in children
also
Making the most of the law: Education and the child with disabilities.

Learning language and loving it, Elaine Weitzman. 1992. A Hanen Centre publication, Toronto.

Little well beings: A handbook on health in family day care. 1994. Canadian Paediatric Society. (Professional)

Management of children with developmental coordination disorder: At home and in the classroom. 3rd printing, 1998. School of Occupational Therapy and Physiotherapy, Building T16, McMaster University, 1280 Main St. W., Hamilton, ON L8S 4K1
Send a cheque for $5, payable to McMaster University, to Cheryl Missiuna at the above address.

Minding the set: Making your television work for you and your family. 1994. The Alliance for Children and Television with Rogers Cablesystems.

The Mother zone: Love, sex, and laundry in the modern family, Marni Jackson. 1992. Macfarlane Walter & Ross, Toronto.

Moving and growing: Exercises and activities for fives and sixes (Booklet). 1997. Fitness Canada and the Canadian Institute of Child Health, Ottawa.

New guide to prescription and over-the-counter drugs, Canadian Medical Association. 1996. Reader's Digest, Montreal, QC.

Nurturing independent learners: Helping students take charge of their learning, Donald Meichenbaum (University of Waterloo) and Andrew Biemiller (University of Toronto). 1998. Brookline Books, Cambridge, MA.

On your own: A book for kids learning to be at home alone, Saskatchewan Safety Council and Canadian Institute of Child Health, Ottawa.

Our promise to children, ed. Kathleen A. Guy. 1997. Canadian Institute of Child Health, Ottawa.

Our strength for tomorrow: Valuing our children. Report on Child Health. May 1997. The CFPC Task Force on Child Health, The College of Family Physicians of Canada, Mississauga, ON.

Out of the garden: Toys and children's culture in the age of TV marketing, Stephen Kline. 1993. Garamond Press, Toronto.

Paediatrics & child health, medical journal, Canadian Paediatric Society, Ottawa. (Professional)

Privacy Playground: The first adventure of three little cyberpigs. 1998. Media Awareness Network. Downloadable from the Web site. <http://www.media-awareness.ca>

Racism in Canadian schools, M. Ibrahim Alladin. 1996. Harcourt Brace & Company Canada, Toronto.

Raising kids without raising Cain, Gary Direnfeld. 1993. University of Toronto Press, Toronto.

Really cookin', Carol Ferguson. 1994. Maxwell Macmillan Canada, Toronto.

Religion, Myrtle Langley. 1996. Eyewitness Books, Stoddart, Toronto.

Sleep problems in children: A parent's guide, The Canadian Sleep Society, Toronto.

Sleep thieves: An eye-opening exploration into the science and mysteries of sleep, Stanley Coren. 1996. Free Press, New York (Prentice-Hall Canada, Toronto).

Speaking of SEX: Are you ready to answer the questions your kids will ask? Meg Hickling, RN. 1996; 3rd printing, 1998. Northstone Publishing Inc., Kelowna, BC.

Surviving your partner's job loss, Jill Jukes and Ruthan Rosenberg. 1992. Murray Axmith, Toronto.

The 3 a.m. handbook: The most commonly asked questions about your child's health, ed. William Feldman, MD. 1997. Produced in conjunction with The Hospital for Sick Children. Key Porter Books, Toronto.

Well beings: A guide to promote the physical health, safety, and emotional well-being of children in child care centres and family day care homes, 2nd ed. 1996. Canadian Paediatric Society, Ottawa. (Professional)

What every babysitter should know: Babysitting course, 2nd ed. 1993. St. John Ambulance.

When girls feel fat: Helping girls through adolescence, Sandra Susan Friedman. 1997. HarperCollins, Toronto.

When in doubt, eat broccoli, Liz Pearson. 1998. Penguin Books, Toronto.

When your child hates school, Greg Anderson. Trilobyte Press, Oakville, ON.

Your child's best shot: A parent's guide to vaccination. 1997. Canadian Paediatric Society, Ottawa.

Youth violence: How to protect your kids, Kevin Guest, Donald Cowper and Andrew Haynes. 1997. Communities against Youth Violence, Toronto.

About the Editor

Christine Langlois is *Canadian Living*'s Health and Family Editor. She has developed and edited three comprehensive books in the *Canadian Living Family Book* series, designed to guide parents through their child's development from pre-birth to leaving the nest. Christine makes regular media appearances on parenting and family health issues. She lives in Toronto with her husband and two teenagers.

About the Writers

Lynne Ainsworth, a writer specializing in education issues, lives in Hamilton, Ontario, with her husband and their two school-age boys.

Cindy Barrett, a writer and frequent contributor to *Canadian Living,* lives in Kemptville, Ontario, with her husband and two children.

Marcia Kaye, an award-winning senior writer with *Canadian Living*, specializes in parenting issues. She lives with her husband and their two children in Aurora, Ontario.

John Keating, a Toronto journalist and father of two, is a frequent contributor to *Canadian Living* on parenting and family issues.

Susan Noakes is a Toronto mother of two, a journalist, and chair of her local school council.

Susan Pedwell is an award-winning Toronto freelance writer, and the mother of two. She is a frequent contributor to *Canadian Living.*

Laura Pratt is a Toronto freelance writer and the mother of two. She is a frequent contributor to *Canadian Living.*

Bramwell Ryan is a Winnipeg freelance writer and the father of three. He is a frequent contributor to *Canadian Living.*

Mark Witten, an award-winning journalist from Toronto, is a frequent contributor to *Canadian Living* on family issues.

Acknowledgments

The writers and editors gratefully acknowledge the assistance of the following people:
Janet Abernethy, head of the Children's Department, Richview Library, Toronto Public Libraries; Reverend Doctor **Leslee Alfano**; **Greg Anderson**, school principal; **Ethel Archard**, manager of marketing and promotions, Canada Safety Council; Dr. **Harvey Armstrong**, child psychiatrist and founder, Parents for Youth Ltd.; **Marion Balla**, director, Adlerian Centre; Dr. **Leslie Balmer**, psychologist, private practitioner, and chair of the professional advisory committee of Bereaved Families of Ontario; **Frances Balodis**, director, Music for Young Children; **Lynn Barnhardt**, speech-language pathologist, Nipissing-Parry Sound Catholic School District; Dr. **Riva Bartell**, psychologist, Department of Educational Administration, Foundations and Psychology, University of Manitoba; **Dianne Bascombe**, executive director, Child and Family Canada; **Angèle Beaulieu**, communications officer, Canadian Fitness and Lifestyle Research Institute; **David Blankenhorn**, president, Institute for American Values; **Gordon Bullivant**, executive director, Foothills Academy; Dr. **Neil Campbell**, psychotherapist, founder and director, DADS CAN; **David Carmichael**, director of research and development, Ontario Physical and Health Education Association; Dr. **Mary Ann Carter**, psychologist, private practitioner; **Nancy Chapple**, coordinator, Thames Valley School Board; Dr. **Ester Cole**, supervising psychologist, Toronto District School Board, and chair of the Psychology Foundation of Canada; **Robert Conn**, president and C.E.O., SMARTRISK Foundation; Dr. **Betty Davies**, professor, School of Nursing, University of British Columbia; **Jeff Deane**, president, The Canadian Principals' Association; **Sharon Dembo**, child psychotherapist, private practitioner; **Sara Dimerman**, individual, marital, and family therapist and director, The Parent Education and Resource Centre; **Julie Dotsch**, coordinator, Early Child Diversity Network Canada; Dr. **Jim Duffy**, associate professor, Department of Psychology, Memorial University of Newfoundland; **Frank B. Edwards**, author, and publisher of Bungalo Books; **Resa Eisen**, family therapist and mediator, private practitioner;

Theresa Ferrari, youth development specialist, University of Florida; Dr. **Graham Fishburne**, professor, Department of Elementary Education, University of Alberta; Dr. **Raymond Foui**, sessional instructor, Department of Sociology, University of Manitoba; Dr. **Mark Genuis**, executive director, National Foundation for Family Research and Education; Dr. **Robert Glossop**, executive director of programs and research, The Vanier Institute of the Family; **Mary Gordon**, parenting expert, administrator of parenting programs, Toronto District School Board; Dr. **Joan Grusec**, professor, Department of Psychology, University of Toronto; **Claudette Gudbranson**, information officer, Learning Disabilities Association of Canada; **Cheryl Hannebauer**, former board member, BC Confederation of Parent Advisory Councils; **Merylie Wade Houston**, coordinator, Early Childhood Education Program, Seneca College; **Helen Jones**, spokesperson and co-founder, Association of Parent Support Groups of Ontario Inc.; **Jill Jukes**, consultant, Murray Axmith and Associates Inc.; Dr. **Miriam Kaufman**, pediatrician, The Hospital for Sick Children, associate professor, Department of Paediatrics at University of Toronto; Dr. **Brenda Kenyon**, director, Centre for Psychological Studies, University of Guelph; **Patti Kirk**, owner, Parentbooks; Dr. **Stephen Kline**, professor, School of Communication, Simon Fraser University; Dr. **Leon Kuczynski**, professor, Department of Family Relations and Applied Nutrition, University of Guelph; **Joanne Lee**, president, Association for Bright Children of Ontario; Dr. **Donna Lero**, professor, Department of Family Relations and Applied Nutrition, University of Guelph; Dr. **Marc Lewis**, associate professor, Department of Human Development and Applied Psychology, Ontario Institute for Studies in Education, University of Toronto; **May Love**, family counsellor, Renascent Centres; **Brian Luhoway**, counsellor, Alberta Alcohol and Drug Commission; **Kathy Lynn**, parenting educator; Dr. **Katherina Manassis**, staff psychiatrist, The Hospital for Sick Children, assistant professor, Department of Psychiatry, University of Toronto; **Pauline Mantha**, executive director, Learning Disabilities Association of Canada; Dr. **Freda Martin**, director, Hincks-Dellcrest Institute; **Kathleen McDonnell**, author of *Kid Culture*; **Sue McGarvie**, clinical sex therapist; Dr. **Harold Minden**, professor emeritus, Counselling and Development Centre, York University; **Faye Mishna**, social worker, clinical director, Integra Foundation; Dr. **Barbara Morrongiello**, professor, Department of Psychology, University of Guelph; Dr. **Deborah Norris**, assistant professor of Family Studies, Department of Human Ecology, Mount Saint Vincent University; Dr. **Caroline Piotrowski**, developmental psychologist and assistant professor, Department of Family Studies, University of Manitoba; **Ellie Presner**, author of *Kidtips* and *Familytips*; **Lee-Ann Boyd Pringle**, doctoral student, Child Clinical Psychology, York University; **Dyanne Rivers**, former teacher; Dr. **Stephen Rivers**, psychologist, Adolescent Substance Abuse Outreach Program, The Hospital for Sick Children; **Morina Reece**, children and youth issue expert, Health Canada; **Heather-jane Robertson**, director of Professional Development Services, Canadian Teachers' Federation; Dr. **Sandy Romanow**, kinesiologist, private practitioner; Dr. **Norman Rosenblood**, psychoanalyst and associate professor, Faculties of Humanities, McMaster University; Dr. **Art Salmon**, National Technical Director, Participaction; **Lori Santyr**, special education resource teacher, Upper Canada District School Board; **Judy Sarick**, owner, Children's Book Store; **Laura Sliwin**, head of public relations, Canadian Association of Psychoanalytic Child Therapists, and private practitioner; **Jerry Smith**, president, Playtoy Industries, and former spokesperson for the Canadian Juvenile Products Association; **Sheila Urban Smith**, program leader, 4H Programs, Michigan State University; Dr. **Rosemarie Tannock**, Department of Psychiatry, The Hospital for Sick Children; **Charlotte Teeple**, executive director, Canadian Children's Book Centre; **Helen Thomas**, associate professor, School of Nursing, McMaster University; **Nico Trocmé**, associate professor, Faculty of Social Work, and director of the Bell Canada Child Welfare Research Unit, University of Toronto; Reverend Doctor **Tracy Trothen**; **Spy Tsoukalas**, research assistant, Canadian Council on Social Development; **Kim Tytler**, director of marketing and communications, Canadian Institute of Child Health; **Susan Whermann**, occupational therapist, private practitioner; Dr. **Judith Wiener**, professor, Department of Human Development and Applied Psychology, Ontario Institute for Studies in Education, University of Toronto; **Kim Zarzour**, author of *Battling the Schoolyard Bully*.

Index

V

W

Z